THE BLACK MALE IN WHITE AMERICA

THE BLACK MALE IN WHITE AMERICA

JACOB U. GORDON
EDITOR

Nova Science Publishers, Inc.
New York

Senior Editors: Susan Boriotti and Donna Dennis
Coordinating Editor: Tatiana Shohov
Office Manager: Annette Hellinger
Graphics: Wanda Serrano
Editorial Production: Jennifer Vogt, Matthew Kozlowski, and Maya Columbus
Circulation: Ave Maria Gonzalez, Vera Popovich, Luis Aviles, Melissa Diaz,
          Nicolas Miro and Jeannie Pappas
Communications and Acquisitions: Serge P. Shohov
Marketing: Cathy DeGregory

Library of Congress Cataloging-in-Publication Data
Available Upon Request

ISBN: 1-59033-370-5

Copyright © 2002 by Nova Science Publishers, Inc.
          400 Oser Ave, Suite 1600
          Hauppauge, New York 11743
          Tele. 631-231-7269   Fax 631-231-8175
          e-mail: Novascience@earthlink.net
          Web Site: http://www.novapubishers.com

Printed in the United States of America

CONTENTS

PREFACE

More than fifty years ago, a Swedish scholar, Gunnar Myrdal wrote *An American Dilemma* (1944). Earlier in the 19th century, another European scholar from France, Alexis de Tocqueville visited America to see what a great republic was like. He later wrote, *Democracy in America*, (1835) on his return to France. This volume has earned the reputation of being both the best ever written on democracy and the best ever written on America. It remains the most often quoted book about the United States.

While Myrdal and Tocqueville were impressed with the America ideals and promises, they were concerned about how some segments of the American population were treated unjustly, especially American Indians and Blacks. They were troubled by the "color line" they observed. The challenge was and still is how to translate the American ideals into reality for all Americans.

Since these two publications, many scholars of American Studies have attempted to reconcile America's promise with its ugly realities – racism, poverty, bigotry, sexism, ageism, and homophobia. Yet, America remains the most powerful and prosperous democracy that the modern world has ever known. In fact, not since the Ancient Kingdoms of Africa and the Empire of Rome has a nation exerted an influence upon the human race equal to that of the United States. Through public and private initiatives, the colossal American economy reaches into every region of the globe. It should be noted however, that on one hand, America promotes democracy and human rights abroad, and on the other hand, it continues to grapple with civil rights problems at home. This hypocracy often diminishes American influence in the international community and the ability to create a more perfect civil society at home. It is in the context of this American dilemma that this volume attempts to examine two related issues: (1) how the black male has coped with the American dilemma, and (2) the relevance of the black male to an emerging area of rigorous scholarship – men's studies.

Much of what we have learned about human history has focused on men, especially great men. For the most part, the role of women in history has been ignored, suppressed, omitted and/or devalued. Yet, the emergence of men's studies in recent years cannot be ignored. This is particularly the case in African-American men studies. Arguably, men studies gained recognition about ten years ago in large measure as a response to the impact of the women's movement in American life. It all began with the 1848 Declaration of Sentiments, a report of the first Women's Rights Convention held at Seneca Falls, N.Y., July 19-20. The women at Seneca Falls declared:

"We hold these truths to be self-evident: that all men and women are created equal; that they are endowed by their creator with certain inalienable rights; among these are life, liberty, and the pursuit of happiness; that to secure these rights governments are instituted, deriving their just powers from the consent of the governed."

The key phrase here is "that all men and women are created equal." By 1920, Congress enacted the 19th Amendment that guaranteed women's right to vote.

Since 1921 when women first voted in America, this nation was never the same again. To say the least, women do not only vote but now serve as elected and/or appointed officials in all aspects of American public and private life. It is important to note here that the history of women's suffrage in the United States began as early as 1776 when Abigail Adams wrote to her husband, John Adams, America's second President, asking him to "remember the ladies" in the new code of laws. Adams replied, the men will fight the "despotism of the petticoat."

A second factor for consideration was the women's studies movement in the 1970's, following the Black Studies movement on college and university campus in the 1960's. In response to these historical developments, American men, in general, became uncomfortable. They were forced by the emerging "women power" to do a number of things. They questioned their declining significance and dominance in the American way of life. They questioned their masculinity and their power relationship to women. Several male organizations emerged, and they began to reassert themselves. In 1991, the American Men's Studies Association was formed. It publishes *The Journal of Men's Studies*, a scholarly journal about men and masculinities. The National Council of African American Men also publishes *The Status of Black Men in America* and *Journal of African American Male Studies*. Gender issues became a dominant factor in American life. For African-Americans, the issues were beyond sexism. The problems of the color line, as predicted by W.E.B. DuBois became even more pronounced at the turn of the 20th century. Blacks had high hopes for their "pursuit of happiness" as the 20th century arrived. Instead, African-Americans had to face the worst type of racial discrimination in human history. The Ku Klux Klan had grown to an organization of more than 100,000 white-hooded knights. They had made more than 200 appearances and seemed to flourish in the South and North Central states by early 1900. The lynching of African-Americans and race riots were common. The African-American was characterized with a turbulent voyage that included joblessness, high illiteracy rate, poor health, poor education, high crime, violent and disproportionate incarceration rates, low life expectancy, and poverty. As black folks challenged the status quo, especially through the civil rights movement, it became imperative that the African-American conditions had to be ameliorated. An understanding of the African-American male was necessary in order to improve the quality of life of African-Americans. Thus, by the 1990's the federal government, foundations, philanthropic organizations, and corporate America began to focus on the problems of African-American boys and men. An important element of this focus is research. Research findings are needed to bridge the existing gap between theories and practices.

This book explores twelve related research topics, each constituting a chapter. These chapters reflect the magnitude of the problems facing the African-American male. The book also documents the success stories of African American men and how they have lived beyond stereotypes and other odds. These problems are not likely to go away in the 21st century. They require government action and individual initiative toward a civil society in which America's promise can be a reality for all Americans, thus making sure that no single American will be left behind.

Chapter 1

AFRICAN AMERICAN MALES IN KINDERGARTEN

Oscar Barbarin
School of Social Work
University of North Carolina, Chapel Hill

ABSTRACT

African American experience significant risk of academic and socio-emotional difficulties in school. This chapter reviews assessment data on emergent reading, math and socio-emotional adjustment during kindergarten. The data show that problems related to achievement and adjustment are more acute for African American males than other groups of children. Moreover, the risks of sub-par achievement originate much earlier than the middle school years as is widely thought. SES, gender, and differential relationships with teacher may be implicated in the differential status of African American males in kindergarten. The data underscore the importance and value of early intervention in the family and school particularly regarding the teacher child relationship.

National studies of educational progress and state-mandated assessment programs in the late elementary, middle school and high school years strongly confirm what experienced school administrators and teachers have long suspected. Namely, the achievement test scores of African Americans consistently fall below those of their Euro-American peers. African Americans score significantly lower than Euro-Americans on tests of vocabulary, reading, math, and scholastic aptitude (Jencks & Phillips, 1998).

As noted in a recent report by the College Board (1999), this means that African Americans are significantly under-represented among children who are the highest achievers in reading, mathematics, science and writing and are disproportionately represented among the lowest achievers in those areas. The implications of such underachievement are troublesome because of what it portends for the future the future of the African American community. A dearth of African American males excelling in elementary and middle school means that as a group they will not be exposed to and have the opportunity to see if they can master a demanding curriculum in high school which is a *sine qua non* condition for admission to selective undergraduate institutions. Failing at this, they stand as much chance as a snowball in hell of admission to selective graduate and professional training programs, which now serve as the gateway to highly valued careers and professional advancement.

Take for example the case of 13 year old Daniel who embodies the dilemmas surrounding the education African American males. Daniel is now in the fifth grade in a predominantly Euro-American suburban school district. He is the 3rd of 4 children growing up in an empoverished female headed household. Although older than all of his classmates he does not stand out because of his small stature. His teachers are concerned that the pace of his academic progress has slowed to a standstill and his classroom behavior is becoming increasingly disruptive. Daniel has significant academic deficits. His skills in reading and math are equivalent to those of first grader. He does not turn in homework though he often claims to have done it. However ineffective, he is quite inventive in his efforts to conceal his problem and the inevitable stress it causes for him. For example, on one exam, he turned in a page that was blank except for his name. When confronted about his failure to attempt the exam, he demurred and to account for the missing information he accused his teacher of erasing his answers. The scene might have evoked laughter were it not so deadly serious.

Daniel's situation is anything but typical. He has already been held back twice: in kindergarten and third grade. Psychological tests administered at school reveal that Daniel is at least average in intelligence, ruling out deficits in intellectual functions as the principal cause of his failure to read and achieve along with other children in his class. These data make his situation all the more puzzling and raise questions about how this could happen. Nevertheless, the facts of his case provoke reflection which may lead to insights what is happening to African American males and reveal why academic and socio-emotional development stalls. When and how do problems of academic achievement arise? What possible explanations might be made for pervasive academic difficulties among children with a documented capacity to learn?

ONSET OF UNDER-ACHIEVEMENT

All the available evidence suggests that the roots of under-achievement can be traced back at least to the beginning of school. For example recent national data from a study of beginning kindergartners show conclusively that African American males start school already behind other groups of children with respect to emergent reading and mathematics skills (ECLS-K, 1998). Thus problems of reading in elementary school may have roots in the pre-school years. For example, data from the 1995 National Household Education Survey (NHES) reveal that African American preschoolers are lower than Euro-Americans on indicators of emergent literacy. On average 3 and 4 year old African Americans score at about the 20th percentile on standardized vocabulary tests (Jencks & Phillips, 1998). Interestingly, African American children are behind on some skill areas but not on others. For example, the NHES data show that African-American children are identical to Euro-Americans in the ability to recognize letters and count to 20. However, they are less able than Euro-Americans to identify primary colors, read or write their names (National Center for Education Statistics, 1995). Perhaps these differences arise from differential emphasis in African American and Euro-American homes on the development of specific skill and in their understanding of the skills children are expected to display by the time the begin formal schooling. Thus African American children may lag in the development of reading skills because they enter pre-school with more limited vocabularies than Euro-American children the kindergarten experience as currently structured is not sufficient to make up the difference. These early differences are important because the gaps they create are somehow never closed by education in elementary school. In fact, it is estimated that about half of the achievement gap observed, for example in middle and high school can be accounted for by these differences detected at when African-American children are in kindergarten (Ferguson, 1998a). To be sure there are many exceptions to this pattern in which individual children grow academically and flourish during the later school years. Nevertheless, the comparative deficits of African American and Latino children to Asian and Euro- American children seem to persist for the most part in the subsequent years of schooling (Ferguson, 1998a).

GENDER, ETHNICITY AND ECLS-K ASSESSMENTS OF EARLY READING AND MATH SKILLS

Across all ethnic groups, a higher proportion of females demonstrate reading competence in the early years of school than do males. Learning to reading involves a progressive process of competence building. The ability to sight read depends upon a accumulation of skills beginning with the recognition of the different sounds in a language, awareness that letter symbols are used to represent those sounds and a fluent blending of beginning and ending word sounds that are represented by alphabet symbols. Gender and ethnic gaps in sight reading an advanced reading skill probably represent continuity with differences observed in the pre-cursor skills such as letter recognition and sound awareness. Boys eventually catch up. Just focusing on males, striking ethnic differences are observed in reading skills and in the pace at which they develop in the early years of schooling. The percent of African American Males demonstrating mastery of early reading skills is generally lower than that of Euro-American males. For example, 18% of African American males demonstrate competence recognizing the beginning sounds of words at the start of kindergarten and 36% do by the end. For Euro-American males, the figures are 18% at the start and 54% by the end. In sight-reading, 1% of African American males demonstrate competence at the start of kindergarten and 7% by the finish compared to 3% and 17% respectively for Euro-American males.

A similar pattern of ethnic differences holds true for math. On skills in judging relative size, addition and subtraction, the proportion of Euro-American children demonstrating mastery is higher than the proportion of African Americans. However, differences between African American males and females are negligible. For example, very few of the African American children (1%) show competencies in addition/subtraction at the beginning of kindergarten and about 8% are proficient by the end. For Euro-Americans these figures are 5% and 22% respectively.

Conclusions about the validity of claims that African American males constitute an especially vulnerable group must be tempered by recognition of these consistent effects for ethnicity and the universal effect of gender on early achievement. Thus to make proper sense of the developmental status of African American males as reflected in these data, it is important to be mindful that boys as a group, not just African American boys, exhibit lower performance on a variety of dimensions compared to girls. Regardless of ethnicity, there are consistent gender differences across all ethnic groups in school performance particularly reading. Boys tend to have lower average scores in reading than girls, are more often among the lowest achievers in reading and writing and are more often classified as eligible for special education services on the basis of difficulty in learning or in the self-regulation of behavior and emotions (College Board, 1999). Their position relative to other groups to whom they have been compared are attributable in part to gender. The reason they may continue to warrant special concern is that their situation reflects the combined downward influence of ethnicity and gender on achievement.

The dual risks of ethnicity and gender on early learning are evident in the case of Daniel as they are for many African American males like him. These early deficits sets the stage for a self-perpetuating process of under-performance that continue in elementary, and high school. For Daniel, there were many warning signs that he would encounter significant problems in adjusting to the instructional program at school. The loss of his father through death in kindergarten and an accidental burning causing serious injury clearly impeded his ability to profit from the training in emergent reading and math skills. Though the circumstance of other children many not be as evident or as severe, for many the pattern and rhythm their lives may distract and divert energies from skill acquisition. Although Daniel was retained in kindergarten and 3rd grade, he never caught up.

THE EMERGENCE OF EMOTIONAL AND BEHAVIORAL SELF-REGULATION

Academic achievement is not the only domain which challenges young children and in which significant differences have been observed between African American males and other groups of children. The pre-school period leading up to kindergarten is an important time for the development and consolidation of several critical socio-emotional competencies often grouped under the rubric of self-regulation (Barbarin, 1993a). Teacher often describe these in terms of the ability to get along with others, to communicate their needs clearly, to follow directions, to work independently, to sit still, to wait one's turn and to solve disagreements verbally and not physically. These domains are capture in the ABLE model proposed by Barbarin (1999). This model includes the following domains of socio-emotional functioning: Self regulation of *A*ttention, *B*ehavior, *L*anguage and *E*motions. As a group, they represent skills the child needs to learn about the environment, to respond to environmental stimulation, to benefit from experiences with others and to respond to the demands/requirement of the environment in ways that are self-affirming. These domains are social in nature but they build on a substrate of physical and neurological development that occurs from birth to age 3. These domains are conceived as capabilities that children develop to an art and refine in the pre-school years (3-5). In truth there is much variation in the rates at which children mature and develop these social competencies. Although many children acquire these competencies during the pre-school period, some children who ultimately reach expected level of self regulation, experience significant delays and may not attain them until they are well into first or second grade.

Like many other African American males, problems with academic skills were just a part of the difficulty Daniel has experienced at school. Daniel's status at school is also mired in a host of behavior and socio-emotional concerns. By the middle school years, Daniel presented with behaviors that were so disruptive that the school could no longer ignore them. Unable to perform the required academic tasks he performed in a different way. He was often restive, talked out loud, made frequent trips to the pencil sharpener, trash can or bath room, anything to get away from his desk and work. He would extend his leg to trip students as they passed his desk. As his performances took on an edge of anger and defiance, the school became alarmed felt that it must act but none of the options available seemed enough. In reviewing the details of his situation and his developmental history it is possible to make a case for a reciprocal if not causal link among the behavioral, socio-emotional and academic difficulties Daniel exhibited. The need for intervention on both the academic and socio-emotional front was just as pressing in kindergarten as it was in the 5th grade, but the signs of Daniel's struggle were not recognized. This is especially true in the behavioral domains such as restlessness, inattention and opposition. Daniel and young males as a group are much more likely than females to exhibit problems of immature of self-regulation and social skills in the form of aggression, disobedience, inattention, hyper-activity (See Barbarin, 1993a).

Although gender differences in behavioral regulation are indisputable, ethnic comparisons of male behavior do not yield such clear cut results. Data from the Child Health Supplement to the National Health Interview Survey (1988) show that young Euro-American male are rated by parents as often mean and aggressive with the same frequency as African-American males. However African American males more often rated as disobedient at school because they do not follow rules and exhibit disruptive classroom behavior. They are more often rated by parents as restless, distractible, oppositional and having difficulty getting along with others (Barbarin & Soler, 1993).

EXPLAINING THE READING GAP AMONG AFRICAN AMERICAN MALES

Conclusions about the relatively disadvantaged position of African American males with respect to reading may be easy to justify on the basis of the data reviewed above. However it is not easy to identify or to formulate empirically supported explanations of the principal causes. Children typically are born healthy and without significant neurological deficits come into the world with the innate capacity to develop competence in math and reading. The ability to read skillfully is closely tied to the development of language skills beginning first with the ability to recognize sounds and then combine them into words. In the first year of life, infants have the capacity to recognize, distinguish and reproduce a much broader array of sounds that are represented in their parents' language. In time this ability contracts to the sounds that employed in their language. So for example, English draws on 44 distinctive sounds or phonemes. Usually by the time the infant is 12 months s/he is able to combine sounds to make simple single syllable words. As vocabulary develops from initial gestures to babbling, to one-syllable utterances, to single words to two words, to sentences and ultimately compound and complex sentences the child acquires the capacity to use speech instrumentally to communicate with others. In time the child also masters language syntax, use of paralinguistic feature such as volume, tone and speed and the rules governing social discourse. But what is going wrong for so many African American males? How can we account for why a disproportionate number of African American children in general and males in particular arrive at school less well equipped with the linguistic skills needed for the academic and social demands of school? What derails or slows their progress as they move along the path to conventional skilled reading?

Table 1. Social, Familial and School Factors thought to have a Role in Explaining Achievement of African American Males Minority Achievement Gap

Qualities of Parental Functioning and Family Life
- SES (Socio-economic Status)
- Familial Poverty and related social risks
- Ethnicity / Culture (practices, roles (e.g. active, energetic advocacy), expectancies, efficacy (exercise influence vs trusting acceptance), relationship)
- The home literacy environment
- Parenting Practices (relationship quality, discipline, expectancies regarding achievement,)
- Parental Emotional Investment in the student's education
- Parental Behavioral Involvement with the child and school around learning

Qualities of the School
- Quality of Early childhood programs
- Class size
- Ability Grouping and Tracking
- Student Course selection
- Teacher expectations and practices
- School resources
- Quality of School leadership
- Proportion of the different ethnic groups making up the school student and staff

Social and Community Factors
- Gender
- Racism
- Neighborhood Poverty
- Integration of the school into the community

Fit / Compatibility among childhood environments: Family, School and Community
- Articulation between role definitions, practices and values of the Home, the School and the Community
- Relationship between the Teacher and the student
- Relationship between Parent and Teacher

Table 1 presents a multi-level list of factors often posited as contributors to the Black Euro-American achievement gap. They range from home life and family functioning to school and community (Phillips, Brooks-Gunn, Duncan, Klebanov & Crane, 1998). Low Socio-economic status emerges as an overriding and powerful determinant in explanations of under-achievement among African-American males. For example in both the National Household Education Survey and the ECLS data presented here, racial differences in early academic skill are highly associated with SES and in the case of the NHES racial differences are wholly accounted for by a combination of low maternal education, poverty and single parenthood. (National Center for Education Statistics,1995). Without doubt, SES is one of the most robust and consistent predictors of academic achievement (McLoyd, 1998). It is also ubiquitous and exerts influence at multiple levels, from the individual to the systemic. Study after study shows a strong relationship between SES and measures of achievement with correlations hovering above.60. Low SES is highly associated with deficits in reading and math achievement. But what does this relationship tell us about the origins of low or delayed achievement? Unfortunately not much! The research supporting these relationships is devoid of details on the mechanisms by which limitations of financial resources or human capital can be linked to low achievement. As a consequence, there are few clues on which to base speculations about the processes or mechanisms that link SES to school performance between the ages of 3 and 5. This is due in part to the fact that SES, itself is probably a proxy for many other potential causes including poverty, adequacy of material resources, human capital in the form of parental education and employment status, family distress or well-being, household structure and relationships, social denigration and stigma, neighborhood quality, community resources, living standards, exposure to toxins, health and access to health services, nutrition, safety and organization. Each of these factors by themselves could be responsible for problems of achievement. But because SES is such a distal and complex variable, it does not by itself clearly delineate the underlying causal mechanism responsible for sub-par achievement. It is probably more accurate to consider the effects of SES as indirect and mediating. In other words SES exerts powerful influence on the achievement outcomes of African American males through its impact on the quality of life and functioning of families, schools and communities.

SOCIO-EMOTIONAL DEVELOPMENT AND ACHIEVEMENT

Problems in the acquisition of social emotional competence are important to note in their own right but may gain in significance when we consider their possible role in academic difficulties. It is argued here and elsewhere that attainment of socio-emotional competence set the stage for and are essential to later academic achievement (See Huffman, Mehlinger, & Kerivan, 2000). The timing of the development of self regulation is important because children who experience delays may also experience delays in academic achievement. Presumably, the extent to which children acquire these socio-emotional competencies, they set the stage for later learning and social development. **Problems in Socio-emotional competence not only diminish academic achievement but they also complicate effort to remediate problems in skill acquisition by males.** Serious or even moderate behavioral, attentional or emotional difficulties are often identified by teachers as significant impediments to achievement. They reduce the ability of children to marshal their intellectual resources to learn and ultimately weaken academic motivation and engagement. Such deficits also divert the energies of teachers from engaging children in needed instructional activity to enforcing classroom order and discipline. In this way, socio-emotional competence is essential to school success because it constitutes a pre-requisite condition for effective instruction and learning.

AFRICAN AMERICAN MALE ACHIEVEMENT AS A FUNCTION OF GENDER AND FAULTY SOCIAL DEVELOPMENT

To what extent can difficulties of African American males be explained by problems of socio-emotional maturation? Along with evidence of lower male achievement there is evidence that African American males exhibit patterns of behavioral and emotional disengagement from school earlier and to a greater extent than girls (Barbarin & Soler, 1993). Barbarin and Soler (1993) using data from the National Health Interveiw – Child Health Supplement found young African American males had more difficulties related to aggression, opposition, conduct problems and school failure than females. The consequences of this early behavioral dysregulation, delayed maturation of social competence may be seen in the intractable pattern of sub-par achievement that follow them though school. In light of the strong relationship that gender has to achievement and conduct problems for all ethnic groups, this is not enough to explain the uniquely disadvantaged position of THE young African American male student. More pertinent to their condition is the finding that **young African-American males were rated by their mothers as having more symptoms of depression than their female peers**. It is not immediately obvious why African-American males should exhibit more depressive symptom than African American females. Upon closer inspection, several reasons emerge. Perhaps the elevated levels of inattention, restless, disruptiveness and misbehavior result in African American boys being subject more frequently to disapproval and sanctions which are also more personally judgmental, harsh and punitive. They may internalize this disapproval in a way that is demoralizing and destructive of a sense of self. As a consequence of how harshly the world sees and judges them, they may have difficulty forming A view of self as competent and worthwhile. The outcome of this internalized punishment and disapproval is depression Thus the elevated level of depression is related to being in environments where they are more likely to be denigrated and to meet with disapproval. Other plausible explanations include gender-differentiated socialization, biological vulnerability early in life which makes young males more susceptible to malnutrition, and early exposure to toxins and metals that severely compromise neurological development necessary for acquisition of self-regulation (Politt & Gorman, 1994). However among adolescence the pattern of depressive symptoms was reversed and more like what occurs among other ethnic groups, namely, females presented with more depressive symptoms than males. In adolescence, African American males often disengage from school as they rely more on peers for affirmation and approval. Once they disinvest from school, its ability to sanction them decreases, the stakes in school are lowered, and they become less depressed.

African American males carry the burden of the risks associated with both race and gender. The gender effect means that they experience a decrement in performance that is shared with many other ethnic groups. Accordingly, they are subject to the delays in social maturation and emotional development that is commonly observed in males. These are expressed in a decreased capacity to deal with set backs, to tolerate frustration, to regulate attention and to cope with emotional difficulties. These gender differences in achievement are well documented. They are not only plagued by the deficits of academic development attributable to low SES, racism and ethnicity, but they must also shoulder the burden of high level of conduct problems that are universally associated with being male. Socio-emotional competence, like achievement in reading and math is highly correlated with SES. Thus the difficulties they face as African Americans is compounded by being male. In light of the demonstrated problems in social competence, early onset problems of achievement in reading, and the negative expectations that others develop because of it, concern about the plight of African American males is well justified.

RACIAL STEREOTYPES

The existence of achievement gap at every SES level and the failure of ethnic minority students who begin with the same level of achievement and skill to succeed at a commensurate level as their academically equivalent Euro-American peers opens up the possibility that racial stereotypes may play a key role in the African American male achievement gap (Ferguson, 1998b). Racial stereotypes may be expressed in low expectation about the ability of African Americans to excel academically and to perform on a par with Euro-Americans. Racial segregation contributes to a deeply ingrained beliefs that denigrated groups such as African Americans because of genetic differences, cultural practices and beliefs, a lack of value for education or insufficient motivation and discipline are incapable of succeeding in school. These beliefs become a reason for not caring, not trying hard and not investing sufficient resources to make a difference. As appealing as such explanations may be, they are not altogether satisfying. Resorting to institutional racism as the cause of the male achievement gap, like SES, is lacking in explanatory punch, because it is difficult to conceive how it is linked concretely to achievement.

Perhaps the predisposition of males to delays in social maturation and conduct problems sets up negative expectancies on the part of teachers about their capabilities and the likelihood that they will be able to adapt to school African American males to more punitive responses and lower expectations from adults across each of these setting. This combined with the observation that young African American males have more depressive symptoms, may explain the persistent underachievement. The achievement gap cannot be explained entirely by low SES since it occurs at every income level. This raises the possibility that race related factors may be involved. African American males' low achievement scores reflect a compounding of the adverse effects of ethnicity and gender on both achievement and socio-emotional competence. Because they contend simultaneously with the gender related delays in social maturation and self-regulation that universally bedevil the early development of boys, and the already heavy burdens of racism and economic adversity, African-American males face imposing challenges to academic achievement.

IMPORTANCE OF EARLY INTERVENTION

The case of Daniel reminds us of the tragic costs of avoiding or failing to heed the signs of early difficulty in school. Early skills are often a foundation for later skill development. Therefore, early underachievement has a predictable relationship to children achievement test scores over their careers in school. Early failure continues unchecked in the higher grades. Thus, achievement scores in math, science or writing early in school are auto-correlated. Many academic skills are acquired in a sequential fashion. Deficiencies in skill development in lower grades set a high barriers to the acquisition of more complex skills required for success as the child matures. Daniel is not alone in experiencing a host of life stressors that take a toll on academic achievement and adjustment to school. There are many African American males in school districts across this country, just like Daniel, are performing marginally and end up not realizing their full potential as students

The onset of ethnic disparities in academic skills by kindergarten underscores the need to act earlier in the child's life. It is impossible to reverse these problems without focused efforts and attention to reform of multiple aspects of schools (e.g. see Crevola & Hill, 1998). Things simply do not get better by themselves without intervention. The pre-school years are not too early to focus on these skill oriented domains since half of the variance in the achievement gap can be accounted for by differences that are observed by the kindergarten year (Ferguson, 1998a). It makes sense that high achievement among African American males has to begin with the development of academic skills for reading and numeracy at ages 3 to 5. Are there programs or practices that have succeeded in closing, reducing or overcoming the achievement gap between African American males and other groups of students? Fortunately, the answer to this question is a resounding yes.

REFERENCES

Barbarin, O. (1993a). Emotional and social development of African American children. *Journal of Black Psychology*, 19 (4), 381-390.

Barbarin, O. (1993b). Social context, psychosocial resilience and psychopathology: Competing frameworks for understanding the emotional adjustment of African-American children. *Journal of Black Psychology*, 19 (3) 478-492.

Barbarin, O. and Soler, R. (1993). Behavioral, emotional and academic adjustment in a national probability sample of African American children: effects of age, gender and family structure. *Journal of Black Psychology*, 19 (4), 423-446.

College Board (1999). *Reaching the Top: A report of the National Task Force on Minority high achievement*. N.Y.: Author.

Crevola, C. A.& Hill,P.W. (1998). Evaluation of a whole-school approach to prevention and intervention in early literacy. *Journal of Education for Students Placed at-Risk*. 3, 133-157.

Ferguson, R. (1998a). Can Schools Narrow the Black-Euro-American Test Score Gap. In C. Jencks & M. Phillips (Eds), pp 318-374 *The Black-Euro-American Test Score Gap*. Washington, D.C.: The Brookings Institution Press.

Ferguson, R. (1998b). Teachers' Perceptions and Expectations and the Black-Euro-American Test Score Gap. In C. Jencks & M. Phillips (Eds), pp 273-317. *The Black-Euro-American Test Score Gap*. Washington, D.C.: The Brookings Institution Press.

Huffman, L.C. Mehlinger, S.L. & Kerivan, A.S. (2000). Risk Factors for academic and behavioral problems at the beginning of school. In *Off to good start: Research on the risk factors for early school problems and selected policies affecting children's social and emotional development and their readiness for school*. Chapel Hill: University of North Carolina, Frank Porter Graham Child Development Center.

Jencks, C. & Phillips, M. (1998). *The Black-Euro-American Test Score Gap*. Washington, D.C.: The Brookings Institution Press.

McLoyd, V.C. (1998) Socioeconomic disadvantage and child development. *American-Psychologist*. 53, 185-204.

National Center for Education Statistics (1995) The National Household Education Survey-October, 1995. *Approaching Kindergarten: A look at preschoolers in the United States*. Washington, D.C.: U.S. Department of Education

Phillips, M., Brooks-Gunn, J. Duncan, G.J., Klebanov, P. & Crane, J. (1998). Family Background, Parenting Practices, and the Black-Euro-American Test-Score Gap. 103-145. In C. Jencks & M. Phillips (Eds), pp 103-148, *The Black-Euro-American Test Score Gap*. Washington, D.C.: The Brookings Institution Press.

Pollitt, E. & Gorman, K. (1994). Nutritional deficiencies as developmental risk factors. In C.A.Nelson (ed.). Threats to optimal development: Integrating biological, psychological, and social risk factors. *The Minnesota Sumposium on Child Psychology. Vol 27*. (pp 121-144) Hillsdale, N.J: Lawrence Erlbaum Associates, Inc.

Chapter 2

AFRICAN AMERICAN MALES IN HIGHER EDUCATION

William B. Harvey
American Council on Education

African American males have had a particularly difficult struggle in their attempts to achieve equity and inclusion in the American society. Structural and psychological obstacles have been consistently placed in their paths to deter their efforts to achieve the inalienable rights of freedom, justice, and equality that America has promised as fundamental elements of citizenship. Few measures, whether they have originated in the legislative, the judicial, or even the religious arena, provided consistent relief from the scourges of racism and discrimination that African American males have been forced to confront. Historically, educational opportunity has offered the most effective route to participation and upward mobility, and the reality continues to be that additional educational attainment raises one's income potential and social standing.

An analysis of the enrollment and completion patterns of African American males in colleges and universities requires not only an examination of the specific indices of this cohort, but also an understanding of their involvement in educational engagements in comparison with other groups. It is considerably more informative to have an understanding of the changes in educational participation for African American males in relationship to other groups, than to examine these data without taking the context into account. For example, an examination of the college enrollment rates for African American males becomes more salient when it is compared with white males as a benchmark group, and with Hispanic males as a group that has also been historically underrepresented. By the same token, an assessment of the progress of African Americans males is more informative when it is compared with the status of African American females during the same time period. This paper attempts to provide a sense of both the absolute and relative progress that has been made by African American males in pursuing and attaining representation in postsecondary education.

HIGH SCHOOL COMPLETION

The numbers of African American males who are eligible to enroll in colleges and universities is, obviously, tied to the numbers of high school completers, since the high school diploma is almost universally considered a prerequisite to entering a postsecondary institution.

Recent data are not encouraging since they indicate that the high school completion rate for this cohort declined to 67.5 percent in 1998, the most recent year for which the figures are available. The 1998 rate is nearly 4 percentage points below the rate for 1997. This figure represents the lowest completion rate by African American men since 1983. While the rate for white males also dropped, from 80.6 to 78.8 per cent, the gap between the two groups actually increased from 9 percentage points to 11. The rate for Hispanic males remains the lowest of the three groups, and it also dropped, from 58.9 percent to 54.3 per cent.

The dichotomy between high school completion rates for men and women is clearly reflected by these data, because the completion rate for African American women rose to 78.4 per cent, up from 77.5 per cent the previous year. While, for African Americans, this gender gap had been as low as 6 percentage points in both 1994 and 1997, it widened in 1998 to nearly 11 percentage points, due to the increase in completion rates among women and the decrease among men. It is important to note that the gender gap is not culturally exclusive to African Americans, but is also manifested among whites and Hispanics, since women in those groups complete high school at higher rates than men. In 1998, among white students, the difference in completion rates between females and males is about six points, while it is nearly 12 points for Hispanic students. (See Table 1)

COLLEGE PARTICIPATION

While, at this particular juncture, the college participation figures for African American males are heartening, this comfort may be short-lived since the high school completion rates for this cohort do not augur well for the near future. The data indicate that, in the freshman class of 2001, the number of African American males will be lower than it was in 1997 as a result of the reduction in the numbers of high school graduates. On a more positive note, however, the most recent data available reveal that a record number of 445,000 African American male high school graduates in the 18-24 year-old category were enrolled in college in 1998, which is definitely a cause for celebration. Further, between 1997 and 1998, college participation among African American men in this age group increased from 35percent to 38.2 percent, ending a trend of stagnation dating back to 1994. In addition, African American male high school graduates attained their second highest "ever enrolled in college" rates in 1998, with 57.5 percent of those in the 14 to 24 age group reported as having been enrolled in college at some point in their lives. This figure falls only slightly short of the record high of nearly 58 percent, which was reached in 1994.

Table 1. High School Completion Rates and College Participation Rates by Race/Ethnicity and Gender: 1978, 1988 and 1996 to 1998

| | 18- to 24-Year Olds | | | | High School Graduates | | | 14- to 24-Year Olds |
Year	All Persons (thousands)	Enrolled In College Rate (percent)	Number Completed (thousands)	Completion Rate (percent)	Number Enrolled In College (thousands)	Enrolled In College Rate (percent)	Ever Enrolled-in College Rate (percent)
All Races							
Men							
1978	13,385	27.1	10,614	79.3	3,621	34.1	52.6
1988	12,491	30.2	9,832	78.7	3,770	38.3	56.6
1996	12,285	34.1	9,815	80.0	4,187	42.6	65.6
1997	12,513	35.0	9,933	79.4	4,374	44.0	64.9
1998	12,764	34.5	9,915	77.7	4,403	44.4	64.9
Women							
1978	14,262	23.7	11,694	82.0	3,373	28.8	50.3
1988	13,242	30.4	11,068	83.6	4,021	36.3	58.3
1996	12,386	37.0	10,317	83.3	4,582	44.4	68.6
1997	12,460	38.8	10,403	83.5	4,820	46.4	69.6
1998	12,743	38.6	10,651	83.6	4,919	46.2	70.7
White							
Men							
1978	11,572	27.6	9,438	81.6	3,195	33.9	52.5
1988	10,380	31.4	8,268	79.7	3,260	39.4	57.9
1996	9,897	34.5	8,000	80.8	3,419	42.7	66.0
1997	10,173	35.7	8,204	80.6	3,633	44.3	65.3
1998	10,400	34.9	8,194	78.8	3,634	44.3	65.5

| | 18- to 24-Year Olds | | | | High School Graduates | | 14- to 24-Year Olds |
| | | | | | | | |
Year	All Persons (thousands)	Enrolled In College Rate (percent)	Number Completed (thousands)	Completion Rate (percent)	Number Enrolled In College (thousands)	Enrolled In College Rate (percent)	Ever Enrolled-in College Rate (percent)
Women							
1978	12,078	23.9	10,088	83.5	2,882	28.6	50.3
1988	10,881	31.2	9,223	84.8	3,399	36.9	59.2
1996	9,778	37.9	8,200	83.9	3,705	45.2	70.7
1997	9,847	39.2	8,352	84.8	3,863	46.3	70.1
1998	10,065	38.8	8,507	84.5	3,907	45.9	71.0
African American							
Men							
1978	1,554	19.6	956	61.5	305	31.9	49.3
1988	1,653	18.0	1,189	71.9	297	25.0	42.8
1996	1,682	25.1	1,199	71.3	422	35.2	53.7
1997	1,701	25.0	1,214	71.4	425	35.0	56.3
1998	1,724	25.8	1,163	67.5	445	38.2	57.5
Women							
1978	1,897	20.6	1,384	73.0	390	28.2	46.7
1988	1,915	23.8	1,492	77.9	455	30.5	49.6
1996	1,956	28.7	1,539	78.7	561	36.4	55.3
1997	1,949	33.8	1,511	77.5	659	43.6	63.0
1998	2,021	33.2	1,584	78.4	671	42.4	65.0
Hispanic							
Men							
1978	781	16.1	420	53.8	126	30.0	46.3
1988	1,375	16.6	724	52.7	228	31.5	48.4

	18- to 24-Year Olds		High School Graduates				14- to 24-Year Olds
	All Persons	Enrolled In College Rate	Number Completed	Completion Rate	Number Enrolled In College	Enrolled In College Rate	Ever Enrolled-in College Rate
Year	(thousands)	(percent)	(thousands)	(percent)	(thousands)	(percent)	(percent)
1996	1,815	16.5	994	54.8	300	30.2	48.8
1997	1,937	19.2	1,140	58.9	371	32.5	49.2
1998	2,109	16.4	1,146	54.3	346	30.2	47.2
Women							
1978	891	14.4	516	57.9	128	24.8	40.0
1988	1,267	17.7	736	58.1	224	30.4	46.0
1996	1,694	24.0	1,026	60.6	406	39.6	58.0
1997	1,669	26.1	1,097	65.7	436	39.7	59.6
1998	1,906	24.9	1,257	66.0	474	37.7	58.7

In regards to high school completion and participation in post-secondary educational experiences, a significant gender gap exists between African American men and women. In comparing the two groups, one finds that in 1998 the gap was reduced to 4 percentage points, down from the 8-percentage point difference recorded in 1997. In this regard, it is worth calling attention to the fact that the enrollment figures for African American women in the 18 to 24 year age group in1998 were at an all time high of 671,000 students.

But, over a longer-term, the twenty-year period from 1978 to 1998, analysis reveals that while the percentage enrollment of African American males in college increased from 31.9 to 38.2 percent, the percentages for African American females rose from 28.2 per cent to 42.4 percent during the same time period. In other words, the figures for females went from being lower than those of their male counterparts at the beginning of the period, to being higher at the end. A cross-racial comparison over that 20-year period reveals that the gains made by African American males were also exceeded by white males in the same age grouping. The percentage figures for white males rose from 33.9 per cent in 1978 to 44.3 per cent in 1998, which tied the record high that was set in 1997, and their 1998 enrollment figures also reached an all time high of 3,634,000. On the other hand, the Hispanic male representation in this age cohort showed only a slight increase over this period, from 30.0 in 1978 to 30.2 in 1998. The 1998 percentages however, compared to a 32.5 enrollment rate in 1997, which represents an actual decline in the enrollment figures for this group by 25,000 students, as the numbers dropped to 346,000 in 1998 from 371,000 in 1997.

A careful review of the involvement of African American males in postsecondary education over the 20-year period from 1978 to 1998 shows an inconsistent pattern of participation. From 1978 to 1988, the percentage rate for18-24 year olds who were enrolled in college fell from 19.6 to 18.0, and for high school graduates from 31.9 to 25.0. During that same period however, the completion rate for high school graduates increased from 61.5 percent to 71.9 percent, but the number of students enrolled in college decreased from 305,000 to 297,000. However, from 1988 to 1998, the circumstances were essentially reversed. Enrollment in college increased from 18.0 to 25.8 percent among 18-24 year olds, and from 25.0 to 38.2 percent among high school graduates, but the completion rate for high school graduates fell from 71.9 percent to 67.5 percent. The number of students enrolled in college increased from 297,000 to 445,000.

The pattern of participation for African American females, though, is one of steady, consistent growth. From 1978 to 1988, the enrollment in college percentage rate for 18-24 year olds grew from 20.6 percent to 23.8 percent, and from 1988 to 1998, it increased from 23.8 to 33.2 percent. Among high school graduates, from 1978 to 1988, the rates grew from 73.0 to 77.9, and from 77.9 percent to 78.4 from 1988 to 1988, while the number of students enrolled in college during the two decades grew from 455,000 to 671,000.

African Americans educators, such as Michael Lomax, the President of Dillard University, are deeply troubled by the growing gap between the participation of African American men and women in postsecondary institutions. The situation raises concern because it creates a pronounced imbalance between college-educated men and women, and may affect the dynamics and relationships between members of the two groups. Assuming that these young women seek will seek partners and mates with a preference for individuals who have similar educational backgrounds, this gap has the possibility of altering the social dynamics of the African American community. Lomax and other college administrators have noted that the surplus of African American women to men has already resulted in a declining quality of relationships, and even in the abuse of women by men.

Why has there been and why does there continue to be a lag in the pursuit of a college education by African American males? These questions clearly have important implications for the future, and have prompted speculation by professional academicians and concerned community leaders alike.

One very fundamental and significant possibility is the obvious realization that African American men, as they complete high school, have simply been unaware of and unfamiliar with the process used to enter a college or university setting. For these young men, the military services are likely to seem a more plausible scenario than college, as evidenced by the relatively high incidence of African American males who enter one of the branches of the service immediately after graduation from high school. Making this choice may very well be an appropriate decision for them at that point in their lives, but their enlistment nevertheless removes them from the pool of potential college attendees.

Within the past few years the exceptionally robust economy has offered unusual opportunities for gainful employment to male African American high school graduates. Individuals with technical skills were in particularly high demand and undoubtedly, some number of young African Americans men decided to take advantage of their employability, and moved into the work force rather than attending college.

Some conservative white social commentators, and even some African Americans, believe that the hip-hop culture, which is indigenous to young African Americans has championed a set of values and attitudes that manifest socially rebellious behavior and discourages academic achievement and intellectual growth. They argue that demonstrating success in the classroom environment is ridiculed as "acting white," and that the effects of this negative pressure reduce the opportunity for African American males to compile the kinds of records of achievement that facilitate college participation. This is a construct that many people find to be offensive because it presents what is essentially a blame-the-victim perspective.

Clearly, there are serious and daunting structural impediments in the social system that African Americans have to deal with, as well as the ongoing restrictions that are posed by the lingering practice of racism. African Americans are dramatically overrepresented on the negative side of many of the indexes that measure quality of life in socioeconomic dimensions, ranging from family income to neighborhood safety. Considering their observations of, and experiences in, the mainstream culture, and given the negative quality of much of their contact with its institutions and representatives, it is not surprising that substantial numbers of young African Americans, particularly males, do not believe that the traditional route to higher education, and on to inclusion in the social and economic mainstream is open to them. To suggest then, that the societal playing field has been leveled, and that the attitudes of African Americans males are the primary factors for their academic achievement levels is to present a perspective that is nieve at best, and mean-spirited at worst.

For example, it certainly has been a consistent mark of the culture, long prior to the development of hip-hop, that a disproportionately high percentage of young African American men have become entangled within the criminal justice system. In recent decades with an acknowledged broadening of opportunities that have been made available as a result of social protest and judicial mandate, some portion of these incarcerated individuals might have gone on to pursue postsecondary education. Collectively, they represent a significant and potentially valuable pool of academic and labor resources, and it is a tremendous loss to the African American community and to the nation that an undetermined number of young men who might have gone to college, have instead, gone to jail.

The combination of economic, cultural, political and social circumstances and conditions that have previously been referred to, have made the pursuit of a college education a difficult journey for many African American men to make. In spite of these hardships, significant increases in the numbers of African American males who participate in each level of higher education have been achieved. As with many aspects of the life circumstances of African Americans, the gains that have been realized are encouraging, but they also show how much progress still needs to be made. (See Table 2)

Taking the ten-year period from 1988-98, and considering all age groups and all types of higher education institutions into account, the numbers of African American males who enrolled in higher education increased steadily over this period. The increase in enrollment from 442,700 in 1988 to 584,745 to 1998 represents a 32.1 percent gain over that period. The enrollment figures for white males actually fell by 4.4 percent during that time, dropping from 4.711,600 to 4,506,381. Hispanic males increased their enrollment figures by 73.9 percent during that same period, going from 310,300 to 539,733. African American women showed an increase of 45.6 per cent during this time period, as their enrollment figures increased from 686,900 to 1,000,157.

WHERE DO AFRICAN AMERICAN MALES GO TO COLLEGE?

Further disaggregation of the enrollment figures provides additional insight into the types of institutions where African American students are matriculating. Considering all types of institutions, significantly larger numbers of African American students enroll in public, rather than private institutions, as is also the case with students from other racial and ethnic backgrounds. About seventy-five percent of African American students are enrolled in public colleges and universities, which is a rate similar to that of the overall college-going population. This enrollment pattern is not surprising, given that attending private colleges and universities is generally considered to be more costly. A fundamental distinction in this pattern is that African Americans continue to matriculate at the Historically Black Colleges and Universities, both public and private, in relatively large numbers. However, the percentage enrollments in these institutions are getting smaller relative to the overall enrollments of African American students in the universe of colleges and universities.

Table 2. Total Enrollment in Higher Education By Control of Institution, Race/Ethnicity, and Sex: Fall 1988 to 1998

	1988	1994	1995	1996	1997	1998	Percent 1988-98	Percent 1994-98	Percent 1997-98
Men	5,998,200	6,371,898	6,342,539	6,352,825	6,396,028	6,379,054	6.3	0.1	-0.3
White (non-Hispanic)	4,711,600	4,650,698	4,594,085	4,552,197	4,548,762	4,506,381	-4.4	-3.1	-0.9
Total Minority	1,051,300	1,451,697	1,484,202	1,533,407	1,582,344	1,617,971	53.9	11.5	2.3
African American	442,700	549,734	555,911	564,146	579,791	584,745	32.1	6.4	0.9
Hispanic	310,300	463,957	480,170	506,574	525,800	539,733	73.9	16.3	2.6
Asian American	259,200	385,043	393,280	405,532	417,717	434,294	67.6	12.8	4.0
American Indian	39,100	52,963	54,841	57,155	59,036	59,199	51.4	11.8	0.3
Nonresident Alien	235,300	269,503	264,252	267,221	264,922	254,702	8.2	-5.5	-3.9
Women	7,044,900	7,906,892	7,919,242	8,014,695	8,106,306	8,150,982	15.7	3.1	0.6
White (non-Hispanic)	5,571,600	5,776,296	5,717,158	5,711,668	5,717,360	5,689,113	2.1	-1.5	-0.5
Total Minority	1,347,400	1,944,164	2,011,972	2,103,989	2,188,866	2,272,967	68.7	16.9	3.8
African American	686,900	898,896	917,761	941,419	971,253	1,000,157	45.6	11.3	3.0
Hispanic	369,600	581,607	613,669	659,534	692,693	719,853	94.8	23.8	3.9
Asian American	237,500	389,252	404,079	422,634	441,489	467,602	96.9	20.1	5.9
American Indian	53,400	74,409	76,463	80,402	83,431	85,355	59.8	14.7	2.3
Nonresident Alien	125,900	186,432	190,112	199,038	200,080	188,902	50.0	1.3	-5.6
Public	10,156,400	11,133,680	11,092,374	11,120,499	11,196,119	11,160,838	9.9	0.2	-0.3
White (non-Hispanic)	7,963,800	8,056,351	7,945,391	7,871,866	7,857,846	7,767,241	-2.5	-3.6	-1.2
Total Minority	1,954,700	2,776,074	2,849,526	2,944,838	3,040,940	3,118,647	59.5	12.3	2.6
African American	881,100	1,144,539	1,160,623	1,177,433	1,205,279	1,220,749	38.5	6.7	1.3
Hispanic	586,900	898,692	937,068	990,722	1,031,618	1,060,259	80.7	18.0	2.8
Asian American	405,700	622,062	637,989	657,913	680,409	714,620	76.1	14.9	5.0

	1988	1994	1995	1996	1997	1998	Percent 1988-98	Percent 1994-98	Percent 1997-98
American Indian	81,100	110,781	113,846	118,770	123,634	123,019	51.7	11.0	-0.5
Nonresident Alien	237,800	301,255	297,457	303,795	297,333	274,950	15.6	-8.7	-7.5
Independent	2,886,700	3,145,110	3,169,407	3,247,021	3,306,215	3,369,198	16.7	7.1	1.9
White (non-Hispanic)	2,319,400	2,370,643	2,365,852	2,391,999	2,408,276	2,428,253	4.7	2.4	0.8
Total Minority	444,100	619,787	646,648	692,558	730,270	772,291	73.9	24.6	5.8
African American	248,500	304,091	313,049	328,132	345,765	364,153	46.5	19.8	5.3
Hispanic	93,100	146,872	156,771	175,386	186,875	199,327	114.1	35.7	6.7
Asian American	91,000	152,233	159,370	170,253	178,797	187,276	105.8	23.0	4.7
American Indian	11,500	16,591	17,458	18,787	18,833	21,535	87.3	29.8	14.3
Nonresident Alien	123,300	154,680	156,907	162,464	167,669	168,654	36.8	9.0	0.6

In 1998, enrollment figures for African American males in HBCUs revealed a slight increase over the previous year, as they grew to 87,167 from 87,097 in 1997. Similarly, female student enrollment at the HBCUs was recorded at 196,978 in 1998, which was slightly higher than the enrollment of 136,798 in 1997. Both male and female enrollment peaked in the mid-1990s, with figures of 91,667 for males in 1994 and 138,733 for females in 1995. (See Table 3) The institutional influence continues to be such a significant force that the top 15 four-year institutions, in terms of the numbers of enrolled African American males among their student bodies, are all Historically Black Colleges and Universities. Further, since African American males are among the various ethnic and racial groups that suffer from the greatest degree of attrition in the postsecondary arena, it is important to note that of the top twenty institutions that grant baccalaureate degrees to African American males, seventeen of them are HBCUs. (See Table 4) About half of the top fifty institutions awarding baccalaureate degrees to African American males are Historically Black Colleges and Universities.

Table 3. African American Enrollment in Historically Black Colleges and Universities by Control of Institution and Sex, Fall 1989 to 1999

	1989	1994	1995	1996	1997	1998	Percent Change 1989-98	Percent Change 1997-98
Number of HBCUs	104	107	107	106	106	106		
All HBCUs	199,974	229,046	230,279	225,886	223,895	224,145	12.1	0.1
Men	79,462	91,667	91,546	88,896	87,097	87,167	9.7	0.1
Women	120,512	137,379	138,733	136,990	136,798	136,978	13.7	0.1
Public HBCUs	137,190	158,888	159,492	156,111	152,362	153,241	11.7	0.6
Men	54,400	63,702	63,607	61,484	59,083	59,310	9.0	0.4
Women	82,790	95,186	95,885	94,627	93,279	93,931	13.5	0.7
Independent HBCUs	62,784	70,158	70,787	69,775	71,533	70,904	12.9	-0.9
Men	25,062	27,965	27,939	27,412	28,014	27,857	11.2	-0.6
Women	37,722	42,193	42,848	42,363	43,519	43,047	14.1	-1.1

Table 4

Enrollment Numbers –
Top 100 Black Male Undergraduate Enrollments (Fall 1999 Preliminary)

Rank	Institution	State	Total Men	Black Men	% Black
1	Florida A&M University	FL	4539	4176	92%
2	Southern University and A&M College	LA	3320	3183	96%
3	Morehouse College	GA	3012	2972	99%
4	North Carolina A&T St. University	NC	3195	2833	89%
5	CUNY New York City Technical College	NY	5456	2439	45%
6	Tennessee State University	TN	2686	2223	83%
7	Morgan State University	MD	2357	2221	94%
8	Norfolk State University	VA	2376	2118	89%
9	Jackson State University	MS	2173	2103	97%
10	Prairie View A&M University	TX	2270	2085	92%
11	Alabama State University	AL	2073	1938	93%
12	Alabama A&M University	AL	2117	1857	88%
13	Hampton University	VA	1981	1801	91%
14	Grambling State University	LA	1862	1782	96%
15	Texas Southern University	TX	2007	1732	86%
16	Howard University	DC	2211	1689	76%
17	Wayne State University	MI	7257	1639	23%
18	South Carolina State University	SC	1701	1602	94%
19	University of Memphis	TN	6417	1554	24%
20	Temple University	PA	7563	1553	21%
21	Georgia State University	GA	6347	1498	24%
22	University of the District of Columbia	DC	2006	1489	74%
23	University of Maryland-College Park	MD	12704	1463	12%
24	Georgia Southern University	GA	5984	1438	24%
25	Virginia State University	VA	1491	1400	94%
26	Florida International University	FL	11427	1380	12%
27	Benedict College	SC	1360	1358	100%
28	University of Houston- University Park	TX	11478	1323	12%
29	North Carolina Central University	NC	1484	1322	89%
30	Chicago State University	IL	1496	1304	87%

Graduation Rates –
Black Male Baccalaureate Degrees in all Disciplines

Rank	Institution	No. of Degrees
1	Florida A&M University	489
2	Morehouse College	482
3	North Carolina A&T St. University	350
4	Southern University and A&M College	347
5	Howard University	290
6	Grambling State University	275
7	Southern Illinois University-Carbondale	273
8	Hampton University	260
9	Tennessee State University	252
10	Norfolk State University	250
11	South Carolina State University	240
12	University of Maryland-College Park	224
13	Prairie View A&M University	224
14	Jackson State University	216
15	Morgan State University	211
16	Alabama State University	191
17	Alabama A&M University	190
18	North Carolina Central University	190
19	Florida International University	188
20	University of Maryland- University College	184
21	University of Florida	180
22	Chicago State University	179
23	Georgia State University	177
24	Florida State University	176
25	University of South Carolina at Columbia	170
26	Virginia State University	170
27	Alcorn State University	168
28	Wayland Baptist University	168
29	Saint Leo University	167
30	Bowie State University	167

31	University of Arkansas	AR	1347	93%
32	CUNY City College	NY	4028	31%
33	DeVry Institute of Technology	GA	1691	71%
34	Southern Illinois University-Carbondale	IL	10181	12%
35	Florida State University	FL	11564	10%
36	University of Cincinnati-Main Campus	OH	10557	11%
37	Fayetteville State University	NC	1476	76%
38	NC State University at Raleigh	NC	12804	9%
39	Clark Atlanta University	GA	1105	100%
40	Eastern Michigan University	MI	7194	15%
41	Ohio State University-Main Campus	OH	18703	6%
42	University of Maryland- University College	MD	4991	22%
43	University of South Carolina at Columbia	SC	6987	15%
44	Michigan State University	MI	15853	7%
45	Bowie State University	MD	1199	88%
46	Tuskegee State University	AL	1062	98%
47	Virginia Commonwealth University	VA	6443	16%
48	Bethune Cookman College	FL	1122	92%
49	Fort Valley State University	GA	1043	95%
50	Old Dominion State University	VA	5775	17%
51	University of Louisiana at Lafayette	LA	6515	15%
52	Southern University at New Orleans	LA	1079	89%
53	CUNY Bernard M Baruch College	NY	5466	17%
54	Alcorn State University	FL	11063	9%
55	CUNY Brooklyn College	MS	968	98%
56	University of South Florida	NY	3927	24%
57	Albany State University	GA	981	95%
58	Mississippi State University	MS	7146	13%
59	University of Akron-Main Campus	OH	8021	11%
60	University of Maryland-Eastern Shore Campus	MD	1168	77%

31	Temple University	165
32	University of Michigan-Ann Arbor	156
33	Fayette State University	154
34	Michigan State University	153
35	Rutgers University-New Brunswick	148
36	Texas Southern University	148
37	Georgia Southern University	147
38	University of Maryland- Eastern Shore	146
39	NC State University at Raleigh	146
40	Park University	144
41	CUNY City College	144
42	Tuskegee State University	142
43	DeVry Institute of Technology-Decatur	141
44	CUNY Bernard M Baruch College	141
45	CUNY York College	141
46	University of Memphis	141
47	CUNY John Jay College Criminal Justice	137
48	Ohio State University-Main Campus	136
49	Clark Atlanta University	135
50	University of Southern Mississippi	135
51	University of North Carolina-Charlotte	130
52	University of Phoenix-So. California Campus	130
53	Mississippi Valley State University	129
54	University of California-Los Angeles	128
55	University of Central Florida	126
56	CUNY Brooklyn College	125
57	Virginia Commonwealth University	125
58	University of Virginia-Main Campus	125
59	University of Illinois at Urbana-Champaign	121
60	Delaware State University	118

REPRESENTATION OF AFRICAN AMERICAN
MALES IN HIGH DEMAND FIELDS

African American male participation in the fields of study that currently are in highest demand has increased substantially over the ten-year period from 1989-90 to 1999-2000, in almost all areas. (See Table 5) The growth in the high tech areas of computer science and engineering has been especially dramatic. The number of African American male computer science majors increased from 1074 to 1762 during that period, making this field unique in that the rate of growth was even higher among males than females, as the number of African American women majoring in computer science increased from 1173 to 1615. African American males continued their gender dominance in engineering over the ten-year period, increasing their numbers from 1416 to 1978. The number of African American women majors increased from 656 to 1089.

In the fields of business and the biological and life sciences, the more common pattern was followed in which the numbers of majors increased among African American males, but were exceeded by the increases among African American females. The number of African American male majors in business increased from 6002 to 8551, while the increase in African American female majors grew from 8905 to 13905. Similarly, the number of African American male majors in the biological and life sciences grew from 658 to 1373, and at the same time the number for females increased from 1994 to 4717.

Increases also occurred at the professional degree level for both African American men and women. The number of males enrolled as law school students increased from 746 to 1014, while the number of women grew from 936 to 1573. However, the number of African American males who are enrolled in medical school is no greater in 1999-2000 than it was ten years earlier. While the number of African American women medical students has increased from 458 to 655, the number of male students remains at 420. Given the state of health care in the African American community, this figure has disturbing ramifications.

DOCTORAL PARTICIPATION OF AFRICAN AMERICAN MALES

Over the ten-year period from 1988 to 1998, African American males showed a significant increase in the number of doctoral degrees earned. (See Table 6) While there were only 321 doctorates earned by the members of this group in 1988, by 1998 the numbers had grown to 520, an increase of 59 percent. The record high number of 535 degrees awarded was reached in 1996, and in the subsequent two years, the numbers decreased to 524 in 1997 and to 520 in 1998. While the trend line of doctoral degrees awarded to African American males moved steadily upwards during the first four years of this period, it was less stable after that and basically moved alternately up and down over the last six years, ending on a slight downward trajectory.

Table 5. Major & Minor Difference: A 10-Year Comparison by Race and Gender

DEGREE LEVEL	Field of Study	Race	1989-90			1999-00*		
			Men	Women	Total	Men	Women	Total
	Computer Science	White	13974	4944	18918	16315	4875	21190
		African American	1074	1173	2247	1762	1615	3377
		American Indian	54	30	84	107	58	165
		Asian American	1335	809	2144	3561	1703	5264
		Hispanic	669	416	1085	1183	567	1750
		Non-Resident Alien	1472	594	2066	1981	902	2883
		Unknown	743	410	1153	1116	428	1544
		Computer Science Total	19321	8376	27697	26025	10148	36173
	Engineering	White	40533	6961	47494	31689	7258	38947
		African American	1416	656	2072	1978	1089	3067
		American Indian	123	23	146	237	89	326
		Asian American	4827	1185	6012	5186	1664	6850
		Hispanic	2035	476	2511	2397	702	3099
		Non-Resident Alien	4427	490	4917	3722	805	4527
		Unknown	1369	182	1551	1313	295	1608
BACHELOR'S		Engineering Total	54730	9973	64703	46522	11902	58424
	Biological and Life Sciences	White	14488	14326	28814	18638	25138	43776
		African American	658	1336	1994	1373	3344	4717
		American Indian	72	58	130	156	223	379
		Asian American	1573	1672	3245	3561	4452	8013
		Hispanic	955	1164	2119	1336	1871	3207
		Non-Resident Alien	431	436	867	544	825	1369
		Unknown	456	418	874	876	1141	2017
		Biological and Life Sciences Total	18633	19410	38043	26484	36994	63478

DEGREE LEVEL	Field of Study	Race	1989-90			1999-00*		
			Men	Women	Total	Men	Women	Total
	Business	White	108524	89158	197682	92966	83561	176527
		African American	6002	8905	14907	8551	13905	22456
		American Indian	369	411	780	607	782	1389
		Asian American	3518	4495	8013	7664	9061	16725
		Hispanic	4881	5875	10756	6509	7552	14061
		Non-Resident Alien	4530	2816	7346	7026	5828	12854
		Unknown	4268	3842	8110	4259	4438	8697
		Business Total	**132092**	**115502**	**247594**	**127582**	**125127**	**252709**
	Business	White	108524	89158	197682	92966	83561	176527
		African American	6002	8905	14907	8551	13905	22456
		American Indian	369	411	780	607	782	1389
		Asian American	3518	4495	8013	7664	9061	16725
		Hispanic	4881	5875	10756	6509	7552	14061
		Non-Resident Alien	4530	2816	7346	7026	5828	12854
		Unknown	4268	3842	8110	4259	4438	8697
		Business Total	**132092**	**115502**	**247594**	**127582**	**125127**	**252709**
	Law	White	18510	12997	31507	15547	12194	27741
		African American	746	936	1682	1014	1573	2587
		American Indian	68	70	138	146	150	296
		Asian American	430	410	840	1031	1174	2205
		Hispanic	791	668	1459	1029	941	1970
		Non-Resident Alien	162	95	257	270	191	461
		Unknown	442	324	766	972	745	1717
		Law Total	**21149**	**15500**	**36649**	**20009**	**16968**	**36977**

FIRST PROFESSIONAL

DEGREE LEVEL	Field of Study	Race	1989-90			1999-00*		
			Men	Women	Total	Men	Women	Total
	Medicine	White	8139	3881	12020	6137	4157	10294
		African American	420	458	878	420	655	1075
		American Indian	30	22	52	64	58	122
		Asian American	859	479	1338	1466	1108	2574
		Hispanic	512	279	791	459	349	808
		Non-Resident Alien	90	54	144	65	48	113
		Unknown	86	50	136	265	199	464
		Medicine Total	**10136**	**5223**	**15359**	**8876**	**6574**	**15450**

Table 6. Doctoral Degrees by U.S. Citizenship by Race/Ethnicity and Sex, 1989 to 1998

	1988	1989	1990	1991	1992	1993	1994	1995	1996	1997	1998	Change 1989-98	Change 1997-98
Total Doctorates[a]	33,501	34,326	36,067	37,522	38,856	39,771	41,017	41,743	42,415	42,555	42,683	24.3	0.3
Men	21,680	21,813	22,962	23,652	24,436	24,658	25,211	25,158	25,267	24,944	24,653	13.0	-1.2
Women	11,819	12,513	13,105	13,870	14,420	15,113	15,806	16,414	16,945	17,251	17,856	42.7	3.5
U.S. Citizens[b]													
All U.S. Citizens	23,290	23,400	24,905	25,543	25,975	26,408	27,129	27,740	27,741	27,934	28,218	20.6	1.0
Men	13,724	13,395	14,166	14,366	14,500	14,493	14,730	14,965	14,700	14,915	14,750	10.1	-1.1
Women	9,566	10,005	10,739	11,177	11,475	11,915	12,399	12,773	13,041	12,990	13,452	34.5	3.6
White	20,786	20,894	22,172	22,419	22,885	23,237	23,805	23,920	23,856	23,035	23,338	11.7	1.3
Men	12,344	11,987	12,690	12,679	12,828	12,852	13,052	13,052	12,744	12,447	12,369	3.2	-0.6
Women	8,442	8,907	9,482	9,740	10,057	10,385	10,753	10,868	11,112	10,586	10,968	23.1	3.6
Total Minority	2,121	2,130	2,359	2,654	2,741	2,951	3,070	3,517	3,542	3,844	4,012	88.4	4.4
Men	1,104	1,129	1,210	1,344	1,416	1,473	1,509	1,702	1,729	1,876	1,873	65.9	-0.2
Women	1,017	1,001	1,149	1,310	1,325	1,478	1,561	1,815	1,813	1,968	2,139	113.7	8.7
African American	818	821	900	1,004	968	1,108	1,095	1,309	1,315	1,336	1,467	78.7	9.8
Men	317	327	351	417	394	439	409	490	535	524	520	59.0	-0.8
Women	501	494	549	587	574	669	686	819	780	812	947	91.7	16.6
Hispanic	595	582	721	731	778	834	884	919	950	1,047	1,190	104.5	13.7
Men	321	307	380	370	410	423	438	460	478	535	606	97.4	13.3
Women	274	275	341	361	368	411	446	459	472	512	583	112.0	13.9
Asian American	614	633	641	789	846	889	949	1,140	1,091	1,296	1,168	84.5	-9.9
Men	414	446	427	483	530	551	591	670	614	740	643	44.2	-13.1
Women	200	187	214	306	316	338	358	470	477	555	524	180.2	-5.6
American Indian	94	94	97	130	149	120	142	149	186	166	189	101.1	13.9
Men	52	49	52	74	82	60	71	82	102	77	104	112.2	35.1
Women	42	45	45	56	67	60	71	67	84	89	85	88.9	-4.5

	1988	1989	1990	1991	1992	1993	1994	1995	1996	1997	1998	Change 1989-98	Change 1997-98
Non-U.S. Citizens[c]	7,817	8,274	9,791	11,169	11,932	12,189	13,154	13,129	13,375	11,406	11,338	37.0	-0.6
Men	6,298	6,583	7,822	8,742	9,255	9,332	9,968	9,748	9,867	8,285	8,080	22.7	-2.5
Women	1,519	1,691	1,969	2,427	2,677	2,857	3,186	3,362	3,497	3,111	3,230	91.0	3.8

[a] Includes doctorates earned by persons with unknown citizenship status and unknown race/ethnicity

[b] Includes doctorates earned by persons with unknown race/ethnicity

[c] Includes doctorates earned by unknown gender

In comparison, African American females who earned doctoral degrees over the ten-year period have demonstrated a similar up-and-down pattern, but the 91.7 percent rate of growth is much greater than that achieved by their male counterparts. In 1988, African American females earned 501 doctoral degrees, but that number increased to 947 in 1998, which represents a record high figure. Further, the one-year increase of 135 in the number of degrees awarded, rising from 812 in 1997 to 947 in 1998, is also a record high, eclipsing the previous one-year increase of 119 from 1994 to 1995.

For Hispanic males, the ten-year period from 1988 to 1998 was also one in which the numbers of doctoral degrees earned moved up and down at the beginning of the time span. But, from 1992 to 1997, the pattern was consistently upward and Hispanic males tied the all-time high number of doctoral degrees earned by African American males in 1997, then surpassed that figure with a record breaking number of 606 degrees awarded in 1998. Doctoral degrees earned by Hispanic males nearly doubled during the ten-years, increasing by a rate of 97.4 percent, and this is one of the few categories in which the "gender gap" disappears. Hispanic males have actually been more successful in negotiating the system to earn doctoral degrees than their female counterparts have been, and the one-year increase of 71 degrees awarded, from 535 in 1997 to 606 in 1998, is the largest in history.

FACULTY REPRESENTATION

Increasing African American representation in the faculty ranks has proven to be one of the most challenging and complicated aspects of the higher education enterprise. Since the desegregation of American institutions of higher education, the change in the racial composition of the faculties at most of the predominantly white colleges and universities has been slight. (See Table 7) While African Americans nominally represented five percent of the full-time faculty in higher education in 1997, this figure is somewhat misleading as it stands because it includes those persons who hold such positions at the Historically Black Colleges and Universities. Obviously then, the level of representation at predominantly white institutions is much lower than five percent.

Further, while the number of African American male faculty members has increased from 12,483 in 1989 to 14,061 in 1997, the rate of growth over this period of time is the lowest of any underrepresented group, as defined by either race or gender. The 12.6 percent rate of increase for African American males compares to growth rates during the same time period, of 27.2 percent for African American females, and 30.2 percent for Hispanic males. But it is white males who remain, overwhelmingly, the dominant group within the academic profession, even though their numbers dropped from 319,330 in 1989 to 306,374 in 1997.

Table 7. Full-Time Faculty in Higher Education, By Race/Ethnicity and Gender: 1989, 1995, and 1997

	1989 Total	Percent	1991 Total	Percent	1993 Total	Percent	1995 Total	Percent	1997 Total	Percent	Percent Change 1989-97	Percent Change 1995-97
Total	514,662	100.0	520,551	100.0	533,770	100.0	538,023	100.0	553,355	100.0	7.5	2.8
Men	358,562	69.7	355,257	68.2	354,302	66.4	350,756	65.2	352,890	63.8	-1.6	0.6
Women	156,100	30.3	165,294	31.8	179,468	33.6	187,267	34.8	200,465	36.2	28.4	7.0
White[a]	455,600	88.5	456,316	87.7	468,770	87.8	468,518	87.1	477,281	86.3	4.8	1.9
Men[b]	319,330	89.1	313,267	88.2	313,278	88.4	307,498	87.7	306,374	86.8	-4.1	-0.4
Women[c]	136,270	87.3	143,049	86.5	155,492	86.6	161,020	86.0	170,907	85.3	25.4	6.1
Total Minority	58,935	11.5	64,235	12.3	65,000	12.2	69,505	12.9	76,074	13.7	29.1	9.5
Men	39,232	10.9	41,990	11.8	41,024	11.6	43,258	12.3	46,516	13.2	18.6	7.5
Women	19,703	12.6	22,245	13.5	23,976	13.4	26,247	14.0	29,558	14.7	50.0	12.6
African American	23,225	4.5	24,611	4.7	25,658	4.8	26,835	5.0	27,728	5.0	19.4	3.3
Men	12,483	3.5	13,107	3.7	13,385	3.8	13,847	3.9	14,061	4.0	12.6	1.5
Women	10,742	6.9	11,504	7.0	12,273	6.8	12,988	6.9	13,667	6.8	27.2	5.2
Hispanic	10,087	2.0	11,424	2.2	12,076	2.3	12,942	2.4	14,772	2.7	46.4	14.1
Men	6,757	1.9	7,347	2.1	7,459	2.1	7,864	2.2	8,795	2.5	30.2	11.8
Women	3,330	2.1	4,077	2.5	4,617	2.6	5,078	2.7	5,977	3.0	79.5	17.7
Asian American	24,125	4.7	26,545	5.1	25,269	4.7	27,572	5.1	31,283	5.7	29.7	13.5
Men	19,006	5.3	20,520	5.8	18,943	5.3	20,285	5.8	22,339	6.3	17.5	10.1
Women	5,119	3.3	6,025	3.6	6,326	3.5	7,287	3.9	8,944	4.5	74.7	22.7

	1989 Total	Percent	1991 Total	Percent	1993 Total	Percent	1995 Total	Percent	1997 Total	Percent	Percent Change 1989-97	Percent Change 1995-97
American Indian	1,498	0.3	1,655	0.3	1,997	0.4	2,156	0.4	2,291	0.4	52.9	6.3
Men	986	0.3	1,016	0.3	1,237	0.3	1,262	0.4	1,321	0.4	34.0	4.7
Women	512	0.3	639	0.4	760	0.4	894	0.5	970	0.5	89.5	8.5

[a] Full-time faculty members in this group as a percentage of all full-time faculty that year.

[b] Full-time faculty members who are men in this group as a percentage of all full-time faculty men that year.

[c] Full-time faculty members who are women in this group as a percentage of all full-time faculty women that year.

The tacit resistance to including greater numbers of African American faculty in the professorial ranks at predominantly white institutions is clearly revealed in a recent study that was conducted among the nation's leading chemistry departments. This study disclosed that of the 1,637 tenured or tenure-track faculty at the top fifty chemistry departments in the United States, eighteen were African American, and that the hiring of African American professors at the institutions dropped even as the number of new African American Ph.D. holders in chemistry increased from 24 in 1990 to 56 in 1999. Since 1991, not a single African American scholar has been hired to tenure-track post at one of the 50 top chemistry departments. This situation occurred in a discipline where there is significant underrepresentation of African Americans, and with institutions that frequently exclaim their interest in becoming more racially diverse. Based on the popular mythology of the day, as promulgated by opponents of affirmative action, these African American scientists are not only highly sought after, but besieged with multiple job offers at starting salaries that greatly exceed those of their white counterparts.

African American male faculty members at predominantly white colleges and universities not only make pedagogical and scholarly contributions in their classrooms and within their campus communities, but their very presence also helps to debunk some of the negative stereotypes that are frequently imposed upon and associated with the members of this cohort. When they are present, students of color have role models whose achievements they can aspire to emulate. Equally as important though, is that they present white students with the opportunity to interact with and learn from academic models who, given the nature of American society, are likely to have had life experiences and personal interactions that are very different from their own.

CONCLUSION

Even with slow, but fairly steady, progress being made in many respects, the place of African American males in higher education remains tenuous. A litany of factors, from the inadequate preparation that African American students often receive in high schools, to the inhospitable atmosphere that African American faculty members must contend with, make it difficult for African American males to succeed in colleges and universities. Still, since we know that there is no freedom without struggle, we must continue to challenge the world of academe to be a place that lives up to both its premise and its promise. Apart from the Historically Black Colleges and Universities, postsecondary institutions have not, historically, been welcoming places for African Americans. But, since higher education is such a critical part of the road to advancement and progress for the African American community, innovative strategies and approaches must be developed and implemented that will result in greater levels of success within these institutions for African American males. This is not a wish, but a necessity. It is not an alternative, but an imperative, if we are to have a peaceful and productive society in the 21st century.

BIBLIOGRAPHY

Allen, W. R. (1992) The Color of Success: African American College Student Outcomes at Predominantly White and Historically Black Colleges. *Harvard Educaional Review,* 62 (1) 26-44.

Brown, M. C. (1999) *The Quest to define college desegregation: Black Colleges, Title VI compliance, and post-Adams litigation.* Bergle and Garvey: Westport, CT.

Davin, R. E. (1991) Social support networks and undergraduate student academic success related outcomes: A comparison of Black students on Black and white campuses. In W.R. Allen, E. Epps, and N. Hanniff (eds) *College in Black and White, African American Students in predominantly white and historically Black universities* (pp. 143-157). Albany, NY: State University of New York Press.

Fleming, J. (1984) *Blacks in College: A comparative study students' success in Black and in white institutions.* San Francisco: Jossey Bass.

Harvey, W. B. (2002) *Minorities in Higher Education, 2000-2001: Eighteenth Annual Status Report.* American Council on Education, Washington, D.C.

_____ K. (1997) Increasing African Americans' Participation in Higher Education. *Journal of Higher Education* (68)5, pp, 523-548.

_____R. (2001) The Black Male Research Agenda. *Black Issues in Higher Education.* May 10, 2001.

Chapter 3

African American Fatherhood

Bridgitt L. Mitchell

Johnson County Community College
Overland Park, KS

Introduction

Mother, father, and child are the traditional components of the nuclear family. The African American family may not always fit this mold. Often the female headed household is the dominant arrangement for some African American families. However, this should not negate the impact that the father has on his children. Research suggest that the absence of a strong paternal presence in the home is the catalyst behind the most disturbing problems that plague American society: crime and delinquency; premature sexuality and out of wedlock birth; poor educational achievement, addiction and alienation among adolescents; and poverty for women and children (Popenoe, 1996). African American men value their families just as others do. Through unique child rearing practices they attempt to pass on the culture and heritage of their African and African American ancestors to their children. Though societal ills have sabotaged some of his efforts, the African American father has demonstrated that he has the capacity to overcome adversity. This paper examines African American fatherhood, within the context of American "best practices" of fatherhood. It also seeks to develop a better understanding of societal barriers, and child rearing practices among African American men.

What is Fatherhood?

According to the American Heritage Dictionary (1982), a father is one who functions in a parental capacity with regard to another. Fatherhood is defined as the condition of being a father (American Heritage Dictionary, 1982). He is also considered the primary male role model, protector, disciplinarian and provider of the family. Fatherhood is typically described in a biological context as opposed to the role of child-rearing. Contemporary research suggest that the term fatherhood is used interchangeably with the term fathering which includes, beyond the procreative act itself, all the child-rearing roles, activities, duties, and responsibilities that fathers are expected to perform and fulfill (Tanfer & Mott, 1997).

FATHERHOOD AND CHILD DEVELOPMENT

Parents have a tremendous impact in the overall development of children. These influences are across three broad domains of development: a) physical development which includes changes in body size, proportions, appearance, and the functioning of various body systems; brain development; perceptual and motor capacities; and physical health, b) cognitive development focuses on a wide variety of thought processes and intellectual abilities, including attention, memory, academic and everyday knowledge, problem solving, imagination, creativity, and language and, c) emotional and social development which deals with emotional communication, self-understanding, ability to manage one's own feelings, knowledge about other people, interpersonal skills, friendships, intimate relationships, and moral reasoning and behavior. (Berk, 2000). Many interpret researcher to suggest that the role of the mother is the most significant in the development of the child especially from infancy through early childhood. However, there is evidence to support that the role of the father is equally important. Urie Bronfenbrenner's (1979) Ecological Systems theory views the child as developing within a complex system of relationships affected by multiple levels of the surrounding environments, from immediate settings to broad cultural values, laws, and customs. The microsystem level emphasizes that reciprocal interactions with adults (mother and father) impact the behavior of the children as well as the behavior of the adults. John Bowlby (1969) found that attachment behaviors in infants are built in social signals that encourage the parent to approach, care for, and interact with the baby. Babies typically form strong bonds with their primary caregivers that are typically mothers but can also be formed with fathers.

According to the U.S. Department of Health and Human Services (2000), there are five benefits of positive relationships between father and their children. First, father involvement is critical even for very young children. This contributes to the development of emotional security, curiosity, and math and verbal skills. Second, high level of involvement by fathers in activities with their children, such as eating meals together, going on outings, and helping with homework are associated with fewer behavior problems, higher levels of sociability, an higher level of school performance among children and adolescents. Third, Active involvement in the child's schooling, such as volunteering at school and attending school meetings, parent-teacher conferences and class events, is associated with higher grades, greater school enjoyment, and lower chances of suspension or expulsion from school. Fourth, father-child relationships affect daughters as well as sons. Girls who live with both mother and father do better academically. They are also less likely to engage in early sexual involvement and in the use of alcohol and drugs. Fifth, Both boys and girls have reduced risk of drugs and alcohol use if their fathers are involved in their lives.

HISTORICAL CONTEXT OF AFRICAN AMERICAN FATHERHOOD

In order to thoroughly understand the magnitude of being an African American Father, it is necessary to revisit his ancestral past. Between 1528 and 1870, approximately fifteen million Africans were brought forcibly to the New World, most to Cuba, Brazil, America, and other areas in the Caribbean and South America (Segal, 1995). They came from several racial stocks and tribes including Mandingo, Efiks, Hausas, Krus, and Yorubas, Ashantis, and Senegalese (Bennett, 1966). It is estimated that from 10 to 20 percent of these captives died during the crossing and that another 4 percent succumbed after they were sold by slavers (Black 1993; Segal, 1995). Once in the New World Africans were forced to give up their names and their native languages. They had to abandoned their children, religions and customs. As slaves they were prohibited from marrying, and extant families were often separated as they were sold to owners of different plantations. McAdoo (1979) cites that Black men were denied their roles as fathers, with limits to the jurisdiction and authority of their households and discipline of their children. Male slaves were expected to breed new laborers, and female slaves were sexually exploited. When slavery ended in the United States, African Americans found themselves locked out of educational and occupational opportunities that American pride themselves on (Muzi, 2000). Consequently, despite their desire to become equal citizens they were plagued with the realities of slavery. Slavery disrupted and impeded the traditional family relationships of African people. However, this did not completely deteriorate their kinship bond. Due to the rigorous nature of the roles of both men and women during this time it was common for children to be cared for by older women and older children. The biological parents had little time to have direct involvement with the child's upbringing. Nevertheless, within this rigid and restrictive environment men established close, affectionate bonds with their wives and children and asserted their domestic authority to the extent possible (Willis, 1997).

BARRIERS TO AFRICAN AMERICAN FATHERS

Fatherhood is in trouble in the African American community and throughout American society. With the prevalence of societal ills such as divorce, teenage pregnancy, substance abuse and unemployment, African American fathers are faced with several barriers to effective fatherhood. There are three major areas that impact African American men and their ability to fulfill their paternal obligations to their children: the composition of the family, economics, and criminal justice system.

The Changing Pattern of the Family

The structure of the family has undertaken a transition from nuclear family in the 1950's. For African Americans the family structure has gone from extended family to a Eurocentric nuclear family. Many fathers are living apart from their biological children. This intriguing phenomenon can be contributed to the increase in divorce and the number of out of wedlock births (Popenoe, 1996). The divorce rate in America is the highest in the world. About half of American marriages end in divorce, three-forths of which involve children (Berk, 2000). So about 1 in 4 American children live in single-parent households. Although the large majority reside with mothers, the number in father headed households has increased over the past decade (Hethering & Stanley-Hagen, 1997). Despite these unfavorable circumstances it is important for fathers to maintain positive relationships with their children. Failure to do so can hinder the progression of the child's development. Fathers absent from the home yield devastating consequences for children. For many children it is equivalent to life without emotional, moral, or economic support of the father (Daniels, 1998). Consequently children can exhibit emotional distress, depression, aggression, and anxiety as well as a decline in their school achievement and social interactions.

Another barrier for African American fathers is the increase in the number of children born out of wedlock. According to Popenoe (1996) about 70 percent of African American births occur outside of marriage. Typically the mother is the primary custodian of these children. Single parent mothers range from teenagers to educated established women. Many young women give birth and remain unmarried, while middle aged women make a conscious decision to exclude the father from the child rearing process (Daniels, 1998). Consequently many of these children are reared in impoverished conditions. According to the Children's Defense Fund (2000) single mothers are three times as likely to be poor compared with other adults, and almost half of poor children live in single parent families.

The African American family is also a victim of the welfare system. This system succeeded in unraveling the fabric of the black family by penalizing the fathers presence. Mothers were either denied or restricted to limited access to this government assistance that included subsidies for food, housing, and medical expenses. As the result of the inability for many of these men to provide the necessary amenities for their families they simply became invisible members of their families.

Economic Factors

Economics is another critical barrier to African American men and their children. Poverty continues to be a threat to the African American family. It has many probable causes. One primary reason is that fathers work sporadically or their wages are too low. Another is simply because of the inadequate skills and/or education for a job or vocation. Some others are unemployment due to disability, loss of job, illness, or the need to care for sick family members or children with special needs (Children's Defense Fund, 2000). Consequently one out of five children live in poverty. The poverty rate for all blacks and hispanics is over 25 percent (U.S. Department of Health and Human Services, 2000).

The unemployment rate of fathers has a direct impact on the quality of life for their children. If fathers are unable to retain gainful employment it can deter child support payments. Child support is a critical supplement to the custodial parents income. According to the Children's Defense Fund (2000) many women are not receiving child support. Those who do are not receiving the compensatory rate. Hence, children are more susceptible to becoming victims of child abuse based on the undoing strains on the family such as providing food, shelter, and clothing. Additionally, children who live in deprived conditions are also vulnerable to developmental delays.

Even when the father is employed and present in the home, inadequate health insurance can impact the children's well being. Children of color are more likely to be uninsured.

Nationally, one in five African American children are uninsured. Compared with insured children uninsured children are less likely to have a regular source of care, three times less likely to have seen a provider in the past year, and five times more likely to use the emergency room as a regular place of care (Children's Defense Fund, 2000, pg 26). As a result of these alarming statistics African American children have an infant mortality rate twice as high as whites. They are also 1.7 times more likely to die from accidental injury than a white child. Consequently these children may not have the same opportunities as their white counterparts to grow up health and strong. Typically low income children are perpetually stuck in a system that does not make accommodations for their physical well being.

Criminal Justice System

Crime impacts many households of the African American family. African American men have become the scapegoat for society. Through the multi-media age of information, he has been stripped of his right as a viable citizen to that of a menace to society. These men are perpetrators as well as victims of crime. This violence obstruct the functioning of the family by removing him from home. According to the U.S. Department of Justice (2000) data on current rates of incarceration, an estimated 28 percent of African American males will enter State or Federal prison during their lifetime compared to 16 percent of Hispanics and 4.4 percent of white males. Accordingly 65 percent of prison inmates belong to racial or ethnic minorities. So this means that many black men are not present in their homes. The U. S. Department of Justice also reports that prior to admission to State or Federal prisons less than half of the parents report living with their children.

When compared to all other racial groups, African Americans had the highest victimization rates (Federal Bureau of Investigation, 1999). The FBI's Uniform Crime report (1998) showed that 47 percent of murder victims were African American. This obviously has a tremendous impact of families because in death they are permanently separated. Consequently, children are at greater risk of maladjusted social and emotional development as well as impoverished environments. Violent crimes include, murder, rape and sexual assault, robbery, and assault.

CHILD-REARING STRATEGIES

There are some controversies associated with the child rearing practices of African American families. The notion that African American parents subject their children to harsh discipline are based on considering white child-rearing practices as standard (Bradley, 2000). The primary concerns lie with the inclusion of physical discipline (i.e. spanking). Hill and Sprague (1999) reports that African American parents relied more on spanking than white parents. Other research has discovered that the child-rearing practices of African American parents are diversified and that the use of physical discipline is context specific or used as a last result.

McAdoo (1979) found that African American men were actively involved in the disciplining of their children. The father expected prompt obedience from their children as well as displays of good behavior. Additionally, these fathers typically explained why behaviors were unacceptable and expressed their expectations. Many of these fathers have been deemed more effective disciplinarians than mothers, because children have a tendency to adhere to their requests (Barnes, 1985). Barnes also noted that several strategies were used for discipline or guidance, including spanking, withdrawal of privileges, and time-out.

African American fathers teach their children by rewarding interactions that will assist them into their transitions to adulthood in mainstream America and clearly opposing practices that will deter their success as a minority in a majority culture. For the most part, this guidance is done in a loving and caring way. African American children typically have a sense of belonging and strong attachment to their care givers despite the disciplinary tactics. It is important to note that the physical punishment that the children encounter is done with the child in mind. It is not intended to belittle or subject the child to any kind of emotional trauma, and should not be confused with child abuse.

Best Practices among Successful Fathers

Though stories of highly successful fathers don't appear to be prevalent, there is evidence to support the assertion that African American men are indeed successful fathers. Both historical and contemporary sources support this notion. A recent study (Greif, et al, 1998) examined African American fathers of high achieving sons. Achievement was based on the admission of sons to colleges or universities. This study interviewed 29 families to determine the common characteristics among their parenting styles. This study identified six specific parenting practices that these families shared. The first, is that fathers consistently showed concern for their children and their interests. Second, fathers clearly set limits and used consistent discipline. Third, they urged their children to strive for the highest possible levels of success. Fourth, they maintained open, consistent, and strong levels of communication with their sons. Fifth, fathers provided positive racial and male identification with their sons, by instilling that stereotypes and biases can not keep them from achieving. Finally, fathers involved the church, family members, and any others in the community that could promote the child's success. The following are cases in point.

CASE 1

Tiger Woods is a great example of a child who had extraordinary guidance and support from his father. We know him today as a golfing prodigy (Strege, 1998). However, his accomplishments are in part the result of a dynamic father. Earl Woods recognized his son's interest and through his own experiences enabled his son to actualize his own potential. Aside from the technical knowledge about the game of golf, his father remained a steadfast advisor and confidant to his son. He also instilled in him the importance of hard work that is obviously a signature quality exemplified by Tiger's character. Tiger Woods is not only the first African American to break down the barriers in the sport of golf, he is the product of a father who sacrificed, and endured many challenges to raise a son that has become an American icon.

CASE 2

Michael Jackson currently known as the "King of Pop," was the child in a family of eight children. His father Joe Jackson, a former Gary, Indiana blue-collar worker, dreamed that his children could have a better life than he did. He sacrificed the family's financial resources and dared to give his children what was thought to be impossible. In the 1960's he had formed one of the most successful black male groups of all time, called the Jackson Five (Campbell, 1993). He encouraged his children to work hard and strive for perfection. Through his relentless determination he created the Jackson dynasty that included his daughters LaToya, Rebee, and Janet. Joe Jackson was not only a dreamer but a visionary, for he recognized that the possibilities were endless if he provided guidance and support and believed in their ability to be great.

CASE 3

Sidney Poitier, in his eloquent account of his life "The Measure of A Man," gives his father credit for the overall development of his character. His father was the template for who he has become. His father's humanistic approach, has carried over in to his phenomenal acting career. Because of a sound upbringing, he has committed his life's work to roles that are indicative of his character and what he believes would have made his parents proud. Poitier attributes his outlook on life to his father who lived as if the whole world was his though they were very poor. He learned a sincere appreciation of nature and to value people. He acknowledges that those enriching experiences with his father has had a tremendous impact on his own parenting style. As a result of his childhood, his general philosophy is to respect, love, and live.

CASE 4

Yvonne Thornton, physician, vividly recounts the impact that her parents had during her childhood, particularly her father. Donald Thornton, a ditch digger in New York, dreamed that his six daughters would become physicians. He strongly urged his daughters to seek educational and professional opportunities that were unavailable to him in the 1940's. Under the auspices of their father the Thornton sisters gave musical performances, including at the Apollo Theater, to help finance their scholarship (Thornton, 1996). Mr. Thornton gave his children the drive and motivation to achieve their goals in the face of hardships such as racial and gender discrimination. Though only two became physicians, each is a highly successful professionals.

CASE 5

Venus and Serena William's, professional tennis players, father predicted that his daughters would someday be tennis champions. Richard Williams, a tennis coach, new that it would be a difficult task to accomplish this feat because typically African-American have not been prominent figures in this athletic arena. Despite negative opinions about the method in which he trained his daughters, he succumbed to the ridicule and raised two very successful daughters. Through undying perseverance, these two young women have made their mark in history as two of the most dynamic tennis players of the century. To date they have made unbelievable accomplishments such as winning the U.S. Open and Wimbledon.

CASE 6

Colin Powell, Secretary of State, has succeeded in becoming one of the most influential people of the 21st century. Before being appointed to this prestigious White House Cabinet position during the George W. Bush administration, he was the Chairman of the Joint Chiefs of Staff. Son of an Jamaican immigrant, Mr. Powell recognizes his father Luther Powell as key figure during his upbringing. Though his father literally came off of a banana boat to this country, he served as a great role model to young Colin. His father was an honest man that devoted himself to providing for his family. As he watched his father strive to support his family, he learned that anything was possible through hard word. By exemplifying this impeccable ethic, Colin Powell has certainly proven this notion to be true.

Though some may call these remarkable stories an exception, they are characteristic of effective fatherhood. These cases represent the attributes that African American fathers exhibit, support, strength, courage, perseverance, determination, compassion and the belief that their children will pass this legacy to their children. It appears that from this review that one can develop a Afrocentric theoretical model for examining the effectiveness of fatherhood. Such a model may be designed as follows:

Afrocentric Fatherhood Model

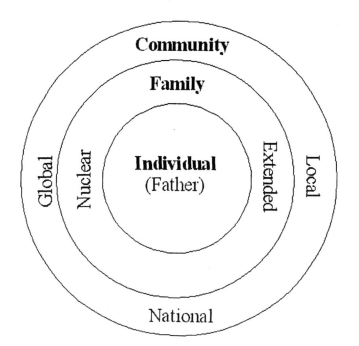

1. **Individual (father)**: Self-identity and respect including race and gender; responsibility; love and compassion; honesty and integrity; character; guidance; nurturing relationship; communication skills.
2. **Family**: Extended or nuclear; values; stability; resilience; support; discipline; education; and spirituality.
3. **Community**: Local and national environments (race relations, systems, institutions, public policy, corporate/private sector values and practices); global environment (economy, demographics, international relations, cultures and religions).

CONCLUSION

There is a myth that African American men contribute little or nothing to the well being of their families. However there is historical evidence and research that dispels this fallacy. African American men may not meet the standard definition of fathers but they have facilitated the overall successful endeavors for the black community for generations. So what is African American Fatherhood?

An African American father is the epitome of resilience. He has paid an enormous price for survival in an environment that continually impedes his success. He is the ancestor of men who through sweat and blood fought for their right as men in a racist society. More importantly he is the strength, discipline, and support that enables the next generation to prosper. The application of the Afrocentric fatherhood model developed in this paper should prove helpful to future researchers and/or service providers.

His presence is undoubtedly beneficial in the development of the child, physically, cognitively, socially and emotionally. The African American father makes a viable and necessary contribution to sustaining the family and ensuring that his children help to promote a productive society. He is not a mere victim of societal ills but a catalyst that forges a bright future for the African American family.

BIBLIOGRAPHY

Bennet, L., Jr. (1966). *Before the Mayflower*. Baltimore: Penguin Books.

Berger, A. S. (1985). *The Black middle class family*. Bristol, IN: Wyndham Hall Press.

Berk., L. E. (2000). *Child Development*. Boston, Massachusetts: Allyn Bacon Press.

Berube, M. (Ed.). (1982). *The American Heritage Dictionary* (2nd ed.). Boston, MA: Houghton Mifflin Company.

Black, C. V. (1993). *History of Jamaica*. Kingston, Jamaica: Carlong Publisher Caribbean Ltd.

Bowlby, J. (1969). *Attachment and loss: Attachment*. New York: Basic Books.

Bradley, C. (2000). The disciplinary practices of African American Fathers: A closer look. *Journal of African American Men, 5* (1), 43.

Bronfenbrenner, U. (1979). *The ecology of human development: Experiments by nature and design*. Cambridge, MA: Harvard University Press.

Campbell, L. D. (1993). *Michael Jackson: The king of pop*. Branden Books.

Children's Defense Fund. (2000). *The state of America's children: Yearbook 2000.* Washington, D.C.

Daniels, C. R. (1998). *Lost fathers: The politics of fatherlessness in America.* New York: St. Martins Press.

Federal Bureau of Investigation. (1999). *FBI Uniform Crime Report.* Washington, D.C.: U. S. Department of Justice.

Greif, G. L., Hrabowski, F. A., & Maton, K. I. (1998). African American fathers of high achieving sons: Using outstanding members of an at-risk population to guide intervention. *The Journal of Contemporary Human Services, 79* (1), 45-60.

Hetherington, E. M., & Stanley-Hagan, M. M. (1997). "The effects of divorce on fathers and their children." In M. E. Lamb (ed.), *The role of the father in child development.* New York, NY: Wiley.

Hill, S. A. and Sprague, H. J. (1999). Parenting in black and white families: The unteraction of gender with race and class. *Gender and Society, 13*, 480-502.

McAdoo, J. L. (1979). Father-child interaction patterns and self-esteem in black preschool children. *Journal of Nursery Education, 34,* 46-53.

Muzi, M. J. (2000). *The experience of parenting.* New Jersey: Prentice Hall.

Popenoe, D. (1996). *Life without father.* New York: Martin Kessler Books.

Poitier, S. (2001). *The measure of a man: A spiritual autobiography.* San Francisco, CA: Harper Collins Publishers.

Powell, C. (1995). *My American journey.* New York, NY: Ballantine Books.

Roberts, D. (1998). "The absent Black father." In C. R. Daniels (Ed.), *Lost fathers: The politics of fatherlessness in America.* New York: St. Martins Press.

Segal, R. (1995). *The Black diaspora.* New York: Farrar Straus and Groux.

Strege, J. (1998). *Tiger: A biography of Tiger Woods.* Broadway Books.

Tanfer, K., & Mott, F. (1997, January). *The Meaning of Fatherhood.* Paper presented at a workshop at the Urban Institute, Washington, D.C.

Thornton, Y. S. (1996). *The Ditch Diggers Daughters.* New York, NY: Penguin Books Ltd.

U. S. Department of Health and Human Services. (2000, June). *HHS Fatherhood Initiative.* Washington, D.C.: HHS Press.

U. S. Department of Justice. (2001, March). *Sourcebook of Criminal Justice Statistics.* Washington, D.C.: Bureau of justice statistics.

Willis, W. (1997). "Families with African American roots." In E. W. Lynch and Marcia J. Hanson (Eds.), *Developing cross cultural competencies.* Baltimore: Paul H Brooks Publishing.

Chapter 4

THEATRE AND THE RE-CREATION OF THE BLACK EXPERIENCE

I. Peter Ukpokodu
University of Kansas

ABSTRACT

Drawing inspiration from the prominent place Africa has taken in the African-American imagination since the 1950s and '60s, and especially the revisiting and exploring by African-American artists of the cultural, spiritual, and historical connections, the paper examines how African-American dramatists have used the art of the theatre to re-create the black experience. Beginning from Olaudah Equiano's *Narratives* to establish remembered history, the paper focuses on the analysis of the eleven episodes of George C. Wolfe's groundbreaking drama, *The Colored Museum*, that uses the "epic" technique of Bertolt Brecht to "historicize" the black experience in the Americas. Wolfe's re-creation covers a wide historical period (from the slave trade in Africa through the devastating middle ages to the contemporary) and various cultural experiences in America. The paper concludes by looking at some theatrical developments that have taken place since the production of *The Colored Museum* and how *Colored Contradictions*, among others, has extended Wolfe's cultural history to the end of the twentieth century.

THEATRE AND THE RE-CREATION OF THE BLACK EXPERIENCE

We are almost a nation of dancers, musicians, and poets. Thus every great event, such as a triumphant return from battle or other cause of public rejoicing, is celebrated in public dances, which are accompanied with songs and music suited to the occasion. The assembly is separated into four divisions, which dance either apart or in succession, and each with a character peculiar to itself. The first division contains the married men, who, in their dances frequently exhibit feats of arms and the representation of a battle. To these succeed the married women, who dance in the second division. The young men occupy the third, and the maidens the fourth. Each represents some interesting scene of real life, such as a great achievement, domestic employment, a pathetic story, or some rural sport;

and as the subject is generally founded on some recent event, it is therefore ever new. This gives our dances a spirit and variety that I have scarcely seen elsewhere. We have many musical instruments, particularly drums of different kinds, a piece of music which resembles a guitar, and another much like a stickado. These last are chiefly used by betrothed virgins, who play on them on all grand festivals. (Olaudah Equiano, p. 36)[1]

In his book, *The Interesting Narrative of the Life of Olaudah Equiano, or Gustavus Vassa, The African*, Equiano, an ex-slave, re-creates his experiences and his native, cultural identity. Generally regarded as "the first great African American slave narrative,"[2] the book is the remembered history of the vicissitudes of Equiano's life, and of the things he had "witnessed" and experienced. Equiano understands the limits of remembered history. He was only eleven years old when sold into slavery. "Such is the imperfect sketch my memory has furnished me with, of the manners and customs of a people among whom I first drew my breath."[3] It is this personal memory or memory as passed on collectively or individually from one generation or person to another, that has been central to artistic creativity by some African-Americans.

In a paper delivered at the Langston Hughes Lecture at the University of Kansas, Lawrence, Kansas in April 2000, the distinguished professor of African and African-American Studies, Emmanuel Obiechina, examines among other things the phenomenon of slaves and ex-slaves like Equiano (Gustavus Vass), Ottobah Cugoano (James Stewart), Samuel Ajayi Crowther, James Wright, Ayuba Suleiman (Job Solomon), Abubakar al-Siddiq (Edward Donlan), Ali Eisami (William Harding), and Ignatius Sancho as authors, narrators, storytellers and performers. He points out that their art came from the continental African heritage of fireside improvisational storytelling and from community gatherings and festivities where raconteurs, griots, minstrels, balladmakers, and epic performers reigned supreme in a participatory affirmation of a people's common culture. It was through this art form which was a part of the "cultural personality" impressed upon them at a young age that children of the African diaspora as slaves and ex-slaves gave vent to their emotional anguish. Says Obiechina:

> They told stories about themselves and their tragedy...mainly because self-dramatization had effects more significantly redeeming to the narrators than simple, overt expectations of sympathy. They told their stories because the telling of them eased their pent-up feelings: talking about their misfortunes had therapeutic use by lightening the pressure upon the heart. Most importantly, the re-enacting brought forcefully back to the faculties a sense of the past, which painfully as it may have been, fulfilled the significant function of reinforcing their sense of human worth in the present. Like Coleridge's ancient mariner, these dispersed children of Africa poured their tales into the ears of their audiences, who were compelled to be attentive by the peculiar authenticities of the tales themselves and the thrill and fascination of vicarious identification. These tales, suffused

---

[1] Olaudah Equiano, *The interesting Narrative of the Life of Olaudah Equiano*, edited with an introduction by Robert J. Allison (Boston and New York: Bedford Books, 1995), p. 36. This edition is different in title from the first American printing, *The Interesting Narrative of the Life of Olaudah Equiano, or Gustavus Vassa, The African* (New York, 1791). In general, Equiano's *Narrative* was first published in 1789.

[2] See Robert J. Allison's introduction, p. 17.

[3] Equiano, p. 44.

with agony and suffering, were distilled from terrors so harrowing that there is nothing to compare with them in recent history, except perhaps the Holocaust.[4]

The slaves and ex-slaves used their remembered African history and culture to forge their art. It is because of them that artistic "Africanisms in America"[5] have survived to be part of the African-American heritage. Centuries separated from *The Interesting Narrative of the Life of Olaudeh Equiano, or Gustavus Vassa, The African* some contemporary African-American playwrights have applied memory or history as a theatrical device through which to gain a glimpse of the African past and of African descendants in America. The memory and the history they dramatize are not pure history, if there is ever pure history, but an agency to interpret the past through dramatic filters. Equiano has warned us that memory furnishes an imperfect sketch. The paper will draw examples from the skits of George W. Wolfe's *The Colored Museum*.

Wolfe approaches his theatrical reflection of African-American history by employing two artistic techniques—the museum and the Epic—in his play, *The Colored Museum*. The two techniques are complementary: the exhibits of a museum, because they are individual pieces of art works, are similar to the individual episodes of the Epic Theatre. Though each individual exhibit piece or episode has its own limited life and story, the whole story is only fully comprehended and most meaningful when all the exhibits and episodes are looked at and "listened" to.

The two techniques work well together in *The Colored Museum*. An Epic style, as developed by Erwin Piscator (1893-1966) and Bertolt Brecht (1891-1956),[6] has a broad sweep of subject matter in which multimedia techniques—narrative, dramatic, and cinematic—are readily used as desired and relevant. The mixture of media in production may render the theatrical event episodic, but the episodes and the "distancing" are necessary to allow the intellectual engagement of the audience both in the historical process and in the ability to see the unity in the episodes and to make informed judgement. Because the intent is to intelligently comprehend the historical, socio-economic and political conditions of real life in the real world that the theatrical event addresses, everything used in the production is expected to be functional, not decorative. The entire purpose is to arrive at an "alienation" (verfremdung) effect. The concept is not to alienate the audience at the theatre but to invite them to have a new, fresh look at what is usually familiar. The fresh look will lead to questions and discussions in which the audience will find the reasons to take sides and pass judgement as in politics, with the ultimate hope that the audience will apply this to make a change in the real world. It is this attitude that Wolfe brings to his play to make the audience examine the history of African Americans.

Wolfe situates *The Colored Museum* in a museum and he refers to the episodes in the play as "the exhibits." A museum, among other things, is a treasury of history, and the

---

[4] Emmanuel Obiechina, "Common Themes in African Diasporan Literature: Something shored up from History's Monumental Wreckage" (unpublished), Langston Hughes Lecture, University of Kansas, Lawrence, Kansas, April 12, 2000, p. 2.

[5] The title of a conference organized by the National Association of African-American Heritage Preservation and held in New orleans from September 26-30, 2000. The conference focused on the shared heritage of two continents. It is noteworthy that New Orleans is fondly referred to as the Voodoo Capital of the United States.

[6] The Epic is now mostly identified with Bertolt Brecht who used both playwriting and theory to popularize it.

playwright does not hesitate to locate the historical place and world as he sets the stage: "THE STAGE: White walls and recessed lighting. A starkness befitting a museum where the myths and madness of black/Negro/colored Americans are stored."[7] The cast of two men and three women is "all black." The importance of this description dawns on the audience as the black performers are placed within white walls. The history that Wolfe is producing is one of blacks in white America, or of a minority in a majority culture. He makes it clear that the minority group he is referring to as "colored" have been known by other names and adjectives over the ages: "black/Negro/colored Americans." It is then, among other relationships, an evolving history of the names of that black being in America currently referred to collectively as the African American. In the true Brechtian spirit, one is invited to reflect on, and investigate, the origins of such names, why it has been necessary to portray oneself in a particular image, and the social, political, and economic climates that have energized the change of name—what Wolfe calls "the myths and madness" of and about such a people.

The museum that Wolfe takes the audience through contains eleven exhibits of African-American history from slavery to the contemporary period. The exhibits do not account for a complete history of the African American, if such a history is ever possible. His selections seem to be guided by an artistic interest primarily, and to this he subordinates his choice of historical subjects and moments. His exhibits express the particular view he has about a particular event or subject that had perhaps helped to shape African Americans in America or en route to America from Africa. The eleven exhibits—Git on Board, Cookin' with Aunt Ethel, The Photo Session, Soldier with a Secret, The Gospel According to Miss Roj, The Hairpiece, The Last Mama-on-the-Couch Play, Symbiosis, Lala's Opening, Permutations, and The Party—are not of equal importance; indeed none of the pieces is as important and far-reaching as the first one.

"Git on Board" is a humorous, brief history of the African-American experience that opens up with "Blackness. Cut by drums pounding. Then slides rapidly flashing before us. Images we've all seen before, of African slaves being captured, loaded onto ships, tortured. The images flash, flash, flash. The drums crescendo. Blackout..." (p. 5). Wolfe's choice of the word "blackness" instead of "darkness" is intended to refer to the continent, Africa. It does not refer to a stage without light that would be described as a dark stage. The stage is not dark, for it is only after the 'drums crescendo" that there is blackout. It is, therefore, the blackness of the African continent where the history begins. Images of Africa and of the African performing arts—the rich cultural heritage that is partly the foundation of African-American performance—are represented by the "blackness" and the pounding drums. The slides the audience is shown confirm its African location and the history of slavery.

When the lights come on stage and Miss Pat welcomes the audience aboard the Celebrity Slaveship that is "departing the Gold Coast and making short stops at Bahia, Port au Prince, and Havana before reaching its final destination of Savannah (p. 5), the vision of a torturous history is set. Gold Coast, Bahia (Brazil), Port au Prince (Haiti), and Havana are historical landmarks in slavery. It is imperative that we discuss the importance of these places, if only briefly.

Gold Coast (now Ghana) was one of the principal West African coastal countries that supplied slaves to Europe and the Americas. The Elmina Castle near Accra, the capital city,

---

[7] George C. Wolfe, *The Colored Museum* in *Black Thunder*, ed. William B. Branch (New York; Penguin, 1992), p. 3. Unless otherwise indicated, all page references to the play use this edition.

where slaves were "processed" and "stored" for shipment overseas still stands today as a monumental historical landmark to the days of the trans-Atlantic slave trade. It was built by the Portuguese in 1482. As Robert J. Allison points out, "slavery to the Europeans was an economic relationship, and a slave a piece of property":

> The slave trade, which had begun before Columbus reached the New World (the Portuguese had brought the first African slaves to Europe in 1441), by the 1750s was well organized and brutally efficient. Of the more than eleven million African slaves brought to America between 1518 and 1850, more than six million were carried over after 1750. Most of the slaves were taken to the Americas to work the sugar plantations of Brazil and the Caribbean and the rice, tobacco, and cotton plantations of mainland North America. Others worked on small farms, as servants in cities, as skilled artisans, or as sailors.[8]

Gold Coast was a principal trader and supplier of slaves. In the Cape Coast (Southwestern Ghana), skirmishes were frequently fought to capture slaves. History has an interesting, gory record of some fights that a certain Thomas Osiat, a grand caboceroe (principal trader) of Cape Coast, conducted against the neighboring Elmina. Osiat took many prisoners in one of such skirmishes. Among them were nine petty caboceroes from Elmina who had competed against him. Osiat had their heads cut off, and he "sent them next day in a bag to his opponents."[9]

Gold Coast could also be interpreted as Wolfe's metaphor for all the countries in Africa where slaves were taken to the Americas. While historians have not agreed on the exact number of African slaves imported to the Americas, there is a consensus that the "aggregate approaches staggering proportions." The figure varies from 13,887,500 (Edward E. Dunbar), 14,650,000 (R. R. Kuczynski), to 9,566,100 (Philip D. Curtin).[10] Basil Davidson's opinion is that it "appears reasonable to suggest that...it cost Africa at least fifty million souls," and that this estimate is "certainly on the low side."[11]

Bahia, Port au Prince, and Havana are representative of places that hold cultural affinity to Africa because of the survival of cultural retentions. Brazil, where Bahia is located, is the second largest black population in the world, and Bahia is fondly referred to as the capital of African culture in the Americas. The three countries—Brazil, Haiti, and Cuba where Bahia, Port au Prince, and Havana are located respectively—are heavily influenced by the Yoruba (Nigeria) traditional religion in their respective practice of Candomble, Voodoo, and Santeria. The music, art, and dance also show the cultural link between those countries and Africa. But it is the practice of religion and in food that the African cultural retentions are most complete. The Orishas (divinities and spiritual beings) hold an important place in the religious and social lives of the people. Eshu (messenger of the gods), Ogun (god of iron and war), Shango (god of thunder and lightning) are among the many gods that have been brought over from Africa and retained. In some cases in which Catholicism and African traditional religion have come together, some form of syncretism has arisen as in Voodoo in Haiti, or as in Candomble in Brazil, where a forced acculturation process has made the African descendants to see the similarities between Catholic saints and African Orishas. The playwright lightly refers to the

---

[8] Allison, p. 3.

[9] Basil Davidson, *The African Slave Trade* (Boston: Little, Brown and Company, 1961), pp. 95-96.

[10] John Hope Franklin and Alfred A. Moss, Jr., *From Slavery to Freedom: A History of Negro Americans*, 40th edition (New York: Alfred A Knopf, 1988), pp. 37-39.

[11] Davidson, pp. 80-81.

religious practice of Christian conversion as the only way to make it through the thunderstorm—"abandon your God and worship a new one" (p. 7). There is a veiled reference to 1452 when Pope Nicholas V authorized the Portuguese, in the name of Christianity, to attack and enslave "the Moors, heathens and other enemies of Christ."[12]

Wolfe leaves no doubt as to the territory most of the slaves are delivered. Savannah, Georgia, thus bears the stamp of arrival in the United States as the final destiny for the slaves. As the home of the first steamship by that name to cross the Atlantic in 1819, Savannah became a metaphor for the fast way of crossing the dreadful "middle passage." It is important to note how the playwright attempts to lessen the horrors associated with the middle passage by humorously pointing out how Miss Pat would come to the people's assistance:

> If there's anything I can do to make the middle passage more pleasant, press the little button overhead and I'll be with you faster than you can say, "Go down, Moses..." Thanks for flying Celebrity and here's hoping you have a pleasant takeoff (p. 6).

There was nothing "pleasant" in the middle passage. The middle passage was the first real indication that the slaves would never return to their homes again. Equiano gives vivid descriptions of the untold suffering while crossing the Atlantic in his *Narrative*:

> [T]he whole ship's cargo [humans] were confined together, it became absolutely pestilential. The closeness of the place, and the heat of the climate, added to the number in the ship, which was so crowded that each had scarcely room to turn himself, almost suffocated us. This produced copious perspirations, so that the air soon became unfit for respiration, from a variety of loathsome smells, and brought on a sickness among the slaves, of which many died—thus falling victims to the improvident avarice, as I may call it, of their purchasers. This wretched situation was again aggravated by the galling of the chains, now became unsupportable, and the filth of the necessary tubs [latrines], into which the children often fell, and were almost suffocated. The shrieks of the women, and the groans of the dying, rendered the whole a scene of horror almost inconceivable.[13]

Equiano points out how some of the slaves preferred death to that form of existence, and when they found a chance jumped into the sea and drowned. Those who were forcefully rescued from drowning were given severe flogging to discourage future attempts at suicide. "Slaves who fell sick were simply pitched overboard," and when British antislaving patrols were instituted in the nineteenth century, slave traders "threw their whole living cargoes into the sea" to escape the impounding of their vessels.[14] Wolfe refers to this history when he writes, "...let me assure you Celebrity has no intention of throwing you overboard and collecting the insurance. We value you!" (p. 6).

Savannah also shared with the other territories the terrifying incidents of slave rebellion. It is for fear of this that Miss Pat prohibits code language that could be used to send messages of revolt. Such codes could be through songs ("call-and-response singing") or by drums. Talking drums are an African invention that send messages in codes and could become an instrument of rebellion. So rebellious were the slaves in Savannah and in Georgia in general

---

[12] Robin D. G. Kelley and Earl Lewis, ed., *A History of African Americans* (Oxford & New York: Oxford University Press, 2000), p. 9.

[13] Equiano, p. 56.

[14] Davidson, p. 94.

that during the war of independence the state had lost an estimated seventy-five percent of her fifteen thousand slaves through defection. Runaway slaves who had fought for Britain in Savannah were in 1786 still referring to themselves as the "King of England's soldiers" as they harassed Georgia countryside in a resistance movement.[15] But the survival instinct would not be limited to creating songs and music of rebellion; from the slave labor and artistic creativity would emerge James Brown and the Fabulous Flames, the Watusi dance, the Funky Chicken, and the athletic feat of basketball millionaires! (p. 7)

Using the "time warp" as a theatrical technique of covering a lot of American history, Wolfe is able to guide the audience through important periods and events. The American Revolution of the 1770s, according to Miss Pat, gave the U.S. the "exclusive rights" to the lives of the people who would later be referred to as African Americans (p. 8). The resultant American Declaration of Independence in 1776 that proclaims that "all men are created equal" would be seized upon by African slaves in Massachusetts and New Hampshire to petition for freedom in 1777. By 1778 black businessman Paul Cuffe and his brother John have initiated a refusal to pay taxes, claiming that there should be no taxation without representation. The Civil War that began in 1861— "which means you [African Americans] would vote Republican until F.D.R. comes along" (p. 8), the Great Depression of the 1930s, the First World War (1914-1918), the Second World War (1939-1945), the Korean War (1950-1953) nd the Vietnam War (1961-1973) are all introduced humorously without the dates. The purpose is clear; it is to reflect on the historical process in which African Americans "play a major role in" (p. 8).

The time warp technique also allows Wolfe to visit the 1960s and reveal some key African-American cultural and political leaders. Martha and the Vandellas—Martha Reeves, Annette Sterling, and Rosalind Ashford—are three female vocalists who, after serving as backup vocalists for Marvin Gaye in a Motown recording, released their own album "Heat Wave" in 1963. The group drew on the gospel and blues traditions of African Americans to create popular dance records such as "Dancing in the Streets," "Nowhere to Run" and "I'm Ready for Love."

Though Diahann Carroll (Carol Diahann Johnson), a Tony award winner for her lead role in the musical *No Strings*, has screen credits for such films as *Carmen Jones*, *Porgy and Bess*, *Paris Blues*, *Hurry Sundown*, *Roots: The Next Generation*, and *I Know Why the Caged Bird Sings*, it is her performance in the *Julia* series that ran from 1968-1971 that *The Colored Museum* places emphasis by referring to it as "'Julia' with Miss Diahann Carroll" (p. 8). This is important to Wolfe and to African-American performance history because *Julia* was the only sitcom since *Amos 'n' Andy* (1951-1953) to star an African American who was not playing the role of a domestic. Carroll's role was that of a widowed nurse raising a son. She also starred in *Dynasty* (1984-1987) as Dominique Devereaux.

The Supremes, made up of Diana Ross, Florence Ballard, and Mary Wilson, were the most successful American singing group at their peak in the 1960s and 1970s. The group captured the imagination of youth when in 1964 and 1965 it produced five consecutive hits that were on top of the charts as number one. Diana Ross would later leave the group for a successful singing and acting career in 1970. Wolfe puts all these cultural success stories amidst the turbulence of the 1960s Civil Rights Movements by bringing in Malcolm X (1925-1965) and Martin Luther King (1929-1968) who represent two different African-American

---

[15] Franklin and Moss, Jr., pp. 70-71.

approaches to civil leadership. The riotous nature of the period is symbolized by the renewed intensity of the drumming that Miss Pat has labelled as rebellious.

Wolfe completes the brief history by making the Celebrity Slaveship touch down at last in Savannah. The image of slaves as goods is reinforced in a final stage direction (p. 9):

(Luggage begins to revolve onstage from offstage left, going past MISS PAT and revolving offstage right. Mixed in with the luggage are two male slaves and a woman slave, complete with luggage and ID tags around their necks.)

Africans have arrived! Episodes from their lives as they become African Americans are frozen for the spectator/audience to see at this museum of African-American history.

"Cookin' with Aunt Ethel" confronts the stereotype of the Aunt Jemima / Mammy figure of the African-American woman. Wolf puts here those things commonly associated with African Americans—jazz, pizzazz, blues, and attitude. He uses the blues to convey various experiences of African Americans from domestic work in white homes to "preoccupation with the texture of [one's] hair" (p. 9). Having created African Americans of any shade from black to yellow, Aunt Ethel reminds everyone:

You have baked
Baked yourself a batch of Negroes
Yes, you have baked yourself
Baked yourself a batch of Negroes
(She pulls from the pot a handful of Negroes, black dolls.)
But don't ask me what to do with 'em now that you got 'em, 'cause, child, that's your problem (p. 10).

Wolfe is reminding the visitor to his museum that African Americans are created by the American society, and that America is responsible for how they turn out. They are America's children and America's problem.

"The Photo Session" is a satire on the African-American middle class. The contradictions between the Ebony Magazine lifestyle of Girl and Guy and their real social life that has been eclipsed by the former are almost schizophrenic. Girl and Guy have given away their life for a pretentious existence, and they are "suffocating" as if they were "not human anymore" (p. 12).

The confused experiences and pains of African-American soldiers engaged in various military actions in foreign territories from the Spanish-American War through the Vietnam War are the focus of the episode, "A Soldier with a Secret." The irony the piece points out is that African Americans, in the name of American patriotism, were fighting abroad in wars for a country and a government that did not recognize their full citizenship and civil rights at home. The African-American soldier thus faced emotional psychological, and physical pains. this is the problem Junie and his friends have to face—that "these colored boys ain't gonna be the same after this war. They aint' gonna have no kind of happiness" (p. 13). In this instance, drugs are the mode of escape from the contradictions of their war experiences as Junie goes "around healin' the hurtin'" by administering the needle so that the soldiers become dead to the pain (14).

"The Gospel According to Miss Roj" addresses gay issues through a parody of snap and drag queens. Miss Roj is an effeminate man, with much sensitivity to the daily problems confronting African Americans in the urban areas like New York. Once s/he is drunk, s/he becomes a fiery proponent of "R.E.S.P.E.C.T" and becomes eloquent and fearless about truth. Note the analysis of societal problems, as in New York:

> A high-rise goes up. You can't get no job. Come on, everybody, and dance. A whole race of people gets trashed and debased.... Some sick bitch throws her baby out the window 'cause she thinks it's the Devil....
> Snap for every time you walk past someone lying in the street, smelling like frozen piss and shit and you don't see it. Snap for every crazed bastard who kills himself so as to get the jump on being killed. And snap for every sick muthafucker who, bored with carrying around his fear, takes to shooting up other people (p. 17).

Miss Roj takes a harsh stance on the plight of African Americans, and is not worried about how people view her/him. S/He neither asks for societal approval nor acceptance. All s/he wants is "Respect."

In "The Hairpiece," Wolfe deals with an issue that has spawned great attention in the African-American community, especially among African-American females. What is "good" or "bad" hair to an African American female? The focus of the skit is on the dialogue between two wigs, one "kinky" (Janine), the other "straight" (LaWanda). They are discussing the reasons that Woman should wear one instead of the other when Woman goes to end the relationship with her lover. In this skit Wolfe draws attention to the fact that in the social consciousness of African Americans, even the trivial could become important in a cultural history. One sympathetically observes that the Woman central to the story no longer has hair:

> LaWanda: What hair! She ain't got no hair! She done fried, dyed, de-chemicalized her shit to death.
> Janine: And all that's left is that buck-naked scalp of hers, sittin' up there apologizin' for being odd-shaped and ugly (p. 18).

Satirizing *A Raisin in the Sun, For Colored Girls who have Considered Suicide / When the Rainbow is Enuf*, and *The Medea*, "The Last Mama-on-the-Couch Play" pokes fun of the stereotypes of African Americans now found in mainstream drama. There is some seriousness directed at various levels of oppression, be they racial, gender, filial, parental, and marital. Son (Walter-Lee-Beau-Willie-Jones) who is African American is oppressed by his boss, a white man. He complains that every day "Mr. Charlie! Mr. Boss Man!...he's wipin' his feet on" him (Son). He is concerned about his ability to be a successful man in the society. He tries very hard to command things around the house only to find that the women in his household—his mother, his wife and his sister—are just as strong as he is, if not stronger. He is particularly threatened by the success of his sister who has a college education and recites poems and dramatic verses that Son does not understand. The skit builds in frustration that is only broken when Mama starts singing and the cast comes dancing. Wolfe seems to be looking at the barriers faced by African Americans, and how to release the overwhelming, nihilistic, suicidal impulse through singing and dancing:

> If we want to live
> We have got to
> We have got to
> Dance...and dance...and dance... (p. 28)

"Symbiosis" gives a heartwrenching and painfully honest story of the coming-of-age of the African-American male. The issue it raises is whether the African American must reject his culture in order to survive in a white world. Says Man, "...my survival depends on it" as he throws away his afro comb, dashiki, afro sheen, autographs from cultural and political leaders, books, and black musical albums (p. 29). It is the question of the melting-pot, assimilationist view of America versus that of multiculturalism.

It is important to see Kid and Man as the same person. The level of adapting to a society here is almost schizophrenic as the character as Man rechecks his cultural heritage in order to survive, and as he as Kid keeps yearning for those very roots he is casting away. Man seems uncompromising in his desire to be somebody: "If I'm to become what I'm to become, then you've got to.... I have no history. I have no past" (p. 29). Sad as Man's statement is, Wolfe points out the impossibility of totally rejecting one's history, one's past because Man, as the skit comes to an end, believes he could be "black only on weekends and holidays." Kid has "a death grip on THE MAN'S arm" (p. 31) that is impossible to loosen. Here is quintessential Wolfe checking the pulse of African Americans at the rise of the "Buppie"—the Black Urban Professional.

The situation between Man and Kid in "Symbiosis" is almost paralleled in the relationship between Lala and Little Girl in "Lala's Opening." The issue that seems to be uppermost in the playwright's mind is the sad history of African-American performing artists and writers who had to leave America to Europe because the international scene was more receptive and hospitable to them than their own country. Ira Aldridge, Paul Robeson, James Baldwin, and Josephine Baker found favors overseas. Wolfe poses the question through Lala:

> Now, before I dazzle you with more of my limitless talent, tell me something, America....
> Why has it taken you so long to recognize my artistry? Mother France opened her loving
> arms and Lala came running. All over the world Lala was embraced. But here, ha! You
> spat at Lala. Was I too exotic? Too much woman, or what?
> [..] But the Paul la Robesons, the James la Baldwins, the Josephine la Bakers, who was
> my godmother, you know. The Lala Lamazing Graces you kick out. You drive... (p. 33).

Here is African-American theatre drawing attention to its own historical suffering in America, and by so doing pays tribute to those pioneers who created the road for others to follow. It is also a note of thanks to those European countries, especially France, that gave home to them. This, the playwright accomplishes by making Lala deliver some lines in French:

> Au revoir je vais partir maintenant
> Je veux dire maintenant
> Au revoir
> Au revoir... (p. 34)

No better tribute could be paid to a country than to speak its language. Language, after all, is a significant primary purveyor of culture.

"Permutations" is very Brechtian. It addresses issues of female sexuality and the growth and development of a new generation of African Americans in a way never thought of as normal and usual. The audience therefore pulls back to think of how the normal and the familiar (it is important to remember that the character central to this sketch is named "Normal") has been rendered strange and vaguely familiar. Human pregnancy and labor take the form of a bird laying an egg. The process is particularly painful to Normal because she is "very young" and naive. She knows, however, that as the only person...who ever lay themselves an egg," she and her egg are "special" (p. 40).

Like a doctor checking on the heartbeats of a pregnant womb, Normal "puts her ear to the egg and listens intently;" she reports of "three...four...five, six" and more hearts, "all alive, beatin' out life inside" her egg (p. 40). The babies that will come out of the egg will be all kinds of shades:

> Any day now, this egg is gonna crack open and what's gonna come out be the likes of which nobody has ever seen. My babies! And their skin is gonna turn all kinds of shades in the sun and their hair a be growin' every which-a-way. And it won't matter and they won't care 'cause it's not everyday a bunch of babies break outa a white egg and start to live.
> And nobody better not try and hurt my babies 'cause if they do, they gonna have to deal with me. (p. 40)

This passage is the heart of "Permutations." Wolfe presents the historical emergence of African Americans of all colors. The focus is a "black" woman laying a "white" egg—his theatrical euphemism for interracial relationships or the miscegenation that began a race of people that come in every color of the spectrum in America. Whatever color, the babies are Normal's and are normal. The emergence of the first product of miscegenation in America must have been regarded with some amount of strangeness, and Wolfe tries to recapture theatrically that level of strangeness. He comforts the audience by letting us know that to a mother who knows the making of the child and therefore holds the history, no baby is strange.[16]

Wolfe ends the historical tour of *The Colored Museum* with "The Party" in which he brings together all the characters of the various sketches. His strong point is that all these various characters and the events identified with them, even in their "colored contradictions," and "madness," are aspects of the African-American history and must be understood and embraced as such. Topsy/Everybody affirms the necessary relationship between history and a dynamic culture: "...I'm not what I was ten years ago or ten minutes ago. I'm all of that and then some. And whereas I can't live inside yesterday's pain, I can't live without it" (p. 42). No history is without its pains and joys, its glory and shame. People must celebrate their "cultural madness" (p. 41).

The Colored Museum ends in the epic style in which it begins, except that this time the focus is no longer on the beginning of the history in slavery in Africa but on the historical experiences of African Americans in the United States. It is therefore a continuing history in which what is not covered in the eleven exhibits is selectively flashed before the audience. It is a history from the beginning to the present:

---

[16] Langston Hughes captures a similar episode of miscegenation in a more realistic mode in *Mother and Child*. There, the African-American women gathered at the monthly meeting of the Salvation Rock Missionary Society are "gossiping as usual" but this time "persistently around a single tense and fearful topic—a certain newborn child." A married white woman has had an affair with an African American and has given birth to a colored baby! Says Mrs. Sam Jones: "Everybody knows can't no good come out o' white and colored love." See *Mother and Child* in Woodie King and Ron Milner, ed. *Black Drama Anthology* (New York: Penguin, 1971), pp. 399-405. It is important to know that the mothers of the babies in both plays (*Mother and Child* and "Permutations") cherish their babies.

(All of a sudden, madness erupts on stage. The sculptures begin to speak all at once. Images of black/Negroid/colored Americans begin to flash—images of them dancing past the madness, caught up in the madness, being lynched, rioting, partying, surviving. Mixed in with these images are all the characters from the exhibits...) (p. 42)

We again hear the voice of Miss Pat who has been "serving" us (p. 5) reminding us to take our baggage "before exiting" (p. 44). The play and the audience have gone full circle.

The tradition of Wolfe's theatrical approach to African-American history would be continued by African-American scholars and playwrights. Indeed, his phrase "colored contradictions" (p. 44) would be used later by two African-American scholars, Harry J. Elam, Jr., and Robert Alexander as the title for an anthology of contemporary African-American plays. As in the groundbreaking drama, *The Colored Museum*, *Colored Contradictions* explores "new ideas as well as issues of historical resonance, new dramatic forms as well as traditional realism;" Elam further explains that:

> These plays evidence new directions and spirit in African-American cultural production. Their range in subject matter, style, structure, and language underscores the recognition that "black experience" can no longer be viewed as a monolith, but must be understood for its variety, its multiple permutations and contradictions.... They press against the externally and internally imposed boundaries placed on African-American cultural expression.[17]

Let me conclude by going back to Equiano's *Narrative*. Equiano remembers the cultural history from which he comes. He remembers coming from a nation of performers and he remembers the horrors of the middle passage. He writes from experience. Wolfe does not live Equiano's experiences and times. Those times and experiences however, have come down to him both as oral and written histories, and from many sources. Over the ages they have become part of the African-American transmitted knowledge existing in the public domain. It is from this body of knowledge and from the experiences that Equiano did not live that Wolfe composes and interprets the African-American experience in theatrical terms. Earlier theatre artists have dramatized aspects of their experience, and newer dramatists have also enriched this creative history, and they continue to do so. Amiri Baraka's *The Slave* and *Junkies are Full of (SHHH...)*, James Baldwin's *Blues for Mister Charlie*, Charles Gordone's *No Place to be Somebody*, and August Wilson's *Joe Turner's Come and Gone*, *The Piano Lesson* and others have isolated aspects of the black experience for dramatization.[18] The collected plays in *Colored Contradictions* continue the exploration and interpretation of the black experience in theatrical terms. Wolfe is the representative choice here because his groundbreaking application of the epic technique allows us to view incidents from centuries of the black experience, at least from slavery and slave trade to 1986.[19] He and Equiano are not afraid to

---

[17] Harry J. Elam, Jr. and Robert Alexander, ed. *Colored Contradictions* (New York: Plume/Penguin, 1996), p. 1.

[18] See, for example, my forthcoming publication entitled "African Heritage from the Lenses of African-American Theatre and Film," *Journal of Dramatic Theory and Criticism*. Haile Gerima's *Sakofa*, August Wilson's *Joe Turner's Come and Gone* and *The Piano Lesson*, and Imamu Amiri Baraka's *Bloodrites* receive extensive interpretation.

[19] *The Colored Museum* was first produced on March 26, 1986, at the Crossroads Theater in New Brunswick, New Jersey.

"re-create" history even though they are aware of the "imperfect sketch that...memory" furnishes.[20] As the historians Robin D. G. Kelley and Earl Lewis have pointed out,

> Africa, and thus the place of African Americans in the world, [has since the 1950s and '60s] held an even more prominent place in the black imagination. Influenced by new political and cultural movements, African-American artists revisited the place of Africa in the black imagination, exploring feelings of community, cultural connection, and spirituality as well as loss and alienation.[21]

Wolfe is part of that new group of African-American artists exploring the cultural connection. It is Wilson, however, who is able to match the anguish of physical separation with the despair of spiritual loss. The "guitars" have replaced the "drums" of rebellion, and the bible the gods as African Americans begin to add to the black experience. All these theatre artists have dramatized to the American public a fictionalized history of African Americans in a refreshing way not possible and permissible in factual history. By bringing humor to tragic experiences, they have made harrowing incidents bearable to audiences. They have also indirectly taught us how and how not to live through the insights provided in their dramas. They continue the legacy of making the African American visible, audible and tactile in the space shared with other human beings.

WORKS CITED

Baldwin, James. *Blues for Mister Charlie.* In *Contemporary Black Drama.* Ed. Clinton F. Oliver and Stephanie Sills. New York: Charles Scriber's Sons, 1971.

Baraka, Imamu Amiri. *Bloodrites.* In *Black Drama Anthology.* Ed. Woodie King and Ron Milner, New York: Penguin, 1986.

_____. *Junkies are Full of (SHHH...).* In *Black Drama Anthology.*

Branch, William B., ed. *Black Thunder.* New York: Penguin, 1992.

Davidson, Basil. *The African Slave Trade.* Boston and Toronto: Little, Brown and Company, 1961.

Elam Jr., Harry J. and Robert Alexander, ed. *Colored Contradictions.* New York: Plume/Penguin, 1996.

Equiano, Olaudah. *The Interesting Narrative of the Life of Olaudah Equiano.* Ed. Robert J. Allison. Boston and New York: Bedford Books, 1995.

Franklin, John Hope, and Alfred A. Moss, Jr. *From Slavery to Freedom: A History of Negro Americans,* 40th edition. New York: Alfred A. Knopf, 1988.

Gerima, Haile. *Sankofa.* Accra, Ghana and Los Angeles: Sankofa Productions, 1993.

Gordone, Charles. *No Place to be Somebody.* In *Contemporary Black Drama.*

Hughes, Langston. *Mother and Child.* In *Black Drama Anthology.*

Kelley, Robin D. G. and Earl Lewis, ed. *A History of African Americans.* Oxford and New York: Oxford University Press, 2000.

King, Woodie and Ron Milner, ed. *Black Drama Anthology.* New York: Penguin, 1986.

---

[20] Equiano, p. 44.
[21] Kelley and Lewis, see unnumbered page facing 302.

Obiechina, Emmanuel. *"Common Themes in African Diasporan Literature: Something Shored up from History's Monumental Wreckage."* Unpublished Lecture: University of Kansas, 2000.

Oliver, Clinton F. and Stephanie Sills, ed. *Contemporary Black Drama*. New York: Charles Scribner's Sons, 1971.

Ukpokodu, I. Peter. "African Heritage from the Kenses of African-American Theatre and Film." *Journal of Dramatic Theory and Criticism* (forthcoming).

Wilson, August. *Joe Turner's Come and Gone*. New York: Penguin, 1988.

_____. *The Piano Lesson*. New York: Penguin, 1990.

Wolfe, George C. *The Colored Museum*. In *Black Thunder*. Ed. William B. Branch. New York: Penguin, 1992.

Chapter 5

CONTRIBUTIONS OF AFRICAN AMERICAN MALES TO THE SCIENCES AND MEDICINE

Robert B. Sanders

ABSTRACT

The scientists included in this document represent the fields of biochemistry, biology, chemistry, computer science, engineering, entomology, genetics, geology, mathematics, medicine, physics, psychology, zoology, and inventions. Described here are African American men and women who have contributed to the advancement of science including medicine, engineering, and inventions. These individuals have contributed in large and small ways that may have been overlooked when chronicling the history of science. All scientists included here are listed in the published literature. I conducted no interviews, and no suggestions were accepted solely on the basis of hearsay. There is no intent to be all-inclusive. The selections are strictly mine. Many important contributions have been omitted, especially those of recent years, because a limit had to be set. This document shows that African Americans made many contributions to the sciences and medicine as slaves and as freed persons. They made contributions during the period of segregation and the modern era. Their contributions had and continue to have an impact on the economy of the United States, and the convenience, health, safety, security, and welfare of its citizens. These contributors improved the economic well being of individuals and groups of individuals. They saved lives, improved the health of persons, and alleviated much pain and suffering. The activities and deeds of George Washington Carver, Ernest Everett Just, Percy Lavon Julian, and Charles Richard Drew, who are arguably the greatest of the African American Scientists, exemplify these characteristics. Some of their research, creations, and contributions will have an influence, at home and abroad, well into the future.

INTRODUCTION

All scientists included in this document are listed in the published literature. I conducted no interviews, and no suggestions were accepted solely on the basis of hearsay. There is no intent to be all-inclusive. The selections are strictly mine. Many important contributions have been omitted, especially those of recent years, because a limit had to be set. African American men included here have made contributions to the fields of biochemistry, biology, chemistry, computer science, engineering, entomology, geology, genetics, mathematics, medicine, physics, psychology, zoology, and inventions. These individuals have contributed in large and small ways that might have been overlooked when chronicling the history of science.

African Americans have made many significant contributions to science and medicine since their arrival in the Americas. Some contributions were made when African Americans were slaves, and others were made during the period of segregation, as well as the modern era. Many of the contributions that the slaves made have been lost, expropriated, unacknowledged, or stolen, and thus the slaves and former slaves have received little or no credit for their contributions. As late as 1858, patents were not given to slaves for their inventions on the grounds that slaves were not citizens. An unknown number of potential contributions of African Americans were not acknowledged and were not accepted by the larger society during the period of segregation. In this period African Americans were denied the benefits and privileges of basis as well as higher education, where scientific contributions are most often made. Thus, in many instances, illiterate African Americans made many contributions and inventions. During the period of segregation an unknown number of African Americans did not acknowledge their status as Negroes. Nevertheless they made contributions, but the number and significance of these remains unknown and are unlikely to be known.

African Americans have discovered, explored, experimented, invented, and passed on to others their expertise in areas of invention, medicine, science, and technology for centuries. The early accomplishments of black men and women were slowed considerably with the advent of the slave trade. Nevertheless, the slaves brought to the Americas their knowledge of the medicinal value of herbs and a variety of plants. These slaves performed as "nurses" and "doctors" not only to the slave population but also, in many cases, to the master's family. As was the custom, however, the white masters often took credit for their slaves' knowledge, and they used it as their own.

Today, as times change, there are many African American achievers in medical, scientific, and technical fields. Although the war is not over, black Americans have won many battles. This document serves as proof of some of the victories that African Americans have made, and in many instances they made them in spite of overwhelming deprivation.

Individuals are listed in alphabetical order in this work. Their birth, death, educational, and career information are given if they were known. A description of their contributions including dissertation, thesis, and titles of books that they authored is given. Information about their published papers, research conducted, inventions, and patents awarded is presented if they were available.

INDIVIDUAL CONTRIBUTIONS

Abraham, Guy Emmanuel

Physician, educator (born 1936, died -). Dr. Abraham published three scientific books: *Handbook of Radioimmunoassay*, edited by Guy E. Abraham, New York, M. Dekkar, 822 p., 1977; *Radioassay Systems in Clinical Endocrinology*, edited by Guy E. Abraham, New York, M. Dekkar, 669 p., 1981; and Guy E. Abraham, *Premenstrual Tension*, Chicago, IL, Year Book Medical Publisher, 39 p., 1981. He was a professor at the University of California School of Medicine, Torrance, and he was a staff physician at Worcester State Hospital and Harbor General Hospital in Torrance, CA. Dr. Abraham obtained the M. D. degree from Montreal University in 1961.

Adams, Walter Anderson

Physician, psychiatrist (born 1900, died 1959). Dr. Adams was the first African American psychiatrist, chief of Provident Hospital Medical Counsel Clinic for Narcotic Addicts in Chicago, IL. He co-authored *Color and Human Nature*, Westport, CT, Negro Universities Press, 301 p., 1970, with Lloyd Warner and Buford Junker. He earned the M. D. degree from Howard University in 1926.

Alcorn, George Edward Jr.

Physicist, inventor, educator (born 1900s, died -). Mr. Alcorn wrote a dissertation entitled *An Electron Impact Study of the Methylamine, Monoethylamine, Dimethylamine, and Trimethylamine*, and he received a Ph. D. degree in atomic and molecular physics from Howard University in 1967. Dr. Alcorn was a professor at Howard University and the University of Columbia. He held eight patents in the United States and Europe on semiconductor technology. Dr. Alcorn conducted research in the following areas: (1) adaptation of chemical ionization mass spectrometers for the detection of amino acids and development of other experimental methods for planetary life detection, (2) missile reentry and missile defense, (3) the design and building of space instrumentation, atmospheric contaminant sensors, magnetic mass spectrometers, and mass analyzers, (4) the development of new concepts of magnet design, (5) and the invention of a new type of x-ray spectrometer.

Alexander, Archibald

Engineer (design, construction) (born 1888, died 1958). Archibald "Archie" Alexander earned a B. S. degree in civil engineering from Iowa State University in 1912. As a designer for the Marsh Engineering Company, Alexander was responsible for the design of the Tidal Basin Bridge and the K Street Freeway in Washington, DC. Mr. Alexander studied bridge design at the University of London in 1921. After several years as a design engineer, Alexander and George Higbee, a former university classmate, formed a general contracting business, which specialized in the design and construction of steel and concrete bridges. Their engineering firm constructed major development projects across the United States. Starting in Iowa, their construction firm built the heating plant and power station for the University of Iowa, a sewage treatment plant in Grand Rapids, Michigan, an airfield in Tuskegee, Alabama, the Tidal Basin bridge and seawall in Washington, DC, the Whitehurst Freeway in Washington, DC. Mr. Archibald Alexander received many awards during the course of his career. In 1954, President Dwight D. Eisenhower honored Alexander with the appointment as the first Republican Territorial Governor of the Virgin Islands, 1954-1955.

Allen, John Henry, Jr.

Electrical engineer, educator (born 1938, died -). Mr. Allen obtained a patent for a Doppler Operation Test Set (DOTS) and a Dissimilar Metal Anti-Corrosion Ground Stub (DMAGS). He was an assistant professor at California State College. Mr. Allen worked as an engineer at Packard Bell Electronics, Lockheed Aircraft, General Dynamics, and Teledyne Systems Company. He obtained the M. S. E. E. degree from California State University at Los Angeles in 1969.

Amos, Harold

Bacteriologist, virologist, educator (born 1919, died -). Dr. Amos conducted research on the Herpes Simplex Virus, and he was an expert on hexose metabolism in mammalian cells. He was a professor in the Department of Microbiology and Molecular Genetics, Harvard Medical School, Boston, Massachusetts. Dr. Amos received the Ph. D. in bacteriology from Harvard University in 1952.

Anderson, Charles Edward

Meteorologist, educator (born 1919, died 1994). Anderson wrote a dissertation entitled *Study of the Pulsating Growth of Cumulus Clouds*, and he received a Ph. D. degree in meteorology from Massachusetts Institute of Technology, Boston, Massachusetts in 1960. Dr. Anderson was staff member at the Chief Cloud Physics Branch at the Air Force Cambridge Research Center in Massachusetts. He was as a captain in the Army Air Forces in World War II and was the weather officer for the Tuskegee Airmen Regiment in Tuskegee, Alabama. Dr. Anderson worked at the Atmospheric Science Branch of Douglas Aircraft Company, California, and he served as Director of the Office of Federal Coordination in Meteorology in the Environmental Science Service Administration of the U.S. Department of Commerce. Dr. Anderson was a professor, department chairperson, and associate dean at the University of Wisconsin in Madison. Charles Anderson was a professor at North Carolina State University in Raleigh, N.C., where he retired in 1990. Dr. Anderson's research focused on cloud and aerosol physics and meteorology of other planets. He was the author of articles contributed to scientific and technical publications.

Antoine, Albert Cornelius

Chemist (organic), educator (born, 1925, died -). Antoine received a B.S. degree from the City College of New York (CUNY) in 1946 and a Ph.D. degree in Chemistry from Ohio State University in 1953. He was a chemist at the Pentone Company in New Jersey and the Aircraft Engine Research Laboratory, now called the NASA Lewis Research Center. He was an Associate Professor of Chemistry at Clark University (1953-54). Dr. Antoine conducted research in the area of photochemistry.

Baker, Thomas Nelson, Jr.

Chemist (organic), educator (born 1906, died -). He earned a B. S. degree from Oberlin College in 1929, a M. S. degree in 1930, and a Ph.D. degree in organic chemistry from Ohio State University in 1941. He wrote a dissertation entitled *The Molecular Size of Glycogen and of Maman A by the Mercaptalation Method*. Dr. Baker taught chemistry at Tougaloo College, Talladega College, and Virginia State College.

Banneker, Benjamin

Inventor, mathematician, surveyor, astronomer (born 1731, died 1806). In 1761, Banneker constructed a wooden "striking" clock, which was probably the first clock constructed in America. He predicted the solar eclipse of 1789. He published an almanac, which contained tide tables, data on future eclipses, a list of useful medicinal products, and formulas, in 1792. This almanac was the first scientific book written by an African American. Banneker wrote a dissertation on bees and did a study of locus plague cycles. Banneker corresponded frequently with Thomas Jefferson, worked with Pierre L'Enfont in a commission appointed by George Washington that planned the city of Washington, D.C., the nation's capital. He later completed the plans after L'Enfont, chairman of the commission resigned and returned to France.

Barnes, Robert Percy

Chemist (organic), educator (born 1898, died 1970). Dr. Barnes conducted research and published on alpha diketones, a class of organic compounds. He obtained a Ph. D. in chemistry from Harvard University in 1930. Barnes was a professor at Howard University, Washington, DC.

Barnes, William Harry

Physician, otolaryngologist, surgeon, inventor (born 1887, died 1945). Dr. Barnes invented an instrument to make the pituitary gland more accessible for surgical and experimental procedure. He was the chief of otolaryngology at Jefferson Medical College Hospital and the president of the National Medical Association, 1935-36. Barnes published monographs and articles in medical journals. Dr. Barnes earned the M. D. degree from the University of Pennsylvania in 1912.

Basri, Gibor Broitman

Astrophysicist, educator (born 1951, died -). Dr. Basri published articles in the *Astronomical Journal*. He wrote a dissertation entitled *Supergiant Chromospheres*. Basri was an assistant professor at The University of California. He earned the Ph. D. in astrophysics from the University of Colorado, Boulder in 1979.

Bates, Clayton Wilson, Jr.

Engineer, physicist, educator (born 1932, died -). Dr. Bates conducted research in electrical and optical properties of crystalline and amorphous solids and surfaces and photoelectric emission. He published more than 50 articles in scientific journals, and he wrote a dissertation entitled *Nonlinear Resonance Effects in Multilevel Systems*. Dr. Bates was a professor at Stanford University, and he received the Ph. D. in physics from Washington University in St. Louis, MO in 1966.

Battle, Joseph

Mathematician, educator (born 1930, died -). Battle published articles in the American Mathematics Society, *Bulletin*. He wrote a dissertation entitled *Imbedding of Graphs in Orientable 2-Manifolds*, and he received the Ph. D. in mathematics at the University of Michigan in 1963. Dr. Battle was a professor at Duke University.

Beard, Andrew Jackson

Inventor (born 1850, died 1921). Beard invented the "Jenny Coupler" for railroad cars, Patent #594,059 in 1897, which was an automatic coupling device. He sold the device to a New York company for $50,000. The "Jenny Coupler" saved the lives of unknown numbers of trainmen. He also invented a rotary engine, Patent #478,271 in 1892.

Berry, Leonidas Harris

Physician, gastroenterologist, internist, pathologist (born 1902, died -). Dr. Berry was an international expert on endoscopy, the president of the National Medical Association, 1965, and a Diplomate, American Board of Internal Medicine and Gastroenterology. He was the co-author of *Gastrointestinal Pan-Endoscopy*, Charles C. Thomas (co-author), Springfield, IL, 632 p., 1974 and the author of *I Wouldn't Take Nothing for My Journey: Two Centuries of an Afro-American Minister's Family*, Johnson Publishing Company, 459 p., 1981. Dr. Berry was a staff physician at Cook County Hospital in Chicago, IL. He received the M. D. degree from Rush Medical College in 1929 and the M. S. in pathology from the University of Illinois in 1933.

Bishop, Alfred A.

Engineer, inventor, educator (born 1924, died -). Dr. Bishop held a patent for a flow distributor for a nuclear reactor core. He conducted research in thermodynamics and reaction rates, and he was a professor at the University of Pittsburgh, Pittsburgh, PA. Bishop was awarded the Ph. D. degree in mechanical engineering at Carnegie-Mellon University in 1974.

Blackburn, A. B.

Inventor (1800s). He held Patent #376,362 in 1888 for a railroad signal used to alert engineers in trains to danger along the route, and he held Patent #380,420 April 3, 1888, for a spring seat for chairs.

Blackwell, David Harold

Mathematician, statistician, educator (born 1919, died -). Dr. Blackwell conducted research in Markoff chains and sequential analysis and was the first African American mathematician of the National Academy of Sciences, 1965. He was the co-author of *Theory of Games and Statistical Decisions,* Dover Publications, New York, 355 p., 1979, c1954 and the author of *Basic Statistics,* McGraw-Hill, New York, 143 p., 1969; and he published more than 40 research articles. Dr. Blackwell was a professor at Howard University and the University of California. Blackwell received the Ph. D. degree in mathematics from the University of Illinois in 1941.

Blair, Henry

Inventor (born 1804, died 1860). Mr. Blair invented a corn-planting machine, and he was the first African American man to receive an U.S. Patent, which was for that device and which occurred on October 14, 1834. He also received a patent for a cotton planter on August 31, 1836.

Blair, Joseph N.

Inventor (born 1904, died 1980). Mr. Blair invented a speedboat in 1942. He invented an aerial torpedo for long range bombing in 1944, and a 5-mm aircraft gun. Blair offered his inventions to the U. S. government several times but was turned down each time until 1958.

Bluford, Guion (Guy) Stewart, Jr.

Astronaut, aeronautic engineer, military officer (born 1942, died -). Guy Bluford, Ph. D., was the first African American to experience space flight, which occurred on August 30, 1983. He flew three missions as a crewmember on the Space Shuttle for the National Aeronautics and Space Administration (NASA). Dr. Bluford wrote a dissertation entitled *A Numerical Solution of Supersonic and Hypersonic Viscous Flow-Fields Around Thin Planar Delta Wings*. In 1978 Bluford received a Ph. D. in aeronautical engineering from the Air Force Institute of Technology.

Bolden, Theodore Edward

Pathologist (dental), dentist, and educator (born 1920, died -). Dr. Bolden conducted research in histology, peridontal disease, and salivary gland pathology. He was a Diplomate, American Board of Oral Pathology. Dr. Bolden was a professor and chairman of oral pathology, School of Dentistry, Meharry Medical College and a professor, chairman of general and oral pathology, and dean of the College of Medicine and Dentistry, New Jersey Dental School. He was the author of *Outlines of Pathology*, 1960 and the co-author (with E. Mobley and E. Chandler) of *Dental Hygiene Examination Review Book*, 4th edition, 1982. Bolden received the D. D. S. degree from Meharry Medical College in 1947 and the Ph. D. degree in pathology from the University of Illinois in 1958.

Bookhardt, A. L.

Physician (1900s). Dr. Bookhardt discovered chloroseptic throat mouthwash (an anesthetic, antiseptic) with Dr. Julian Wheatley Giles at the Veterans Administration Hospital in Tuskegee, Alabama.

Bouchet, Edward Alexander

Physicist, educator (born 1852, died 1918). Dr. Bouchet was the first African American to receive a Ph. D. degree from an American university, when he received a Ph. D. in physics from Yale University in 1876. He wrote a dissertation entitled *Measuring Refractive Indices*. Bouchet was a science teacher and school principal in Philadelphia, PA; St. Louis, MO; Lawrenceville, VA; and Gallipolis, OH.

Boykin, Otis

Inventor (born 1920, died 1982). Mr. Boykin invented an electrical device that was used in all guided missiles and IBM computers, plus 26 other electronic devices including a control unit for an artificial heart stimulator (a pacemaker). Otis Boykin held 11 patents. He attended Fisk University and the Illinois Institute of Technology. Boykin was self-employed as a consultant.

Bradley, Benjamin

Inventor, slave, freedman (1800s). Benjamin Bradley is credited with developing a working steam engine for a sloop-of-war in the 1840s. A master in Annapolis, Maryland owned Benjamin Bradley. While a slave working at the U. S. Naval Academy, Benjamin used a piece of gun-barrel, some pewter, a couple of pieces of round steel, and some materials to construct a working model of a steam engine. He sold his steam engine to a Midshipman at the Naval Academy in Annapolis. With the proceeds, and money he saved (his master allowed him five dollars a month out of his wages), Benjamin built an engine large enough to drive the first cutter of a sloop-of-war at the rate of about sixteen knots an hour. Bradley was unable to patent his steam engine inventions because United States law forbade a slave from patenting his inventions. However, Benjamin Bradley was able to purchase his freedom with the proceeds of his work.

Brady, St. Elmo

Chemist, educator (born 1884, died 1966). Dr. Brady was the first African American to receive a Ph.D. in chemistry, which was awarded at the University of Illinois in 1916. He was a professor and head of the chemistry department, Fisk University. Brady published articles in *Science* and *Industrial and Engineering Chemistry*. He wrote his dissertation on *The Divalent Oxygen Atom*.

Branson, Herman Russell

Physicist, chemist, biochemist, educator (born 1914, died -). Dr. Branson conducted research in the field of mathematical biology and protein structure. He was a professor and chairman of the physics department at Howard University, Washington, DC. Branson was the president of Central State University, 1968-70 and the president of Lincoln University, 1970-85. He received a Ph. D. in physics from the University of Cincinnati in 1939. He wrote a dissertation entitled *Part I: The Differential Action of Soft X-Rays on Tubifex. Part II: The Construction and Operation of an X-Ray Intensity Measuring Device. Part III: On the Quantization of Mass.*

Briscoe, Edward Gans

Physician, anesthesiologist, educator (born 1937, died -). Dr. Briscoe was an expert on and conducted research on the control of pain. He was a professor at Charles R. Drew Postgraduate School and a physician specialist at Tripler Army Medical Center, Honolulu, HI. Briscoe completed the M. D. degree at Howard University in 1963.

Briscoe, Madison Spencer

Parasitologist, entomologist, educator (born 1905, died -). Dr. Briscoe conducted research on the distribution of parasites. He taught at New Orleans College and Storer College. Dr. Briscoe was a professor in the School of Medicine, Howard University, Washington, DC. Briscoe obtained a Doctor of Science degree from Catholic University in St. Louis, MO, in 1950. His dissertation was entitled *Some Ecological Aspects of Liberia as Interpreted from the Vegetation on Ground and Aerial Photography with Special Reference to the Distribution of Parasites*.

Bryant, J. Edmond

Physiologist, physician, educator (born 1901, died 1955). Dr. Bryant was an instructor of physiology at Howard University Medical College. He published approximately ten articles in medical journals on aspects of tuberculosis. Bryant was a member of the Editorial Board of the National Medical Association *Journal*. He completed the M. D. at Howard University in 1937.

Buggs, Charles Wesley

Bacteriologist, biologist, educator (born 1906, died -). Dr. Buggs was a professor and head of the microbiology department, College of Medicine, Howard University, Washington, DC. He wrote a dissertation entitled *Cataphoretic Phenomena*. Buggs conducted research on the resistance of bacteria to antibiotics, and he was the author of *Premedical Education for Negroes*, 1949. Buggs received the Ph. D. degree from the University of Minnesota in 1934.

Butler, Henry Rutherford

Physician, surgeon, pediatrician (born 1862, died 1931). He authored *Acute Gastro-Infection of Infants and Children*, 1912; and he published papers, pamphlets, and articles on medical subjects. Dr. Butler obtained the M. D. degree from Meharry Medical College, Nashville, TN in 1890. Butler was a physician in private practice in Atlanta, GA.

Calloway, Nathaniel Oglesby

Chemist (organic), physician, military officer, educator (born 1907, died 1979). Dr. Calloway obtained a Ph. D. degree in organic chemistry from Iowa State College in 1934 and a M. D. degree from the University of Illinois in 1943. He was a professor at the University of Illinois Medical School. He wrote a dissertation entitled *Condensation Reactions of Furfural and Its Derivatives*. Dr. Calloway was the author or co-author of more than 30 scientific articles and publications in scientific journals. He conducted research to expand the knowledge of condensation reactions of furfural and its derivatives.

Campbell, Haywood

Bacteriologist, microbiologist, virologist, biochemist (born 1934, died -). Dr. Campbell was a biologist at the National Institutes of Health, and a bacteriologist and a vice president at Eli Lilly Research Laboratories, Indianapolis, IN. He wrote a dissertation entitled *Complement Fixing Antigenicity of Coxsackie B Viruses Grown in Tissue Culture* and received a Ph. D. in bacteriology at the University of Iowa in 1961.

Cannon, Joseph Nevel

Engineer (chemical) (born 1942, died -). Dr. Cannon was a professor of chemical engineering at Howard University. He wrote a dissertation entitled *A Model Study of Transpiration from Broad Leaves* and received a Ph. D. in chemical engineering from the University of Colorado in 1971.

Cansler, Charles W.

Mathematician, educator (born 1871, died 1950). Mr. Cansler published *Cansler's Short methods in Arithmetic* in 1895. He was a teacher and school principal in Knoxville, TN. Cansler attended Maryville College in Maryville, TN.

Cardoza, William Warrick

Physician, pediatrician (born 1905, died 1962). Dr. Cardoza obtained the M. D. degree from Ohio State University in 1933. He was a professor of pediatrics at Freedmen's Hospital in Washington, DC. Dr. Cardoza was a pioneer investigator of sickle cell anemia. He published his research in the *Archives of Internal Medicine* and the *Journal of Pediatrics*.

Carroll, Edward Major

Mathematician, educator (born 1916, died -). Carroll wrote a dissertation entitled *Competencies in Mathematics of Certain Prospective Elementary School Teachers*, and he obtained the D. Ed. degree in mathematics from Columbia University in 1952. Dr. Carroll was a professor of mathematics education at New York University. He was the author of *Wax Paper Geometry*, Watertown, MA, Educational Services, Inc., 1965, and the co-author of *Modern School Algebra 1*, Morristown, N. J., Silver Burdett, 1971.

Carruthers, George R.

Astrophysicist, physicist, aeronautical engineer, inventor (born 1939, died -). Dr. Carruthers wrote a dissertation entitled *Experimental Investigations of Atomic Nitrogen Recombinations*, and he obtained the Ph. D. degree in aeronautical and astronomical engineering from the University of Illinois in 1962. He was a research physicist at the Naval

Research Laboratory. Dr. Carruthers invented lunar surface ultraviolet cameras, and he conducted research in experimental investigations of atomic nitrogen recombination. He was the editor of the *Journal of the National Technical Association*.

Carson, Benjamin Solomon

Physician, neurosurgeon (pediatric), educator (born 1951, died -). Dr. Carson was a Diplomate, American Board of Neurological Surgery, and an expert with hemispherectomies and the separation of Siamese twins. He was the contributor of many articles to medical journals, including the *Journal of the American Medical Association*. Carson was a professor at Johns Hopkins University School of Medicine. He earned the M. D. degree from the University of Michigan.

Carter, Thomas J.

Chemist, inventor (1900s). Mr. Carter received the B. S. degree from Benedict College. He was a chemist for the U. S. Bureau of Standards. Carter perfected a leather-testing machine that tested the durability of leather in various kinds of weather.

Carver, George Washington

Agricultural chemist, botanist, educator (born 1864, died 1943). Dr. Carver did most of his work at Tuskegee Institute, Tuskegee, AL, where he was a professor. Carver made many contributions to agricultural research and the agricultural sciences, and he made more than 300 products from the peanut, ranging from instant coffee to soap and ink. He made 118 products from the sweet potato, including flour, shoe blacking, and candy. Carver produced 75 products from the pecan. He made synthetic marble from wood shavings; dyes from clay; and starch, gum, and wallboard from cotton stalks. He developed a new type of cotton known as Carver's hybrid. He started the fungus collection, which grew to about 20,000 species, at Iowa State University, where he received a masters degree. Dr. Carver received three patents for the production of paints and stains. He revolutionized the agriculture of the southern United States. His discoveries convinced southern farmers to grow peanuts, pecans, and sweet potatoes in place of cotton to provide a new source of income. Dr. Carver also taught methods of soil improvement. In recognition of his accomplishments, the National Association for the Advancement of Colored People (NAACP) awarded Carver the Spingarn Medal in 1923. In 1935 he was appointed collaborator in the Division of Plant Mycology and Disease Survey of the Bureau of Plant Industry of the U.S. Department of Agriculture. In 1940 he donated all his savings to the establishment of the George Washington Carver Foundation at Tuskegee for research in natural science. Carver died at Tuskegee, on January 5, 1943. His birthplace, near Diamond, Missouri, was established as the George Washington Carver National Monument in 1943.

Cassell, Albert I.

Engineer, architect, educator (born 1895, died 1969). Cassell obtained a B. A. degree in architecture from Cornell University in 1919. He designed many of the building at Howard University including Founders Library in 1938. Cassell was a professor and head of the department of architecture at Howard University.

Cesar (Slave)

Medical practitioner, freedman (1700s). Cesar was a South Carolina slave who was given his freedom by the General Assembly of South Carolina for the discovery of a cure for rattlesnake bite. Cesar described the symptoms as well as how to prepare and administer the antidote.

Clark, Kenneth Bancroft

Psychologist, educator (born 1914, died -). Clark wrote a dissertation entitled *Some Factors Influencing the Remembering of Prose Material*, and he received a Ph. D. degree in psychology from Columbia University in 1940. He was a professor at the College of the City of New York and a visiting professor at Harvard University. He was the founder and director of the Northside Center for Child Development in New York, NY. Dr. Clark was the author of more than 16 books on education and psychology. He published *Prejudice and Your Child*, Boston, MA, Beacon Press, 247 p., 1963.

Cobb, William Montague

Physician, surgeon, anthropologist (physical), anatomist, educator (born 1904, died -). Cobb wrote a dissertation entitled *Human Archives*, and he received the M. D. degree from Howard University Medical College in 1929 and a Ph. D. degree from Case Western Reserve in 1932. He was a professor and director of Howard University Medical School. He was the editor of the *Journal of the National Medical Association* and the president of the National Medical Association, 1963-64. Dr. Cobb contributed numerous publications including the following: Index of the *American Journal of Physical Anthropology*, Physical Anthropology of the American Negro, *The First Negro Medical Society*, 1939, more than 500 monographs, and over 200 biographies of black doctors.

Cobb, Price Mashaw

Physician, psychiatrist, educator (born 1928, died -). Cobb received the M. D. degree from Meharry Medical College in 1958. He was an assistant clinical professor at the University of California San Francisco, and he was a staff member at Langley Porther Neuropsychiatric Institute, and Digital Equipment Corporation. He was the president of Pacific Management Systems. Dr. Cobb was the co-author of *The Jesus Bag* (with Wm. H.

Grier) New York, McGraw-Hill, 259 p., 1971, and *Black Rage* (with Wm. H. Grier) New York, Basic Books, 213 p., 1968.

Coffin, Alfred O.

Biologist, zoologist, educator (born 1861, died 1900s). Coffin wrote a dissertation entitled *The Mound Builders*, and he received a Ph. D. degree in zoology from Illinois Wesleyan University in 1889. He was the first African American to obtain a Ph. D. degree in a bioscience field. He was a professor of Romance languages at Langston University. He was the author of *The Origin of the Mound Builders*, Cincinnati, OH, Elm Street Print. Co., 1889 and *A Land Without Chimneys Or The Byways Of Mexico*, Cincinnati, OH, Editor Publishing Co., 1898.

Comer, James Pierpont

Physician, psychiatrist, surgeon, public health administrator, educator (born 1934, died -). Comer obtained the M. D. degree from Howard University in 1960 and the M. P. H. degree from the University of Michigan in 1964. He was a professor and associate dean at the Yale University Medical School. He was the author of *Beyond Black and White*, New York, Quadrangle Books, 272 p., 1972. He was the co-author of *Black Child Care: How to Bring up a Healthy Black Child in America*, New York, Simon and Schuster, 408 p., 1975 and *School Power: Implications of an Intervention Project*, New York, Free Press London, 285 p., 1980.

Cooper, John R.

Chemist, inventor (born 1930, died -). He was a chemist at E. I. Du Pont de Nemours. Cooper held several patents in the development of fluorine-rubber compounds, which were resistant to heat for applications and use for seals in jet engines. Dr. Cooper conducts research to develop synthetic rubber and to discover new applications for synthetic rubber.

Cornely, Paul Bertau

Physician, public health officer, educator (born 1906, died -). Cornely wrote a dissertation entitled *A Survey of Post-Graduate Medical Education in the United States and an Inquiry into the Educational Needs of the General Practioner*, and he received a Ph. D. degree in public health from the University of Michigan in 1934. He was awarded the M. D. degree from the University of Michigan in 1931. He was a professor at Howard University College of Medicine and a staff member at Health Services Evaluation Systems Science, Inc. He conducted research on black health problems, student health programs, and health motivation among low-income families. He was the first African American to receive a Ph. D. degree in public health. He contributed more than 100 articles to scientific journals and popular media.

Cotton, Donald

Chemist (born 1935, died -). Cotton wrote a dissertation entitled *A General Theory of Interfacial Tension and Its Application to Adsorption Phenomena*, and he received a Ph. D. degree from Howard University in 1967. He was a research chemist for the U. S. Naval Propellant Plant and the U. S. Naval Ship Research and Development Laboratory. He held several patents.

Cox, Elbert Frank

Mathematician, educator (born 1895, died 1969). Cox wrote a dissertation entitled *The Polynomial Solutions of Difference Equations, AF (X+1)+BF (X)=Phi (X)*, and he received a Ph. D. degree in mathematics from Cornell University in 1925. He was the first African American to earn a Ph. D. degree in pure mathematics. He was a professor at Shaw University, West Virginia State College, and Howard University.

Craig, Arthur Ulysses

Engineer (electrical), educator (born 1871, died 1959). Craig received a B. S. degree in electrical engineering from the University of Kansas School of Engineering. He was the first African American to receive a degree in electrical engineering from the University of Kansas and the first African American to receive a degree in electrical engineering in the United States. Craig taught at Tuskegee Institute and old M Street (Dunbar) High School in Washington, DC. He was the Principal of Armstrong Manual Training Night School, and he introduced mechanical and architectural drawing in black schools in Washington, DC. He retired after 18 years with the Board of Transportation of New York.

Crossley, Frank Alphonso

Engineer (metallurgical) (born 1925, died -). Crossley wrote a dissertation entitled *Grain Refinement by the Paritectic Reaction in Aluminum and Aluminum Base Alloys*, and he received a Ph. D. degree in metallurgical engineering from the Illinois Institute of Technology in 1950. Crossley was the first African American to receive a Ph. D. degree in metallurgical engineering. He was an engineer at Lockheed Missile Systems and the Illinois Institute of Technology Research. He conducted research on submarine launched intercontinental ballistic missiles and on titanium science and technology.

Crosthwait, David Nelson, Jr.

Engineer (electrical, mechanical), educator (born 1898, died 1976). Crosthwait received a B. S. degree and a Masters of Engineering degree from Purdue University in 1913 and 1920, respectively. He was an expert on heat transfer, ventilation, and air conditioning. Crosthwait was a research engineer, director of research laboratories at C. A. Dunham Company, the technical advisor for Dunham-Bush, Incorporated, and president of the Michigan City Redevelopment Commission. He designed the heating system in the Radio City Music Hall in New York, NY. Mr. Crosthwait was the author of a manual on heating and cooling with water and guides, standards, and codes for heating, ventilation, refrigeration, and air conditioning systems. He received 34 United States patents and 80 foreign patents referring to the design, installation, testing, and servicing of HVAC power plants, heating, and ventilating systems. After he retired from industry, Crosthwait taught at Purdue University.

Crummie, John H.

Military officer (captain, U. S. Air Force), engineer (electrical), inventor (born 1936, died -). Crummie conducted research on high altitude, space balloons. He developed a locating system for tracking launched balloons.

Dailey, Ulysses Grant

Physician, surgeon, educator (born 1885, died 1961). Dailey obtained the M. D. degree from Northwestern University in 1902. He established Dailey Hospital and Sanitarium in 1926, and he was its Surgeon-in-Chief for six years. Dr. Dailey was a lecturer at Northwestern University. He was the president of the National Medical Association, and he was the Editor-in-Chief of the National Medical Association *Journal*. Dr. Dailey was the author of numerous articles in the *Journal* of the National Medical Association.

Daniel, Walter Thomas

Engineer (structural), educator (born 1908, died -). Mr. Daniel wrote a dissertation entitled *Deflection in Rigid Frames Stressed Beyond the Yield Point*, and he received a Ph. D. degree in engineering from Iowa State University in 1932. He was the first African American to earn a Ph. D. degree in engineering, and he was the first African American engineer to receive a license in Louisiana. Dr. Daniel was a professor at Prairie View State College and Howard University.

Darity, William Alexander

Health administrator, educator (born 1924, died -). Darity wrote a dissertation entitled *Contraceptive Education: The Relative Cultural and Social Factors Related to Applied Health Education with Special Reference to Oral Contraceptives*, and he received a Ph. D. degree in public health from North Carolina Central University in 1964. He was a community health educator in Charlotte, NC, Danville, VA, and Norfolk, VA. Dr. Darity was a consultant for the World Health Organization. He was a professor and administrator at the University of Massachusetts.

Darlington, Ray Clifford

Pharmacist (born 1908, died -). Darlington wrote a dissertation entitled *An Investigation of Bentonite as a Major Component of Ointment Bases*, and he earned a Ph. D. degree in pharmacy from Ohio State University in 1948. He was the first African American to receive a Ph. D. degree in pharmacy in the United States.

Davidson, Shelby J.

Inventor, lawyer (1800s). Davidson earned a B. A. degree from Howard University in 1893. He invented a mechanical tabulator (adding machine), and he was the author of several published articles on adding machines.

Davis, Stanley Peter

Physicist (born 1900s, died -). Davis wrote a dissertation entitled *Measurements of Time Dilation in Gamma-Ray Bursts by Analysis of Temporal Structure*, and he received a Ph. D. degree in physics from The Catholic University of America in 1995. He conducted research in the areas of high-energy astrophysics, astroparticle physics, and cosmology. Dr. Davis was the author or co-author of several articles and reports in scientific and technical journals. He was a physicist at the National Academy of Sciences/National Research Council Resident Research Associate, NASA/Goddard Space Flight Center-Laboratory for High Energy Astrophysics in Greenbelt, MD.

Delaney, Martin Robison

Physician (born 1812, died 1885). Delaney studied as an apprentice physician under A. N. McDowell, J. P. Gazzan, and F. J. Lemoyne. He attended Harvard Medical School, 1850-51, but he left due to the protests of fellow students. He practiced medicine the remainder of his life. Delaney was the first African American major in the U. S. Army, 1865. Dr. Delaney was instrumental in putting down a cholera epidemic in Pittsburgh, PA, where he practiced. He was the author of *Blake; or the Huts of America*, Beacon Press, Boston, MA, 1970, reprint, and *Principia of Ethnology: The Origin of Races and Color*, 1879, and *The Condition, Elevation, Emigration, and Destiny of the Colored People of the United States, Politically Considered*, in 1852. Delaney published a newspaper, *The Mystery* in 1843 and co-edited Frederick Douglass' *The North Star*. He explored the Niger Valley in Africa in 1854 with an eye toward the recolonization of African-Americans and signed a treaty with eight African kings who offered inducements to African-Americans to emigrate. During the Civil War, as a major, he was the first black officer commissioned by the U.S. Army. As the first major black nationalist, Delany warned his people, "no people could gain respect unless they retained their identity."

Derham (Durham), James

Physician (born 1757, died 1800s). Derham was born a slave in Philadelphia, PA, May 1, 1757. He was the first African American man to practice medicine in America. He learned medicine by working with Dr. John Kearsley, who taught him how to prepare medicines and to perform other minor chores. Dr. George West, a surgeon, purchased him and allowed him to perform many duties of a doctor. Derham was sold to Dr. Robert Dove, who employed him as an assistant and was so pleased with his progress that he freed him. As a freed man, Derham secured a license and practiced medicine in New Orleans during the 1780s. He was fluent in English, French, and Spanish. Dr. Benjamin Rush read his paper entitled "An Account of the Putrid Sore Throat" before the College of Physicians of Philadelphia in 1789.

Donaldson, James Ashley

Mathematician, educator (born 1941, died -). He wrote a dissertation entitled *Integral Representations of the Extended Airy Integral Type for the Modified Bessel Function*, and he received a Ph. D. degree in mathematics from the University of Illinois in 1965. Donaldson was a professor at the University of Illinois and the University of New Mexico. He was a professor and chairperson of the department of mathematics at Howard University. Dr. Donaldson conducted research on the perturbation theory, and he published articles in the *Journal of Mathematics and Physics*.

Dooley, Thomas Price

Geneticist, zoologist, educator, administrator (born 1904, died -). Thomas Price Dooley earned a B. A. degree from Morehouse College in 1927 and a M. S. degree from the University of Iowa in 1931. Dooley wrote a dissertation entitled *Influence of Colchicine on the Germ Cells of Insects, Gryllus Assimilis and Melanoplus Differentialis, with Special Reference to the Mitochondria and Dictysomes*, and he received a Ph. D. degree in zoology from the University of Iowa in 1939. Dr. Dooley was a professor, head of the department of natural science, and dean of the school of arts and sciences at Prairie View A and M College.

Dorman, Linnaeus Cuthbert

Chemist (organic), inventor (born 1935, died -). Dorman wrote a dissertation entitled *Synthesis of Heterocyclic Nitrogen Compounds of the Tetrahydroimidazole and Hexahydropyrimidine Series – Reduction of Aromatic Ketones with Alloys of Magnesium*, and he earned a Ph. D. degree from Indiana University in 1961. Dorman was a research chemist at Dow Chemical Company in Midland, Michigan. He published articles in professional and scientific journals.

Dorsette, Cornelius Nathaniel

Physician, teacher (born 1852, died 1897). Dorsette was born a slave. He obtained a B. A. degree from Hampton Institute in 1878, and he was a teacher of Booker T. Washington. Dorsette earned the M. D. degree from the University of Buffalo Medical School in 1882. Dr. Dorsette was the first African American licensed to practice medicine in Alabama. He founded the Hale Infirmary, which operated from 1890 to 1958. He was a member of the Board of Trustees of Tuskegee Institute from 1883 to 1897.

Douglas, William

Inventor (1800's). He held six patents for inventions of self-binding harvesting machinery.

Drew, Charles Richard

Physician, surgeon, scientist, educator (born 1904, died 1950). Dr. Drew developed techniques for separating and preserving blood, and he did research in the field of blood plasma at Presbyterian Hospital in New York, NY. He showed that blood plasma lasted longer than blood. He set up the first blood bank in London, England, during World War II (1939-1945). Dr. Drew received a patent for an apparatus for preserving blood. The device prevented the diffusion of potassium from the red blood cell into the plasma. This medical breakthrough made the storage of blood in blood banks possible. Born in Washington, D.C., Drew graduated from Amherst College in 1926 with a B.A. degree and from McGill University with M.D. and C.M. (master of surgery) degrees in 1933. He received a doctorate in medical science from the College of Physicians and Surgeons, Columbia University in 1940. In 1941 Drew became the first director of the American Red Cross Blood Bank, and thereafter he tried to make the public aware that blood banks do not need to be segregated by race. He practiced medicine and taught surgery throughout his career. He received many honors and awards, including the Diplomate of surgery by the American Board of Surgery of Johns Hopkins University in 1941, and the Spingarn Medal of the *National Association for the Advancement of Colored People* (NAACP) in 1944.

Duke, Charles Sumner

Engineer (structural and architectural) (born 1879, died 1952). Mr. Duke earned a B. A. degree from Harvard University in 1904 and a C. E. degree from the University of Wisconsin in 1913. He was an engineer with GSA in the Virgin Islands, the Pennsylvania Railroad, Missouri Pacific Railroad, Chicago & Northwestern Railroad, George W. Jackson, Incorporated, and in independent practice. Duke designed the Seventh Day Adventist Church at 46th and St. Laurence in Chicago, IL and the Walter AME Church at 38th and Dearborn in Chicago, IL.

Dumas, Albert W., Sr.

Physician, inventor (born 1876, died 1900s). He earned the M. D. degree from the Illinois Medical College in 1899, passed the Mississippi State Board, and practiced medicine in Natchez, MS for 40 years. Dr. Dumas invented a nonstopping Trocar and Canula, which was manufactured by Max Wocher Company, Cincinnati, OH. He was president of the National Medical Association in 1939-40.

Earls, Julian Manley

Engineer, physicist (born 1942, died -). Earls wrote a dissertation entitled *Volume I. Radiation Protection Guides for Long-Range Space Missions. Volume II. Radiological Health Aspects of Fabricating Operations with Thoriated Metals*, and he earned a Ph. D. degree from the University of Michigan in 1973. Dr. Earls earned a P. M. D. (administration) degree from the Harvard Business School in 1979. He was a physicist and administrator for the National Aeronautics and Space Administration and the Nuclear Regulatory Agency.

Edwards, Gaston Alonzo

Architect (born 1875, died 1900s). He obtained a B. S. degree from North Carolina A & T College in 1901, and he received a M. S. degree from Cornell University in 1909. Edwards was the president of Kittrell College and the principal of Hillside Park High School in Durham, N. C. Mr. Edwards was the first African American to design and construct buildings for the American Baptist Home Mission Society, and he was the first African American architect that was licensed to practice in North Carolina.

Edwards, Robert Valentino

Engineer (chemical), educator (born 1940, died -). Edwards wrote a dissertation entitled *The Temperature Dependence of the Collision Induced Predissociation Rate Constant of 1 Sub 2*, and he was awarded a Ph. D. degree from Johns Hopkins University in 1968. Dr. Edwards was a professor and chairperson of the chemical engineering department at Case Western Reserve University. He contributed more than 100 scientific articles and lectures.

Elder, Clarence L.

Inventor (born 1935, died -). He graduated from Morgan State College. Elder invented and held a patent for an "Occustat" energy conservation system that was designed to obtain up to 30% in energy savings. Mr. Elder invented and held 12 patents for electronic devices, trade marks, and copyrights. Clarence L. Elder was the head of his own research and development firm in Baltimore, Maryland (Elder Systems Incorporated). In 1976, Clarence Elder was awarded a patent for a monitoring and energy conservation control system, which was called an *Occustat*. This control system was designed to reduce energy use in temporarily vacant homes and buildings, which was especially useful for schoolrooms and hotels. The system monitored the incoming and outgoing traffic in order to gauge occupancy of the structure. When the people left the building or room, the *Occustat* system into went into action, to reduce heat and light demand, and it facilitated energy savings up to 30 per cent.

Elkins, T.

Inventor (1800s). He invented a refrigerating apparatus with metal cooling coils and a chamber that kept perishable food at a temperature that was lower than that of the outside. Elkins obtained patent #221,222 for this device in 1879.

Elliott, Irvin Wesley, Jr.

Chemist (organic), educator (born 1925, died -). Elliott wrote a dissertation entitled *I. Hydrogenation Studies on Reissert Compounds. II. Synthesis of Some Hexadecanes and Octadecanes*, and he earned a Ph. D. degree in chemistry from the University of Kansas in 1952. Mr. Elliott also earned a B. S. degree in 1947 and a M. S. degree in 1949 from the University of Kansas. He taught at Southern University, and he was a chemist at Eastman Kodak Company and the Kansas Geological Survey. Dr. Elliott was a professor at Fisk University and Florida A and M University, and he conducted research on isoquinoline and dibenzopyrrocoline alkaloids. Professor Elliott was the author of Dibenzopyrrocoline Alkaloids, which was published in *The Alkaloids*, Academic Press, 1987.

Ellis, Wade

Mathematician, educator, administrator (born 1909, died -). Mr. Ellis wrote a dissertation entitled *On Relations Satisfied by Linear Operators on a Three Dimensional Linear Vector Space*, and he earned a Ph. D. degree in mathematics at the University of Michigan in 1944. Ellis was a teacher in the segregated schools of Oklahoma, at Fort Valley State College, and Fisk University. Dr. Ellis was a mathematician at the Radiation Laboratory at the Massachusetts Institute of Technology and the Air Force Laboratories in Cambridge, MA. Dr. Wade Ellis was a professor at Oberlin College and a professor and associate dean of graduate studies at the University of Michigan. Professor Ellis was the vice chancellor of academic affairs at the University of Maryland Eastern Shore and the interim president of Marygrove College in Detroit, MI.

Epps, Charles Harry, Jr.

Physician, surgeon (born 1930, died -). Mr. Epps received the M. D. degree from Howard University in 1955. Dr. Epps was the chief of orthopedic surgery at Howard University and an examiner for the American Board of Orthopedic Surgeons. He was the author of *Complications in Orthopaedic Surgery*, 2 vols., Lippincott, Philadelphia, PA, 1206 p., 1978.

Esogbue, Augustine Onwuyalim

Engineer (industrial), educator (born 1940, died -). Esogbue completed a dissertation entitled *Optimal and Adaptive Control of a Stochastic Service System with Applications to Hospitals*, and he earned a Ph. D. degree in operations research and systems engineering from the University of Southern California in 1968. Dr. Esogbue was a professor at Case Western Reserve University, the Georgia Institute of Technology, Morehouse College, and Howard University. Esogbue was the author of *Integrative Procedures for Coordinated Urban Land and Water Measurement*, School of Industrial and Systems Engineering, Georgia Institute of Technology, Atlanta, GA, 219 p., 1975. He was the co-author (with Bellman, Richard Ernest) of *Mathematical Aspects of Scheduling and Applications*, Pergamon Press, Oxford, New York, 329 p., 1982.

Ferguson, Lloyd Noel

Chemist, educator (born 1918, died -). Mr. Ferguson wrote a dissertation entitled *Absorption Spectra of Some Linear Conjugated Compounds*, and he received a Ph. D. degree in chemistry from the University of California in 1943. Dr. Ferguson was a research assistant for the National Defense Project at the University of California in Berkeley, a professor and head of the chemistry department at Howard University, and a professor at California State University in Los Angeles. Furgeson was the author of *Electron Structures of Organic Molecules*, Prentice Hall, New York, 335 p., 1952, *Modern Structural Theory of Organic Chemistry*, Prentice Hall, Englewood Cliffs, NJ, 600 p., 1963, and *Textbook of Organic Chemistry*, Van Nostrand, New York, 755 p., 1965.

Ferrell, Frank J.

Inventor (born 1800s, died -). Mr. Ferrell was born in New York, and he obtained twelve patents for improvements to valves for steam engines.

Fisher, D. A.

Inventor (1800s). D. A. Fisher invented furniture casters so that heavy furniture could be moved easily by rolling it. Prior to that event all furniture had to be lifted up to be moved. He received patent #174,794 in 1876 for his invention.

Fitzbutler, William Henry

Physician, educator (born 1842, died 1901). William Henry Fitzbutler attended the Detroit Medical College in 1871, and he was the first African American to attend. Mr. Fitzbutler earned the M. D. degree from the University of Michigan in 1872, and he was the first African American to accomplish this. Dr. Fitzbutler practiced medicine in Louisville, KY, and he was the first African American to do so. Dr. William Henry Fitzbutler founded and was the dean of Louisville National Medical College. He trained many of the successful physicians of Kentucky.

Flipper, Henry Ossian

U. S. Army Officer, engineer, translator, writer (born 1865, died 1940). Mr. Flipper was born a slave, attended Atlanta University, and graduated from the U. S. Military Academy at West Point, NY. He was commissioned a Lieutenant in 1877. He was dishonorably discharged in 1881, and these charges were reversed and his name was cleared in 1976. When he left the army, he pursued a successful career as an engineer, surveyor, and translator in the southwestern United States. He was the chief engineer for several companies, and he opened his own civil and mining engineering office in Arizona in 1887. He was the editor of the Nogales *Sunday Herald* in Arizona in 1887. He was a special agent of the U. S. Justice Department Court of Private Land Claims, where he researched and translated thousands of land-grant claims in Mexican archives and surveyed hundreds of acres in southern Arizona. He was a translator and interpreter for the U. S. Senate Committee on Foreign Relations. He was the author of *The Colored Cadet at West Point*. H. Lee and Company, 1878. He was the translator of *Spanish and Mexican Land Laws*, U. S. Government Printing Office, 1895.

Ford, Leonard A.

Chemist (analytical) (born 1904, died 1967). Leonard A Ford earned a B. A. degree from Morgan State College and a M. S. degree from Howard University. Mr. Ford was the first African American to hold a position as an analytical chemist in the U. S. Department of Agriculture.

Fort, Marron William

Engineer (chemical), chemist (born 1906, died -). Marron William Fort earned a B.S. degree in 1926, a M. S. degree in 1927, and a Ph. D. degree in chemical engineering in 1933 from the Massachusetts Institute of Technology. Mr. Fort wrote a dissertation entitled *Heat of Dilution of Hydrochloric Acid by Continuous Flow Calorimetry*. Dr. Fort was the chief chemist and plant superintendent of A. G. Caldwell Company in Massachusetts. Fort was the deputy chief, Industrial and Transportation Division, U. S. Operations Mission, International Co-op Administration in Turkey and the chief in Pakistan.

Forten, James, Sr.

Inventor (born 1766, died 1842). James Forten, Sr. was born free in Philadelphia, PA. He invented a device for handling sails while he was working in a sailmaking factory, which he later owned. Forten made a fortune of $100,000 from his work and his invention.

Frank, Rudolph Joseph

Engineer (electrical) (born 1943, died -). Rudolph Joseph Frank earned a B. S. degree from Seattle University in 1966, and he earned a M. S. degree from Oregon State University in 1970. Mr. Frank wrote a dissertation entitled *A Feasibility Study on the Use of Arithmatic-Memory Registers in the Design of Digital Computer Systems*, and he received a Ph. D. degree in electrical engineering from Oregon State University in 1972. Frank earned a M. S. degree in business management from Stanford University. He was the director of 5ESS, an electronic switching telecommunications system at AT&T Bell Laboratories in Naperville, IL.

Gallimore, Alex B.

Engineer (aerospace), educator (born 1900s, died -). Dr. Gallimore conducted research in electric propulsion. He was the director of the Plasmadynamics and Electrical Propulsion Laboratory (PEPL) at the University of Michigan. The PEPL developed and tested electric propulsion engines. He earned a Ph. D. degree from Princeton University.

Gourdine, Meredith C.

Physicist, engineer, inventor (born 1929, died 1998). Meredith C. Gourdine received a B. S. degree in engineering physics from Cornell University in 1953. Mr. Gourdine wrote a dissertation entitled *On Magnetohydrodynamic Flow over Solids*, and he received a Ph.D. degree in engineering physics from the California Institute of Technology in 1960. Dr. Gourdine pioneered the research of electrogas dynamics, and he was responsible for the engineering technique termed **Incineraid** for aiding in the removal of smoke from buildings. His work on gas dispersion led to the development of techniques for dispersing fog from airport runways. Dr. Gourdine was on the technical staff of the Ramo-Woolridge Corporation, a senior research scientist at the Caltech Jet Propulsion Laboratory, a laboratory director of the Plasmodyne Corporation, and chief scientist of the Curtiss-Wright Corporation. He established a research laboratory, Gourdine Laboratories, in Livingston, New Jersey, with a staff of over 150. Dr. Gourdine received 27 patents on gas dynamic products as a result of his work. Dr. Meredith C. Gourdine served as president of Energy Innovation, Incorporated of Houston, Texas.

Gregory, Frederick Drew

Astronaut, pilot, military officer (born 1941, died -). Gregory became the first African American astronaut to pilot a space shuttle for the National Aeronautics and Space Administration (NASA) when he piloted the *Challenger* on the Spacelab 3 mission in 1985. He commanded the crew of the orbiter *Discovery* in 1989 and orbiter *Atlantis* in 1991. He served in several administrative positions at NASA headquarters. He has authored and co-authored several published papers on aircraft handling qualities and cockpit design. Gregory completed the M. S. degree at George Washington University in 1977.

Hall, Lloyd Augustus

Chemist, food technologist, inventor (born 1894, died 1971). His flash-dried salt crystals, introduced in the 1930s, combined the preservative effect of sodium chloride with the curative action of sodium nitrate and sodium nitrite. These products helped to revolutionize the meat-packing industry. Hall introduced the use of antioxidants to prevent the spoilage of fats and oils in bakery products, and later pioneered a special process that used ethylene oxide gas to control the growth of molds and bacteria in spices, gums, and cereals. Variations of the process, known as Ethylene Oxide Vacugas treatment, were later used to sterilize disposable hospital goods, in aseptic packaging for dairy and pharmaceutical products, and in the treatment of cosmetic powders, eye makeup, and baby talc. Hall helped develop hydrolyzed plant protein, which proved to be a versatile and highly effective food flavor fortifier. The United States, Canada, and Great Britain granted Dr. Hall more than 100 patents for processes used in food manufacturing and packaging. Hall began his career as a chemist for the City of Chicago, IL. He served as chief chemist for John Morrel and Company of Ottuma, IL, and he was the technical director and chief chemist at Griffith's Laboratories in Chicago, IL. Lloyd August Hall received the B. S. degree from Northwestern University in 1914, a M. S. degree from Northwestern in 1916, and a Doctor of Science (D.Sc.) degree from Virginia State College in 1944.

Harris, James Andrew

Nuclear chemist (born 1932, died -). Mr. Harris received a B. S. degree in chemistry from Houston-Tillotson College in Austin, Texas in 1953, and he earned a masters degree in public administration from California State University, Hayward, CA, in 1975. Mr. Harris did some graduate studies in chemistry and physics. He was the head of the Engineering and Technical Services Division of the Lawrence Berkeley Laboratory, where he was still active in nuclear chemistry research. In the course of several years, the Lawrence Berkeley Laboratory produced a number of new elements by bombarding atomic targets in an accelerator. The research team, of which Mr. Harris was a member, purified and prepared target material and, after exposing the target to a bombardment stream for hundreds of hours with carbon atoms, the research team detected the new *element 104* for just a few seconds in 1969. *Element 105* was produced in 1970 when the same target was bombarded with nitrogen. The new *element 104* was named **Rutherfordium** and *element 105* was named **Hahnium**, in honor of two atomic pioneers, Ernest Rutherford and George Hahn. Harris' alma mater, Houston-Tillotson, conferred an honorary doctorate upon him in 1973, predominantly due to his work in the co-discovery of *elements 104* and *105*.

Henson, Matthew Alexander

Explorer (born 1867, died 1955). Henson was the co-discoverer of the North Pole, April 6, 1909. Admiral Robert Peary (the leader of the expedition) and Matthew Henson, an African American, were the first men to reach the North Pole. An article in *Liberty*, a weekly white magazine, stated that "Admiral Robert Peary's assistant, a Negro, was the first to reach the North Pole, 45 minutes ahead of Peary". Henson published *Negro Explorer at the North Pole*, Fred A. Stokes and Company, New York, 200 p., 1912.

Hill, Henry Aaron

Chemist (organic), administrator (born 1915, died 1979). Henry Aaron Hill wrote a dissertation entitled *Test of the Van't Hoff's Principle of Optical Superposition*, and he earned a Ph. D. degree in chemistry from the Massachusetts Institute of Technology (MIT) in 1942. Dr. Henry Hill was as a research chemist for Atlantic Research Associates, the director of research, and vice president in charge of research at Atlantic Research Corporation. Henry Hill served as a civilian employee at the Office of Scientific Research and Development. Dr. Hill was as supervisor of research for the Dewey & Almy Chemical Company. Hill served as the assistant manager of National Polychemicals, Incorporated. Dr. Henry A. Hill was the founder and president of the Riverside Research Laboratory. He served as director for the Rohm & Haas Company. Dr. Henry Aaron Hill conducted research on fluorocarbons.

Hinton, William Augustus

Physician, pathologist, bacteriologist, educator (born 1883, died 1959). Dr. Hinton developed the "Hinton Test", a reliable method for detecting syphilis. On October 1, 1944, the Maryland State Department of Health approved his test as the only test to be used for diagnosing the disease. The U. S. Army used the Hinton Test extensively during World War II. Dr. Hinton collaborated with Dr. J. A. V. Davies on what is now called the "Davies-Hinton Test". He was the first African American to become a professor at Harvard Medical School. Hinton published *Syphilis and Its Treatment*, Macmillan, New York, 321 p., 1936. This was the first medical textbook by an African American to be published. Dr. Hinton earned the M. D. degree, with honors, from Harvard Medical School in 1912.

Hodge, John Edward

Chemist, educator, administrator (born 1914, died 1996). John Edward Hodge was born in Kansas City, Kansas on October 12, 1914. He obtained the B. A. degree in 1936 and the M. A. degree in 1940 from the University of Kansas, where he was elected to the Phi Beta Kappa scholastic society and the Pi Mu Epsilon honorary mathematics organization. He did postgraduate studies at Bradley University, and he obtained a diploma from the Federal Executive Institute, Charlottesville, VA, in 1971. Mr. Hodge was an oil chemist for the Kansas Department of Inspections in Topeka, KS. He was a professor of chemistry at Western University, Quindaro, KS. In 1941 Hodge began 40 years of service at the USDA Northern Regional Research Center, in Peoria, retiring in 1980. Mr. Hodge was an expert on and conducted research on the chemistry of browning reactions in foods. He contributed articles to the *Journal of the American Chemical Society*, *Journal of Agricultural and Food Chemistry*, *Cereal Foods World*, and *Carbohydrate Research*.

Hunter, John McNeile

Physicist, chemist, educator, administrator (born 1901, died -). John McNeile Hunter received a B. S. degree from the Massachusetts Institute of Technology in 1924 and a M. S. degree from Cornell University in 1927. John Hunter wrote a dissertation entitled *The Anomalous Schottsky Effect for Oxygenated Tungsten*, and he earned a Ph.D. degree in physics from Cornell University in 1937. He was a professor, head of the physics department, director of the division of graduated studies and research and dean of the college at Virginia State College during the period from 1925 to 1967. Of the more than 4000 students taught by Professor John Hunter, more than 50 became physicists and engineers. Ten of those were teachers and one was a university president. Dr. John Hunter conducted research in the area of thermoionics.

Imes, Elmer Samuel

Chemist, physicist, educator (born 1883, died 1941). Elmer Samuel Imes earned the B. A. degree from Fisk University in 1903 and the M. A. degree from the University of Michigan in 1910. Elmer Imes wrote a dissertation entitled *Measurements of the near Infra-Red Absorption of Some Diatomic Cases*, and he earned a Ph. D. degree in physics from the University of Michigan in 1918. Dr. Imes was the second African American to earn a Ph. D. degree in physics. The first was *Edward Bouchet*, who earned the degree from Yale University in 1876. Dr. Imes served as a consulting chemist in New York, and he was a research physicist for the Federal Engineer's Development Corporation. Imes worked with the Burrows Magnetic Equipment Corporation and the E.A. Everett Corporation as a research engineer. Dr. Elmer Imes was a professor of physics and head of the physics department at Fisk University from 1930 until his death in 1941.

Jay, James M.

Biologist, bacteriologist, ecologist, educator (born 1927, died -). Dr. Jay conducted research contributing to the understanding of Chlortetracycline action on microorganisms. He published two books: *Negroes in Science, Natural Science Doctorates, 1876 – 1969*, Balamp Publishing Company, Detroit, 1971 and *Modern Food Microbiology*, Van Nostrand, New York, 1970. He was a professor at Southern University, Baton Rouge, LA and Wayne State University, Detroit, Michigan. He earned a Ph. D. degree from Ohio State University in 1956.

Johnson, Campbell C.

Engineer (quality control) (born 1921, died -). Campbell C. Johnson received the B. S. degree in chemical engineering from Rensselaer Polytechnic Institute in Troy, New York, in 1942. Mr. Johnson worked with the U.S. Army Signal Corps, where he was first introduced to quality control. The remainder of his career was spent with Aerojet General Corporation, where he assured that the corporation produced quality solid rockets. As a quality engineer, Johnson manufactured special purpose test equipment such as electronic switches, power supplies, oscilloscopes, test jigs, test racks, T-V center frequency generators, IF generators, FM generators, marker generators, signal generators and amplifiers. For twenty years, Aerojet relied upon his expertise to guarantee a quality product. Campbell Johnson wrote quality control procedures for Aerojet Cape Canaveral, and Vandenburg Missile Operations, and he directed the propellant quality program for Polaris. Mr. Johnson played a leadership role in establishing registration criteria for professional engineers in quality engineering. He served as chairman of the Expert Examiners in Quality Engineering for the State of California.

Jones, Frederick McKinley

Inventor (born 1892, died 1961). Frederick McKinley Jones was largely self-taught, through work experience and the inventing process. With his experience as a mechanic, he developed a self-starting gasoline motor. Frederick Jones designed a series of devices for the movie industry, which adapted silent movie projectors to use talking movie film. Jones developed a device for the movie box office that delivered tickets and returned coins to ticket purchasers. Frederick McKinley Jones was granted more than 40 patents for refrigeration devices. In 1935 Jones invented the first automatic refrigeration system for long-haul trucks. This invention was adapted to a variety of other common transport carriers, including ships and railway cars. The system eliminated the problem of food spoilage during long shipping periods. His inspiration for the refrigeration device was from a conversation he had with a truck driver, who had lost a shipment of chickens because the trip took too long and the truck's storage compartment overheated. Jones developed an air-conditioning unit for military field hospitals and a refrigerator for military field kitchens. Frederick McKinley Jones received more than 60 patents during his career.

Julian, Percy Lavon

Chemist, inventor, educator (born 1899, died 1975). Dr. Julian helped create derivatives of drugs which are in widespread use today by sufferers of arthritis. He studied the chemistry of steroid hormones. He perfected methods for the extraction and production of sterols, including cortisone, progesterone, and testosterone. In 1935, he synthesized the drug physostigmine, which is useful in the treatment of glaucoma. Julian held 130 patents. He was an expert on the chemistry of indoles, conjugated systems of unsaturated linkages, soya sterols, proteins, and phosphatides. He isolated a soya protein that became the basis of a fire extinguisher used by the U. S. Navy in World War II. He published articles in *Journals of the American Chemical Society*. Dr. Julian taught at Fisk University, West Virginia State College, Howard University, and De Pauw University. He was a chemist and director of research at the Glidden Company, and he was the president of Julian Laboratories Incorporated. He completed the Ph. D. degree in organic chemistry at the University of Vienna, Austria in 1931.

Just, Ernest Everett

Marine biologist, physiologist, zoologist, educator (born 1883, died 1941). Dr. Just studied the structure of cells, marine biology, and egg fertilization. He wrote two major books: *Basic Methods for Experiments in Eggs of Marine Animals*, Philadelphia, Blaikston, 89 p., 1939, and *Biology of the Cell Surface*, Philadelphia, Blaikston, 329 p., 1939 and more than 60 scientific articles relating to his field. Dr. Just was the editor of the journal *Protoplasm*, the journal of *Physiological Zoology*, and the journal of *Biological Zoology*, and he was a professor of biology and of physiology and the head of the department of physiology, Howard University, Washington, DC. He wrote a dissertation entitled *Studies of Fertilization in Platynereis megalops*, and he completed the Ph. D. degree in physiology and zoology at the University of Chicago in 1916.

Kountz, Samuel Lee, Jr.

Biochemist, physician, surgeon, kidney specialist, educator (born 1930, died 1981). He received the B. S. degree from Arkansas Mechanical and Normal College (now the University of Arkansas at Pine Bluff) in 1952. Kountz obtained a M. S. degree in biochemistry from the University of Arkansas, Fayetteville, and he earned the M. D. degree from the University of Arkansas for Medical Sciences, Little Rock in 1958. He was a professor at Stanford University and the University of California, San Francisco School of Medicine. He was a professor and chairman of the department of surgery at the State University of New York Downstate Medical Center, Brooklyn, NY. Professor Kountz was the author or co-author of 172 articles published in scientific and technical journals. Dr. Kountz was one of the world's most distinguished surgeons and a pioneer in the field of kidney transplantation. While working with Dr. Roy Cohn at the Stanford University Medical Center, Dr. Kountz performed the first successful kidney transplant between humans who were not identical twins. In 1967 Dr. Kountz and a team of scientists and physicians at the University of California San Francisco developed the prototype for the Belzer kidney perfusion machine, an apparatus that could preserve kidneys for up to 50 hours from the time they were taken from a donor's body. This device is now standard equipment in hospitals and research laboratories. Kountz discovered that the administration of large doses of the steroid methylprednisolone reversed the acute rejection of a transplanted kidney, and that reimplantation – the implantation of a second donor kidney at the earliest indication that the first might be rejected – could mean the difference between death and the survival of a patient with a transplant. He conducted research in the area of tissue typing, and his groundbreaking discoveries helped improve the results of kidney transplantation and led to the increased use of kidneys from unrelated donors. When Dr. Kountz died, he had personally performed 500 kidney transplants, the most performed by any physician in the world at that time.

Latimer, Lewis Howard

Inventor, draftsman, engineer (born 1848, died 1928). Mr. Lewis Howard Latimer made the patent drawings for the first telephone, which was invented by Alexander Graham Bell.

Howard Latimer invented the "water closet for railroad cars" in 1873. In 1881, Latimer invented and patented the first incandescent electric light bulb with a carbon filament. He wrote the first textbook on the lighting system used by the Edison Company: *Incandescent Electric Lighting, a guide for lighting engineers*, Van Nostrand, New York, 140 p., 1890. Lewis Howard Latimer was an engineer for the Edison Company, and he held seven patents for his inventions.

Lawless, Theodore Kenneth

Physician, dermatologist, educator (born 1892, died 1971). Dr. Lawless worked to develop cures for syphilis, sporotrichosis, and leprosy. He helped devise a treatment for early syphilis, which was known as electropyrexia, a technique that involved the artificial raising of a patient's temperature followed by injections of therapeutic drugs. He developed special treatments for skin damaged by arsenical preparations, which were widely used during the 1920s in the battle against syphilis. He was one of the first physicians to use radium in the treatment of cancer. Lawless was an instructor at Northwestern University School of Medicine in Evanston, IL, where he had received the M. D. degree in 1919.

Leffall, LaSalle Doheny, Jr.

Physician, surgeon, oncologist, educator (born 1930, died -). Dr. Leffall contributed to research on cancer diseases and their treatments. He was a distinguished professor and chairman department of surgery, Howard University College of Medicine, Washington, DC. He completed the M. D. degree at Howard University in 1952.

Lu Valle, James Ellis

Chemist, educator, administrator (born 1912, died 1993). James Lu Valle received the B. A. degree from the University of California at Los Angeles in 1936 and the M. A. degree in 1937. Lu Valle wrote a dissertation entitled *An Electron-Diffraction Investigation of Several Unsaturated Conjugated Organic Molecules*, and he received a Ph. D. degree from the California Institute of technology in 1940. Dr. Lu Valle taught at Fisk University and Stanford University. James Lu Valle worked for the Kodak Research Laboratory, and during World War II, Lu Valle worked with the Office of Scientific Research and Development (OSRD) at the University of Chicago and the California Institute of Technology. Returning to Kodak, Dr. Lu Valle became senior chemist for the Eastman Kodak Research Laboratory and a project director for Technical Operations, Incorporated. Later he became director of basic research for Fairchild Camera and Instrument in Syoset, New York. Dr. Lu Valle conducted research in the areas of photochemistry, electron diffraction, and magnetic resonance.

Massey, Walter Eugene

Physicist, researcher, educator, administrator (born 1938, died -). Dr. Massey conducted research in theoretical and solid state physics on the many-body problems, quantum liquids and quantum solids, which attempts to explain the properties of systems of interacting particles in various states, liquid and solid helium, and superfluid helium. He was the director of the National Science Foundation during the period 1991-1993. Walter E. Massey was a professor at the University of Illinois, Brown University, and the University of Chicago. He was a scientist and director at Argonne National Laboratory. On June 1, 1995, Dr. Walter Eugene Massey, class of 1958, was named ninth president of Morehouse College. Massey served previously as provost and senior vice president academic affairs. Dr. Massey completed the Ph. D. in physics at Washington University, St. Louis, MO in 1966. He wrote a dissertation entitled *Ground State of Liquid Helium-Boson Solutions for Mass 3 and 4*.

Massiah, Frederick McDonald

Engineer (born 1886, died 1975). Frederick McDonald Massiah was born in Barbados, West Indies, and he emigrated to the United States in 1915. Massiah studied architecture at the Pennsylvania School of the Fine Arts, and he earned a Bachelor's degree in civil engineering from Drexel Institute, which is now Drexel University. Massiah was a leader in the use of reinforcements in concrete for construction strength, flexibility, and to minimize construction costs. The construction of the Walnut Park Plaza Apartments in 1927 established Massiah's reputation as a leader in reinforced concrete. In recognition of the outstanding beam and girder work on the Walnut Park Plaza Apartments project, which cost approximately $10 million, Frederick Massiah was awarded the Harmon Foundation Medal for Engineering. During a forty-five year span of activity stretching into the late 1960s, Massiah was responsible for building numerous structures. These included the following: the elliptical dome of the Ascension of Our Lord Church (which was the first structure of its kind in this country), the William Donner X-Ray laboratory at the University of Pennsylvania, the Trenton (NJ) Sewage Disposal Plant, a U. S. Army barracks at Fort Meade (MD), United States Post Office buildings (in Coatesville, PA, Camden, NJ, and Germantown, PA), and the Morton Housing Development.

Massie, Samuel Proctor, Jr.

Chemist (organic), educator, administrator (born 1919, died -). Dr. Massie conducted research on organic compounds and wrote a dissertation entitled *High-Molecular Weight Compounds of Nitrogen and Sulfur as Therapeutic Agents*. Dr. Samuel P. Massie was a professor, Chair of Excellence Endowed Chair, and chairman of the chemistry department at the United States Naval Academy, Annapolis, MD, and he was the first African American professor at the Academy. Dr. Massie was the president of North Carolina College, Durham, NC. Massie taught at Arkansas Agricultural Mechanical and Normal College, Fisk University, Langston University, and Howard University. Dr. Massie was a program director at the National Science Foundation during the 1960s. Samuel Procter Massie, Jr. earned the

Ph. D. degree in chemistry from the University of Iowa in 1946. Dr. Massie was the author or co-author of publications appearing in the *Journal of the American Chemical Society*, *The Journal of Organic Chemistry*, *Chemical Reviews*, and other scientific and technical publications.

McBay, Henry Cecil Ransom

Chemist, educator (born 1914, died 1955). Henry Ransom Cecil McBay received a B. S. degree from Wiley College in 1934 and a M. S. degree from Atlanta University in 1936. Henry McBay wrote a dissertation entitled *Reactions of Atoms and Free Radicals in Solution. I. The Methyl Free Radical as a Tool for Organic Syntheses. II. The Relative Reactivites of Some Low Molecular Weight Aliphatic Free Radicals*, and he earned a Ph. D. degree in chemistry from the University of Chicago in 1945. McBay was an Instructor of Chemistry at Wiley College and Western University in Kansas City. He won the Elizabeth Norton prize at the University of Chicago for outstanding research in chemistry, and in 1948-1949 he was awarded a $5,000 grant from the Research Corporation of New York for research on chemical compounds. Dr. McBay served as a technical expert on a United Nations Educational Scientific and Cultural Organization mission to Liberia in 1951. Henry McBay was a professor at Morehouse College, beginning as an instructor and advancing to full professor and chairman of the chemistry department. Professor McBay was appointed Fuller E. Callaway Professor of Chemistry at Atlanta University and became professor emeritus of chemistry at Clark Atlanta University. More than 45 students of Professor McBay went on to receive doctorate degrees in chemistry. He was the author or co-author of numerous articles that were published in scientific journals.

McCoy, Caldwell, Jr.

Engineer (electrical) (born 1933, died 1990). Caldwell McCoy, Jr., earned a B. S. degree in electrical engineering from the University of Connecticut. Mr. McCoy received a M. S. degree in mathematics and Doctor of Science degrees in telecommunications from George Washington University, Washington, D.C., in 1975. He wrote a dissertation entitled *Improvements in Routing for Packet-Switching Networks*. Mr. McCoy served in the United States Air Force, where he was a combat flyer with the Strategic Air Command. Dr. McCoy was a project engineer with the Naval Research Laboratory in Washington, D.C., where he conducted research on state-of-the-art computer equipment for underwater signaling and detection and designing, testing, and evaluating systems for long-range detection and localization of submarines. For his achievements in developing long-range anti-submarine systems at the Naval Research Laboratory, Dr. McCoy was awarded the Laboratory's Thomas Edison Fellowship in 1968.

McCoy, Elijah,

Inventor, engineer (born 1844, died 1929). Elijah McCoy was born in Colchester, Ontario, Canada on May 2, 1844. He was the son of former slaves, who fled from Kentucky before the U.S. Civil War. McCoy was educated in Scotland as a mechanical engineer, and he returned to the United States and settled in Detroit, Michigan. McCoy experimented with a cup that would regulate the flow of oil onto moving parts of industrial machines. Elijah McCoy invented a lubricator for steam engines, patent #129,843, July 12, 1872, which was the first of his inventions. The "real McCoy" applies to his oiling device. He held 57 patents, and his other inventions included an ironing table and a lawn sprinkler. He was the vice president of McCoy Manufacturing Company in Detroit, Michigan.

McNair, Ronald Ervin

Astronaut, physicist (born 1950, died 1986). Dr. McNair was a mission specialist astronaut for the National Aeronautics and Space Administration (NASA), during the period 1978-1986. In 1984, African American Ronald McNair helped deploy two satellites during a mission on the space shuttle *Challenger*. He was killed January 28, 1986 in an explosion of the *Challenger* Space Shuttle. He did graduate studies at the Massachusetts Institute of Technology (MIT), where his research on *lasers* earned him a Ph.D. degree in physics in 1977. He was an expert in laser excitation, including chemical and high-pressure lasers. His work was published in technical journals.

Mitchell, James Winfield

Chemist (analytical) (born 1943, died -). Dr. Mitchell published *Contamination Control in Trace Element Analysis*, Wiley Interscience, New York, 262 p., 1975 and fifty-six journal articles. He held three patents and was a member of the National Academy of Engineering. He was an analytical chemist at the Bell Laboratories, Murray Hill, NJ. Mitchell completed the Ph. D. in analytical chemistry at Iowa State University in 1970.

Morgan, Garrett Augustus

Engineer (traffic) (born 1877, died 1963). Garrett Augustus Morgan received wide recognition for his outstanding contributions to public safety. Firefighters in many cities in the early 1900s wore the safety helmet and gas mask that he invented in 1912 and for which he received a patent in 1914. Garrett Morgan was awarded a gold medal for his invention at the Second International Exposition of Safety and Sanitation in New York in 1914. In 1923, Morgan received a patent for a traffic signal to regulate vehicle movement in city areas. Garrett Morgan also invented the first hair straightener and marketed the preparation under the name *G. A. Morgan Hair Refining Cream*. Garrett Augustus Morgan held four patents.

Murray, Robert F., Jr.

Geneticist, physician, surgeon (born 1931, died -). Robert F. Murray, Jr. earned a B. S. degree from Union College in Schenectady, NY in 1953, and he earned a M. D. degree from the University of Rochester School of Medicine in 1958. Robert Murray did a fellowship in medical genetics, while working on a master's degree in genetics at the University of Washington. Dr. Robert Murray was a senior surgeon for the U.S. Public Health Service, National Institutes of Health (NIH). Dr. Murray was a professor of pediatrics and medicine, a professor of genetics, a professor of oncology, and chairman of the Department of Genetics and Human Genetics at Howard University. He was a fellow and member of the board of directors of the Hastings Center. Dr. Murray was the co-editor of *Genetic, Metabolic, and Developmental Aspects of Mental Retardation* with P. L. Rosser and the co-editor (with Thomas H. Murray and Mark A. Rothstein) of *The Human Genome Project and the Future of Health Care*, Indiana University Press, Bloomington, 1996. Dr. Robert F. Murray, Jr. was the co-author (with James E. Bowman) of *Genetic Variation and Disorders in People of African Origin*, The Johns Hopkins University Press, Baltimore, MD, 1990.

Onesimus (Slave)

Medical practitioner (1700s). Onesimus was a slave who provided Americans with an antidote for smallpox in 1721. He explained to Cotton Mather, his master, how he had been inoculated against smallpox, a common practice in Africa. Cotton Mather wrote about it to Dr. Boylston who tried it on his son and two slaves. Boylston described the process and was called to London, England and honored by being made a fellow of the Royal Society.

Papan (Slave)

Medical practitioner, freedman, physician (1700s). Papan's treatment of skin and venereal disease was so effective that the Virginia Legislature bought him from his master in 1729 and freed him from slavery. After obtaining his freedom, he practiced medicine in Virginia, where he was born.

Parker, John P.

Inventor, slave, freedman (born 1827, died 1900). John P. Parker was born in Norfolk, Virginia. He was the son of a white father and a slave mother. Parker was one of a few African Americans to obtain patents in the United States before 1900 for a screw for tobacco presses in 1884 and a similar one a year later. He established a business named Ripley Foundry and Machine Company in Ripley, Ohio.

Person, Waverly J.

Geophysicist, seismologist (born 1927, died -). Person authored and co-authored many publications on earthquakes in scientific journals and chapters in textbooks in the earth sciences. He was probably the first African American to become an earthquake scientist. He was the director of the U. S. Geological Survey's National Earthquake Information Center (NEIC) in Golden, Colorado. Person obtained a B. S. degree from St. Paul's College in Lawrenceville, VA in 1949.

Pierre, Percy Anthony

Engineer (electrical), mathematician (born 1939, died -). Percy Anthony Pierre received a B. S. degree in electrical engineering in 1961 and a M. S. degree in electrical engineering in 1963 from Notre Dame University. Pierre wrote a dissertation entitled *Properties of Non-Gaussian, Continuous Parameter, Random Processes as used in Detection Theory*, and he earned a Doctor of Science degree in electrical engineering in 1967 from The Johns Hopkins University, Baltimore, Maryland. Dr. Pierre served a postdoctoral appointment at the University of Michigan. Dr. Pierre was a systems engineer for the RAND Corporation. Dr. Pierre served as a White House Fellow for the Executive Office of the President during 1969-1970. Dr. Percy Pierre was dean of the School of Engineering at Howard University. Professor Pierre was appointed Assistant Secretary for Research, Development, and Regulation for the U.S. Department of the Army. Dr. Pierre served as an engineering management consultant. Dr. Pierre was appointed President of Prairie View A&M University from 1983-89 and Vice President for Research and Graduate Studies at Michigan State University, East Lansing, Michigan (1990-1995). Dr. Pierre conducted research in electrical engineering theory.

Rabb, Maurice F., Jr.

Physician, ophthalmologist (born 1932, died -). He received the M.D. degree in 1958 from the University of Louisville. Dr. Rabb was the director of the Illinois Eye Bank and Research Laboratory of the University of Illinois Medical School, and he was the director of the Fluorescein Angiography Laboratory of the Michael Reese Hospital in Chicago, Illinois. He served as co-director of the Sickle Cell Center at the University of Illinois Medical Center. Dr. Maurice Rabb was chief of ophthalmology for Mercy Hospital in Chicago, Illinois. He was the editor of *Macular Disease*, Little Brown, Boston, MA, 1981. Dr. Rabb conducted research on the physiology of the inner eye.

Rillieux, Norbert

Sugar chemist, inventor (born 1806, died 1894). Norbert Rillieux, who was born in New Orleans, Louisiana, was the son of a French planter/inventor and a slave mother. He was educated at the L'Ecole Central in Paris, France in 1830, where he studied evaporating engineering and served as an educator. Norbert Rillieux was revolutionary in the sugar industry by inventing a refining process that decreased the time, cost, and safety risk involved in producing sugar from cane and beets. When Rillieux returned to New Orleans, he observed that the methods for refining sugar from beets and cane were dangerous, crude, and required backbreaking labor. The methods threatened the slaves who were required to ladle boiling cane juice from one scalding kettle to another to produce a dark sugar. Rillieux designed an evaporating pan, which enclosed a series of condensing coils in vacuum chambers. He received a patent U.S. 4,879 for the apparatus in 1846. Rillieux's system took much of the hand labor out of the refining process. It saved fuel because the juice boiled at lower temperatures, and the new technique produced a superior final product. The Rillieux device was used widely on sugar plantations in Louisiana, Mexico, Cuba, and the West Indies. The invention increased sugar production and reduced operating costs for the plantation system. Rillieux's invention of the sugar-processing pan was considered to be one of the greatest inventions in the history of American chemical engineering.

Roberts, Louis W.

Physicist, mathematician, educator, inventor (born 1913, died 1995). Louis W. Roberts received a B. A. degree from Fisk University in 1935 and a M. S. degree from the University of Michigan in 1937. Roberts was a research assistant for Standard Oil of New Jersey and a graduate assistant while at the University of Michigan. He was a professor at St. Augustine's College, and he was an associate professor at Howard University. During Robert's career he served as chief of the Optics and Microwave Laboratory in the Electronics Research Center of the National Aeronautics and Space Administration, and he was a manager at Sylvania Electric Corporation. Louis Roberts served as director of research for Microwave Associate. He was the director of energy and environment at the Transportation System Center in Cambridge, Massachusetts. Roberts held eleven patents for electronic devices and was the author or co-author of papers on electromagnetism, optics, and microwaves.

Roddy, Leon Raymon

Entomologist, educator (born 1922, died -). Leon Raymon Roddy received a B. S. degree from Texas College. Mr. Roddy wrote a dissertation entitled *A Morphological Study of the Respiratory Horns Associated with the Puparia of Some Diptera, Especially Ophyra Anescens (WIED)*, and he received a Ph. D. degree from Ohio State University. Dr. Roddy was a professor at Southern University in Baton Rouge, Louisiana. His research focused on the classifications of spiders, and he was an expert on the life and times of the spider.

Russell, Edwin Roberts

Chemist, inventor, educator (born 1913, died -). Edwin Roberts Russell received a B. A. degree from Benedict College in 1935 and a M. S. degree from Howard University in 1937. Mr. Russell was an instructor at Howard University, a research chemist at the Metallurgical Laboratories for the University of Chicago, and a staff member involved in the University of Chicago's Manhattan Project during World War II. Mr. Russell served as chairman of the Division of Science at Allen University. Beginning in 1953, Edwin Russell was a research chemist for the E.I. Du Pont de Nemours & Company, Incorporated at the Savannah River Laboratory in Aiken, South Carolina. Mr. Russell conducted research involving bioassay, radioactive tracer, gas absorption and ion exchange absorption, monomolecular films, and radioactive waste treatment. Eleven patents were assigned to Edwin Roberts Russell for inventions at the Savannah River Laboratory in Aiken, South Carolina.

Shaw, Earl D.

Physicist, inventor, educator (born 1937, died -). Earl D. Shaw received a B. S. degree in physics from the University of Illinois in 1960 and a M. A. degree from Dartmouth College in 1964. Mr. Shaw wrote a dissertation entitled *Nuclear Relaxation in Ferromagnetic Cobalt*, and he received a Ph.D. degree in physics from the University of California at Berkeley in 1969. Dr. Shaw was a research scientist for the Bell Laboratories in Murray Hill, NJ, where he was the co-inventor of the spin-flip tunable laser. Tunable lasers allow a range of sensitivity for exploring the physical world, such as biological systems and materials science. A frequency that could destroy the surface of a cell wall could be adjusted to a lower frequency to avoid damage with the tunable device. Dr. Earl D. Shaw held a patent for this device. Dr. Shaw was a professor in the department of physics and astronomy at Rutgers University in Newark, NJ. Professor Shaw was the author or co-author of articles published in the *Physical Reviews*, *Physical Review Letters*, and other scientific and technical publications.

Slaughter, John Brooks

Educator, engineer (electrical), physicist, administrator (born 1934, died -). John Brooks Slaughter received a B. S. degree in electrical engineering from Kansas State University in 1956. Mr. Slaughter earned a M. S. degree in engineering in 1961 and a Ph. D. degree in engineering science in 1971 from the University of California at San Diego. Slaughter wrote a dissertation entitled *The Solution of a Class of Optimal Control Problems by Linear and Piecewise Linear Programming Techniques*. John Slaughter was an electronics engineer for General Dynamics, the physical science administrator for information systems at the Naval Electronics Laboratory Center, and the director of the Applied Physics Laboratory at the University of Washington. Dr. Slaughter was an assistant director for the National Science Foundation and the academic vice president and provost of Washington State University. Dr. John Brooks Slaughter was, by appointment by President Ronald Reagan, the first African American director of the National Science Foundation, 1980-1982. Dr. Slaughter served as Chancellor of the University of Maryland, College Park. John Slaughter was the editor of the *International Journal of Computers and Electrical Engineering*.

Sullivan, Louis Wade

Physician, educator, hematologist, federal cabinet officer (born 1933, died -). Dr. Sullivan published more than 70 articles in medical journals and magazines. He is the author of The *Education of Black Health Professionals*, 1977. He was the first African American appointed to a cabinet position in the administration of President George Bush, which occurred in 1989. He was the first dean and president of Morehouse College School of Medicine. Sullivan completed the M. D. degree at Boston University in 1958.

Stokes, Rufus

Inventor (born 1924, died 1986). Rufus Stokes was born in Alabama, and he moved to Chicago, IL, where he worked as a machinist for an incinerator company. In 1968, Stokes was granted a patent (U. S. Patent # 3,378,241) for an air-purification device to reduce the gas and ash emissions of furnace and power plant smokestack emissions. The filtered output from the stacks was almost transparent. The exhaust purifier benefited the respiratory health of people and diminished the health risks to plants and animals. A side effect of reduced industrial stack emissions was the improved appearance and durability of buildings, automobiles, and objects exposed to outdoor pollution for lengthy periods.

Taylor, Moddie Daniel

Chemist, educator (born 1912, died 1976). Moddie Daniel Taylor received a B. S. degree from Lincoln University in Missouri in 1935 and a M. S. degree from the University of Chicago in 1938. Taylor wrote a dissertation entitled *Acid-Base Studies in Gaseous Systems; The Dissociation of the Addition Compounds of Trimethylboron with Aliphatic Amines*, and he earned a Ph. D. degree from the University of Chicago in 1943, where he worked on the University of Chicago's Manhattan Project during World War II. Dr. Taylor was a professor and chairman of the chemistry department at Howard University. Moddie D. Taylor was the author of *First Principles of Chemistry*, Van Nostrand, New York, NY, 1960. He was the author or co-author of articles published in the *Journal of Inorganic and Nuclear Chemistry*, the *Journal of Thermal Analysis*, *Proceedings Rare Earth Res. Conference, 10th*, and the *Journal of the American Chemical Society*.

Thomas, Herman H.

Geophysicist, astrophysicist, chemist (born 1900s, died -). Herman H. Thomas received a B. A. degree in 1958 from Lincoln University in Pennsylvania. Herman Thomas wrote a dissertation entitled *Trace Element Contamination in Tholeiitic Basalts and a Garnet Peridotite as Determined by an Acid Leaching Technique*, and he received a Ph. D. degree from the University of Pennsylvania, Philadelphia in 1973. Dr. Herman Thomas was a chemist for the U.S. Geological Survey, Fairchild-Hiller, and Melpar. Dr. Thomas was an astrophysicist and a geophysicist for the National Aeronautics and Space Administration GSFC. He was the co-author of *Chemical Composition of Apollo 14, Apollo 15 and Luna 16 Material*, (with C. C. Schnetzler, J. A. Philpotts, D. F. Nava, M. L. Bottino, and J. L. Barker) *Proceedings of the Third Lunar Science Conference, 2*, M. I. T. Press, 1972. He was also the co-author of many articles that appeared in scientific and technical publications. The research interest of Dr. Thomas included tectonics, geomagnetism, and isotope and trace element geochemistry.

Turner, Charles Henry

Zoologist, entomologist, educator (born 1867, died 1923). Charles Henry Turner received a B. S. degree from the University of Cincinnati in 1891 and a M. S. degree in 1892. He wrote a dissertation entitled *The Homing of Ants: An Experimental Study of Ant Behavior*, and he received a Ph. D. degree from the University of Chicago in 1907. Dr. Turner was a professor of biology at Clark College in Atlanta, GA, and he made a career change and became a high school biology teacher. This change allowed him time to carry out his insect research. Dr. Turner was credited with being the first scientist to prove that insects can hear and distinguish pitch. Turner found that roaches could learn by trial and error, as do other animals. His exploration into insect learning systems made Turner an authority on the behavioral patterns of ants and spiders. Charles H. Turner was the author or co-author of forty-nine articles on invertebrates that were published in scientific and technical journals.

Warner, Isiah M.

Chemist (analytical), educator (born 1946, died -). Isiah M. Warner completed the Ph. D. in analytical chemistry at the University of Washington in Seattle, WA in 1976. Warner was a professor at Texas A & M University and the Samuel Candler Dobbs Professor at Emory University. Dr. Warner was the Philip W. West Professor and chairman of the chemistry department at Louisiana State University. Professor Warner has published more than 180 research articles and has trained more than 20 Ph. D. scientists. His articles appeared in *Analytical Chemistry*, the *Journal of the American Chemical Society*, the *Journal of Chromatography*, and others. Dr. Warner's research focused on analytical and environmental chemistry and on studies of cyclodextrin complexation.

Wilkins, J. Ernest Jr.

Physicist, mathematician, engineer (chemical, nuclear) (born 1923, died -). J. Ernest Wilkins, Jr. received a B. S. degree (at age 17) in 1941, a M. S. degree in 1941, and a Ph.D. degree (at age 19) in mathematics in 1942 from the University of Chicago. He received a B. M. E. degree in 1942 from New York University, followed by a M. M. E. degree in 1960. Wilkins wrote a dissertation entitled *Multiple Integral Problems in Paramagnetic Form in the Calculus of Variations*. Dr. Wilkins was an instructor at the Tuskegee Institute. Wilkins was a physicist on the Manhattan Project from 1944 to 1946. He taught mathematics and did research at the University of Chicago's Metallurgical Laboratory, where Enrico Fermi's research group worked on the atomic bomb project. J. Ernest Wilkins was a mathematician for the American Optical Company, and he was a senior mathematician, the manager of the physics and mathematics department, and the manager for the Nuclear Development Corporation of America. Dr. Wilkins served as assistant chairman of the Theoretical Physics Department, General Atomic Division of General Dynamics Corporation and assistant director of the laboratory. In 1970, Dr. Wilkins was appointed as Distinguished Professor of Applied Mathematical Physics at Howard University. Dr. Wilkins was a co-owner of a company, which designed and developed nuclear reactors for electrical power generation.

Wilkins' primary achievement was the development of radiation shielding against gamma radiation, emitted during electron decay of the sun and other nuclear sources. He developed mathematical models by which the amount of gamma radiation absorbed by a given material could be calculated. His technique of calculating radioactive absorption is widely used among researcher in space and nuclear science projects.

Williams, Daniel Hale III

Physician, surgeon, educator, hospital administrator (born 1856, died 1931). Dr. Williams was a pioneering heart surgeon. In 1893 he became the first physician to successfully perform open-heart surgery by entering the chest cavity of a stabbing victim and repairing the heart sac. The young man on whom he operated went on to outlive his surgeon by 12 years. He founded Provident Hospital and Medical Center in 1891 in Chicago, IL. It was the oldest freestanding black-owned hospital in America. He was a founder and the first vice president of the National Medical Association. He graduated from the Chicago Medical School, which later became Northwestern University Medical School, in 1883.

Williams, Luther Steward

Biochemist, microbiologist, educator, administrator (born 1900s, died -). Dr. Williams contributed more than 81 publications to scientific journals on topics in biochemistry and microbiology. He was the dean of the Graduate School at Washington University, 1980-83, the vice president for academic affairs at the University of Colorado, 1983-84, the president of Atlanta University, 1984, and an assistant director of the National Science Foundation during the 1990s.

Wright, Louis Thompkins

Physician, internist, surgeon, researcher (born 1891, died 1952). Dr. Wright was the first black doctor appointed to a municipal hospital (Harlem Hospital) position in New York City, NY and the first black police surgeon, which occurred in 1929. He headed the team, which was the first to use aueromycin, the wonder drug and antibiotic. He was the founder of the Cancer Research Center, Harlem Hospital in New York, NY. Dr. Wright originated the intradermal method of vaccination against smallpox. He was the author of more than 90 articles in medical journals, and Chapter XXII Head Injuries, in *The Treatment of Fractures*, by Charles L. Scudder. Wright completed the M. D. degree at Harvard University Medical School in 1915.

CONCLUSIONS

This document shows that African Americans made many contributions to the sciences and medicine as slaves and as freed persons. They made contributions during the period of segregation and the modern era. Their contributions had and continue to have an impact on the economy of the United States, and the convenience, health, safety, security, and welfare of its citizens. These contributors improved the economic well being of individuals and groups of individuals. They saved lives, improved the health of persons, and alleviated much pain and suffering. The activities and deeds of George Washington Carver, Ernest Everett Just, Percy Lavon Julian, and Charles Richard Drew, who are arguably the greatest of the African American Scientists, exemplify these characteristics. Some of their research, creations, and contributions will have an influence, at home and abroad, well into the future.

The contributions of George Washington Carver revolutionized the agricultural practices and the economy of the southeastern region of the United States. His contributions lead to the replacement of the one crop cotton economy with other plants including the peanut and sweet potato. Carver was a man who started as a slave with so little, and yet he contributed so much to Alabama, the United States, and the world. He was a great though humble man.

The legacy of Dr. Ernest Everett Just's research was the contributions on the physiology of development. He worked on a variety of subjects including fertilization, experimental parthenogenesis, hydration, cell division, dehydration in living cells, the effect of ultra violet rays in increasing chromosome number in animals, and altering the organization of the egg with special reference to polarity. During his time, Dr. Just was a leading, internationally acclaimed biologist. If we were to judge the accomplishments of Dr. Just by the standards set up by the men and women of science, it must be said that Dr. Just was an eminent scientist. His genius has enriched humankind regardless of place, time, race, or nationality.

Dr. Percy Lavon Julian was a world-renowned chemist and humanitarian. His discoveries led to the development of medications for the alleviation of suffering and disease. In addition to his many scientific accomplishments and his numerous chemical discoveries, Dr. Julian was the holder of 19 honorary degrees and 18 civic citations. He was a great chemist and a great man. In 1950 Julian was named "Chicago Illinois' Man of the Year" in a *Chicago Sun-Times* poll, but his home was bombed and burned when he moved into the all-white suburb of Oak Park, IL, in 1951. This fact illustrated that even great individuals like Dr. Julian were not immune to the evils of racism and segregation. Julian was an active fund-raiser for the National Association for the Advancement of Colored People (NAACP) for their project to sue to enforce civil-rights legislation.

Dr. Charles Richard Drew designed, organized, and ran the blood plasma bank in the Presbyterian Hospital in New York, NY, which served as one of the models for the system of blood banks now in operation for the American Red Cross and blood centers in the United States and elsewhere. During his appointment as full-time medical director of the plasma project for Great Britain, Drew solved many of the technical problems, which arose in this first great experiment in the gross production of human plasma. As a final report of the project, he wrote a very complete summary of the organizational, technical and medical problems that occurred. His report was published and served as a guide for the later developments in the United States for the U.S Army and for the armies of its allies. When the American Red Cross decided to set up blood donor stations to collect blood plasma for the

American armed forces, Dr. Drew was appointed as the first director, and he set up the first collection unit with full time people. These projects represented a great advance for medical and surgical treatments and led to the savings of untold numbers of human lives and the alleviation of much human suffering.

REFERENCES

Christa Brelin (editor) and William C. Matney, Jr. (consulting editor), *Who's Who Among Black Americans, 7th Edition*, Gale Research Inc., Detroit, 1992/1993.

Shirelle Phelps (editor) and William C. Matney, Jr. (consulting editor), *Who's Who Among Black Americans, 8th Edition*, Gale Research Inc., Detroit, 1994/95.

Herbert M. Morais, *The History of the Negro in Medicine*, International Library of Negro Life and History, Publishers Company Inc., New York, 1967.

Esther M. Branch and Rosalind B. Coles, *Black Americans in Science*, School of Basic Health Sciences, Medical College of Virginia, Virginia Commonwealth University, 1990.

Ivan Van Sertima (editor), *Blacks in Science ancient and modern*, Transaction Books, New Brunswick (U.S.A.), 1991.

Vivian Ovelton Sammons, *Blacks in Science and Medicine*, Hemisphere Publishing Corporation, Taylor and Francis Group, New York, 1990.

L. Mpho Mabunda (editor), *Contemporary Black Biography, v. 1 –10,*Gale Research Inc., Detroit, MI, 1996.

http://www.africana.com

http://britannica.com

http://encarta.msn.com

http://web.mit.edu

Jet, Mar. 20, 1958, p. 22-28.

Hattie Carwell, *Blacks in Science: Astrophysics to Zoologist*, Exposition Press, Hicksville, NY, 1977.

Rayford W. Logan and Michael R. Winston (editor), *Dictionary of American Negro Biography*, Norton, New York, p. 413-14, 1982.

James Haskins, *Outward Dreams: Black Inventors and Their Inventions*, Walker, New York, NY, 1991.

Afro-American Encyclopedia (1974) Miami, Florida: Educational Book Publishers.

Faragher, John Mack (1997) *The American Heritage, Encyclopedia of American History*. New York: Henry Holt and Company.

Chapter 6

THE AFRICAN-AMERICAN MALE
IN AMERICAN JOURNALISM

Jacob U. Gordon
The University of Kansas

One of the cornerstones of American democracy is the freedom of speech and the value of the free press. Yet, it took more than the Civil War for a large segment of the American society to share this freedom. From the very beginning, African-Americans were denied this precious commodity — the freedom of speech. Legislative actions and intimidations were effective instruments for making sure that African-Americans had no voice in American life. African-Americans refused to accept the status quo. They insisted in making their voices heard. First, they communicated by word of mouth through the "grape vine" and later through resistance activities and ultimately the American media. In order to understand the present role of African-Americans in communications in America, it is necessary to investigate the past. In this context, this chapter focuses on the African-American male and his impact in the politics of communications in the 20th century, especially at the fourth quarter of the century. It was the declaration of African American independence in White America. In a national context, it was the second declaration of independence, the first in 1776 was against the British.

The role of the African American male in American journalism dates back to the 19th century when John B. Russwurm founded the first black newspaper, *The Freedom Journal* in 1827. It was co-edited by Samuel Cornish. The desire for black people to speak on their own behalf was the driving force behind the founding of the newspaper. As the first editorial title indicated, "Too Long Have Others Spoken For Us". The editorial went on to say, "we wish to plead our own cause. The civil rights of a people being of the greatest value, it shall ever be our duty to vindicate our brethren, when oppressed, and to lay the cure before the publick" [sic] (*The Freedom Journal*, March 16, 1827). In the March 7, 1829 issue of *The Freedom Journal*, Russwurm wrote another editorial entitled, "Our Rightful Place is in Africa." This editorial demonstrated just how African-Americans must have felt about their oppression. Not long after the editorial, Russwurm went to Liberia, having been appointed superintendent of schools there by the American Colonization Society. On the whole, articulate black men of the late twenties and beyond advocated collective action to advance the race and achieve equality within the United States. One of these was David Walker, whose *Appeal* urged slaves to break their "infernal chains" by armed rebellion. Walker also advocated race pride for African-Americans. Another African-American was Frederick Douglass who escaped slavery in 1838 and published his autobiography, *Narrative of the Life of Frederick Douglass*, in 1845. His Journalistic contribution was the publication of the North Star in Rochester, New York, December 3, 1847. He later renamed the North Star as the Frederick Douglass's Paper in 1851. His second autobiography, *My Bondage and My Freedom* was published in 1855. A third important influence in American journalism in the 19th century was Ida B. Wells Barnett (1862-1931). She was also one of the great political reformers in the first quarter of the 20th century. Through a fierce and relentless rhetoric, Barnett attempted to persuade American society of the necessity of protecting its citizens, regardless of gender or race (Gates, Jr. and West, 2000). Completely engaged with the political issues of the day, Barnett created her own newspaper, *Free Speech and Headlight*, in Memphis, Tennessee in 1891. She was forced by a lynching mob to flee Memphis for her life. Barnett began one of the first black feminist organizations, wrote books and columns for T. Thomas Fortune's *New York Age*, the *Chicago Weekly*, the *Conservator*, the *Gate City Press*, the *Little Rock Sun*, and the *Detroit Plain Dealer*. In her busy schedule, Barnett still found time to work with new jobless and homeless African-America immigrants in her adopted home of Chicago. She died in 1931, leaving a legacy of transformational journalistic style that helped to change America forever. These three early developments, the publication of the first African-American newspaper in 1827, the *North Star* in 1847, and Barnett's newspaper in stimulated black interest and commitment to the American concept of freedom of speech and the free press. These events and the constant challenge for African-Americans to achieve the status of full-citizenship in America led to the development of black professional organizations in journalism.

This chapter explores the development of black professional organizations in communication and the impact of African-American men in American journalism. Nine African-American men have been selected for this study. The works of these men reflect the tradition of the black struggle for freedom and equal opportunity in America. They helped in many ways to shape the present and create the future of the black press. In short, these men and many other African-American journalists have played a significant part in preparing America for the 21st century.

PAUL H. BROCK (1932-)

Born in Washington, D.C., Paul H. Brock attended Howard University. Paul Brock is President of Estellar Productions and the public relations consulting firm of News & Information Management Systems. He is a former radio news journalist (18 years), and has served as Deputy Director of Communications for the Democratic National Committee (DNC) in Washington, D.C.; Vice President for News and Operations at the Mutual Black Network (later the Sheridan News Network, and now American Urban Radio Network); a Senior Fellow for Public Affairs at Howard University's Institute for the Study of Educational Policy; and national Director for Public Information and Communications at the National Association for the Advancement of Colored People (NAACP) - under former Federal Communications Commission (FCC) Commissioner Benjamin L. Hooks.

Mr. Brock has also been a television producer and news anchor at stations WBNB-TV in St. Thomas, Virgin Islands and WETA-TV in Washington, D.C. - where he is credited with producing the first "live" coverage of a Congressional hearing ever aired.

As originator, producer and chief fundraiser for the "NAACP Nightly Convention Highlights" programs that aired nationally over the PBS network from 1978 through 1983 (hosted by syndicated columnist and television personality Carl Rowan), and winning over 17 different awards in public affairs programming; as Coordinator and Associate Producer for the very successful Post-Newsweek television series "Ben Hooks Presents" - which aired in over 100 cities and received numerous individual awards; as producer, writer, film editor and distributor of the award-winning public service announcements on the NAACP voter Education program and the Membership Drive campaign; and as fundraiser, assistant producer and Vice President of the film company responsible for producing the American Playhouse films "Denmark Vesey's Rebellion", "Solomon Northup's Odyssey" and "Charlotte Forten's Experiment in Freedom" - Brock's film and video experience is both lengthy and comprehensive.

Mr. Brock was responsible for publicity and distribution for both the Tony Brown feature film "The White Girl," as well as the long-running PBS television series, "Tony Brown's Journal". He produced the 1992 and 1993 national ACT-SO Awards show for ABC-TV, and worked on the 24th, 25th, and 26th annual "NAACP/IMAGE Awards" television show that aired on NBC-TV. He also served as media and communications consultant to the Chairman of the NAACP -and to two Executive Directors.

Recently, Mr. Brock has turned his attention more to issues such as urban empowerment initiative, community reinvestment in low-income neighborhoods - and demonstrating how revitalization and preservation planning work in concert to produce affordable residential housing.

During Mr. Brock's distinguished career he was recognized as Man of the Year by *Jet* and *Ebony* magazines (1975); listed in *Who's Who in Black America* (1976-1992); received the Unity in Media Award (1975, 1976, and 1980) from Lincoln University; and received the Black Filmmakers 1983 Award as Producer of the Year.

The American Playhouse film, "Denmark Vesey's Rebellion" received over 17 Image Award nominations. The three films also garnered several Emmy nominations, a Peabody Award and two Columbia-Dupont Awards.

As a longtime media and communications practitioner, Mr. Brock was a member until recently of the Public Relations Society of America (in both New York and Ohio); a founder of the National Association of Black Journalists (receiving their "Outstanding Member Award in 1979); and a founder of the National Black Public Relations society N/BPRS), as well as the first President of the Black Public Relations Society of Southern California (BPRS/SC).

Mr. Brock is the father of four children and currently divides his time between Los Angeles, Washington, D.C., Atlanta and New York City.

BERNARD SHAW (1941-)

Mr. Shaw was born on May 22, 1941, and studied history at the University of Illinois. Before retiring on February 28, 2001 from CNN as its principal Washington, D.C. anchor and co-anchor of "Inside Politics", to write his autobiography, Mr. Shaw had developed an illustrious career in the mainstream media. As a black man, this singular accomplishment was inconceivable.

Bernard Shaw joined CNN in 1980. Admittedly, the Cable News Network (CNN) has changed journalism in America and Mr. Shaw played a leading part in the change. A winner of numerous journalism awards, he was live on the scene during the Allied Forces bombing of Baghdad, Iraq, at the start of Operation Desert Storm in 1991. Shaw also provided live coverage of such events as the student demonstrations in Beijing's Tiananmen Square, the 1994 earthquake in Los Angeles, the funeral of Diana, Princess of Wales in 1997, President Clinton's impeachment trial by the U.S. Senate, the Vice Presidential Debate in 2000, and the famous 1988 presidential election between Vice President George Bush and Democratic challenger, Michael Dukakis. Shaw, moderating the debate, forced the candidates to speak about the death penalty. Dukakis had said he was against the death penalty, but Shaw took a direct angle to test his claim, "If Kitty Dukakis (Dukakis' wife) were raped and murdered, would you favor an irrevocable death penalty for the killer?" That was the end of Dukakis in the debate and the actual election. George Bush won the election.

Bernard Shaw's award winning career as a journalist was not one that could be defined by a single moment, but a series of defining moments. It began when he first met Walter Cronkite, a former CBS anchor person in Hawaii. Shaw was stationed there as a sergeant in the Marine Corps. He began his career in 1964 as a reporter for WUS - Chicago, one of the country's first all-news radio stations. Here he had the opportunity to interview Dr. Martin Luther King Jr., who encouraged him to pursue a career in journalism. He later got his wish to work with Cronkite's network at CBS. He helped cover Watergate for CBS before moving to ABC, bringing to American audiences stories such as the mass suicide at Jonestown, Guyana. During Shaw's two day tribute in his honor at the Corcoran Gallery of Art in Washington, D.C., his colleagues and well wishers, including Connie Chung, Mike Chinoy Sandy Kenyon, Colin Powell, Former President George Bush, Dan Rather, Peter Jennings, Tom Brokaw, Senator John Breaux and Judy Woodruff, praised him for four decades of exceptional career in journalism. Former President George Bush noted, "I don't know what they're going to do there at CNN, but I think that they must know, in losing Bernie Shaw, they've lost an iron."

The highlights of Shaw's career have been well reported by the CNN and other media. The following is a summarized version of these highlights and awards: In July 1991, he received the Eduard Rhein Foundation's Cultural Journalistic Award, marking the first time that the foundation presented this award to a non-German. In October 1991, the Italian government honored him with its President's Award, presented to those leaders who have actively contributed to development, innovation, and cooperation. Shaw also received the 1991 David Brinkley Award for Excellence in Communication from Barry University in Miami. As part of CNN's team that covered the outbreak of the Gulf War, Shaw received the 1990 George Foster Peabody Broadcasting Award for distinguished service and the 1991 Golden Award for Cable Excellence (ACE) - the cable industry's most prestigious award - from the National Academy of Cable Programming. Shaw received the ACE for Best Newscaster of the Year. The NAACP presented him its 1991 Chairman's Award for Outstanding Journalistic Excellence. As part of CNN's team covering the 1995 bombing of the Alfred P. Murrah Federal Building in Oklahoma City, Shaw received the 1996 National Association of Television Arts and Sciences' New and Documentary Emmy Award for Instant Coverage of a Single Breaking News Story. In April 1997, Shaw and the CNN team were presented with the 1996 Edward R. Murrow Award for Best TV Interpretation or Documentary on Foreign Affairs by the Overseas Press Club of America for CNN Presents...Back to Baghdad.

Shaw's reporting and anchoring has taken him to 46 countries on five continents. He has been elected a Fellow of the Society of Professional Journalist (SPJ), the highest distinction the society gives to journalists for public service. In June 1995, he was inducted into the SPJ Hall of Fame. In October 1996, Shaw received the 1996 Paul White Life Achievement Award from the Radio-Television New Directors' Association - One of the industry's most coveted awards. One month later, he and his co-anchor Judy Woodruff shared the 1996 ACE for Best Newscaster of the Year for "Inside Politics".

In April 1997, Shaw was inducted into the Chicago Journalists Hall of Fame. In September 1997, he was the inaugural recipient of the Medal of Honor Society's Tex McCrary Award for Journalism, which honors the distinguished achievements of those in the field of journalism. In June 1999, he was inducted into the broadcasting and Cable Hall of Fame.

Among his other honors: the 1997 Candle in Journalism Award from Morehouse College in Atlanta; the 1997 Trumpet Award from Turner Broadcasting System, Inc.; the 1995 Sol Taishoff Award for Excellence in Broadcast Journalism from the National Press Foundation; the 1994 Walter Cronkite Award for Excellence in Journalism and Telecommunciation from Arizona State University; the 1994 Best Newscaster of the Year ACE for Prime News; the 1994 William Allen White Medallion for Distinguished Service from the University of Kansas; the 1994 National Headliner Award from the National Conference of Christians and Jews-Miami Region; the 1993 Best Newscaster of the Year ACE for "Inside Politics" '92; the 1993 Dr. Martin Luther King Jr., Award for Outstanding Achievement from the Congress of Racial Equality (CORE); the 1992 Missouri Honor Medal for Distinguished Service in Journalism from the University of Missouri; and the 1992 Emmy Award presented to CNN in the National News and Documentary competition. He was also an Alfred M. Landon lecturer at Kansas State University in 1992. In 1988, Shaw received the Lowell Thomas Electronic Journalist Award and the ACE for Best News Anchor from the National Academy of Cable Programming.

Shaw received the 1990 ACE for Best News Anchor and the 1989 National Association of Television Arts and Sciences' News and Documentary Emmy Award for an anchor in the Outstanding Coverage of a Single Breaking News Story category. He was awarded the Gold Medal for Best News Anchor at the 32nd annual International film and TV Festival of New York, as well as being named Journalist of the Year for 1989 by the National Association of Black Journalists.

On April 27, 1991, the University of Illinois Foundation announced the establishment of the Bernard Shaw Endowment Fund, creating scholarships in his honor at the University's Chicago campus. Shaw has personally contributed nearly $300,000 to the fund. Grants are awarded to qualified students needing financial aid, with preference given to minority and women liberal arts majors who best represent those values and interests exemplified by Shaw. In May 1993, the university awarded Shaw an honorary doctor of humane letters degree for his outstanding contributions and endeavors. He also received honorary doctorate degrees from Northeastern University in Boston in 1994 and Francis Marion College in Florence, South Carolina, in 1985.

GORDON PARKS (1912-)

Gordon Parks was born in Fort Scott, Kansas, the youngest of fifteen children. He left Kansas when he was sixteen years old, a few days after his mother's funeral and burial. In his own narrative, "A Look Back" in Gordon (1993), Parks noted as he departed from the land he loved, "For, although I was departing from this beautiful land, it would be impossible to ever forget the fear, hatred and violence we Blacks had suffered upon it."

Parks moved to St. Paul, Minnesota where he completed high school, waited on tables, and did janitorial work in order to help out his family. Following several months of unsuccessful attempts to become a musician, he decided in 1937 to become a photographer. He later moved to Chicago where he became associated with the South Side Community Art Center. Here he was awarded a Rosenwald Fellowship for his exhibit of ghetto photographs in 1941. During World War II, Parks was a correspondent for the overseas division of the Office of War Information. After the war, Parks made several documentaries for a large New Jersey oil firm. In 1949, he joined the staff of Life magazine as a photo-journalist, and has won many professional and academic honors on subject matter ranging from ghetto problems to the Black Muslim and international issues.

Parks is the first black man to direct full length movies for a major Hollywood studio. He wrote, scored, directed, and produced the film, "The Learning Tree" (1963) adapted from his novel. His autobiography, *A Choice of Weapons*, reflects the story of his life - a man who grew out of nowhere in Kansas to become a national and international figure. His other works include: *A Poet and His Camera* (1968); *Gordon Parks: Whispers of Intimate Things* (1971); *Half Past Autumn: A Memoir* (1997); *Harlem Document: Photographs* (1981); *Photographs of Gordon Parks* (1983), *Shannon* (1981); *Born Black, With Photos* (1971); *Arias in Silence* (1994), and *Glimpses Toward Infinity* (1996).

Parks is the recipient of numerous awards and honors. He was voted the "Magazine Photographer of the Year" in 1961; the Newhouse Award from Syracuse University (1963); and the Springam Medal-NAACP Award (1972). He is also the recipient of several honorary degrees: Lincoln University, Kansas State University, Boston University, Fairfield University, and Colby College. Park's contributions to photo journalism and films have made a significant difference in American life. His works also have international impact.

VERNON JARRETT (1921-)

Vernon Jarrett was born in Saulsburg, Tennessee. He is one of the nation's foremost newspaper, television, and radio commentators on race relations, politics, urban affairs, and African American history. A Senior Fellow at the Great Cities Institute of the University of Illinois at Chicago, he recently left the *New York Times'* New American News Syndicate to become a features columnist for the *Chicago Daily Defender*.

Under the title "Vernon Jarrett, Piedpiper of Youth Excellence," he recently was featured in a cover story of the May-June, 2000, issue of the NAACP's 90-year-old *New Crisis Magazine*. In 1999, Jarrett was inducted into the National Literary Hall of Fame at the Gwendolyn Brooks Center of Chicago State University. On June 1, 2001, the National Academy of Television Arts and Sciences, Midwest Division, presented to Jarrett its prestigious Silver Circle Award for his 30 years of contributions to television.

He began his professional journalism career over 50 years ago at the *Chicago Defender* newspaper, followed by a stint with the Associated Negro Press. From 1948 through 1951, he and young composer Oscar Brown, Jr., introduced the nation's first black daily radio newscast with their 7:15 AM "Negro Newsfront" over Marshall Field's WJJD AM.

In 1970, Jarrett became the first black syndicated op-ed columnist for the *Chicago Tribune*. In September, 1983, he joined the *Chicago Sun-Times* as op-ed columnist and member of its editorial board, from which he retired in 1996.

During his aggregate 26 years at the *Tribune* and *Sun-Times*, he wrote over 3,900 scholarly commentaries on the great issues of our time. During his more than 30 years as a host at WLS-ABC TV, Channel 7, he produced nearly 1,600 television shows and commentaries. His commentaries are heard today on "The Jarrett Journal" over WVON-AM, Chicago's only black-owned station.

Jarrett also is the creator of the Freedom Readers, a youth reading society sponsored by the Great Cities Institute of the University of Illinois at Chicago, the Chicago public Schools, the Woodlawn Organization, the Jane Adams Association, the James Jordan Boys and Girls Clubs, and a consortium of church organizations and schools. The program was launched on September 3, 1998, the 160th anniversary of Frederick Douglass' escape from slavery with two books in his knapsack.

Jarrett is curator of the Oral History Department of the Rosa Parks Pathways to Freedom Program for Youths (Detroit) and he is a member of the national Advisory Board of the Rosa and Raymond Parks Institute for Self Development (Detroit), and the Advisory Board of the Fisk University Institute on Race. He is also a member of the editorial board of the NAACP's 89-year-old *Crisis Magazine* founded by Dr. W.E.B. DuBois.

Along with an autobiography, he is completing *The Jericho Continuum*, a book of essays on the postures of black leaders during the mounting racism at the turn of the century.

In 1997, Jarrett and 20 other veteran journalists were the guests of the Neiman Foundation and Harvard University as members of The Trotter Group, at which time he appeared on the Arco forum sponsored by Harvard's John F. Kennedy School of Government. The Trotter Group is named in memory of the black journalist and Harvard alumnus Monroe Trotter who graduated Phi Beta Kappa in 1895.

Jarrett is an on-camera source in two lauded Public Broadcasting System documentaries: *Harry Truman* (1997), *The Life and Times of Eleanor Roosevelt*, both produced by the American Experience. Jarrett was featured in the 1995 British Broadcasting Corporation (BBC) production of *The Promised Land,* which documented the great southern black migration to the North during and following World War II, and he is a special commentator in the current Stanley Nelson documentary, *Soldiers without Swords - - a History of the Black Press in the 20th Century.*

The national regard for the veteran newsman also is indicated by the MacNeil-Lehrer Report's selection of him as one of five journalists chosen to analyze the final 1992 presidential campaign debate between President George Bush, Arkansas Governor Bill Clinton and Businessman Ross Perot.

He also has been a guest on ABC-TV's *Nightline* with Ted Koppel; the *NBC Evening News* with Dan Rather; NBC's *Meet the Press*; *60 Minutes* on CBS; *CBS Night Watch*; and *Good Morning, Canada.*

In 1994, The American Bar Association chose Jarrett as a keynote speaker for its National Summit on Racial and Ethnic Bias in the Legal System which was held in

Washington, D.C. His views on post-World War II urban America have been featured in *The London Observer*.

Jarrett has received over 100 awards and special recognitions from professional, civic, religious, and educational institutions, including the following: the first recipient of the NAACP's James Weldon Johnson Achievement Award given in memory of the NAACP's first black executive secretary and composer of the black hymn "Lift Every Voice"; one of the three keynote speakers at the 1999 kickoff for the 100th Anniversary of the parliament of the World's Religions which held its founding meeting in Chicago at the 1899 Colombian Exposition; in 1979, named one of the nation's top five communicators in a national poll of black leaders conducted by Ebony magazine; an episode in Jarrett's childhood in Tennessee is featured in Pulitzer Prize-winner Studs Terkel's best-selling book, *The American Dream-Lost and Found*, and Terkel's latest book (1997), *My American Century*. The Jarrett chapter was one of six dramatized on a legitimate stage in Chicago; recipient of the 1990 Annual National Black Book Business and Professional Award presented by *Dollars and Sense* magazine; the 1988 American Civil Liberty Union's James P. McGuire Award; in 1977, Jarrett and his NABJ cabinet were the White House guests of President Jimmy Carter, and in 1978 he headed a delegation of black journalists to the United Nations for a two-day orientation on foreign affairs; presented the 1991 NABJ Life-Time Achievement Award, the highest honor given by the 3,000-member National Association of Black Journalists; during its 20th anniversary convention in Philadelphia, the NABJ also presented to him its Award of Merit as a founder and its second president, and in 1997 at Chicago, he received the Annual NABJ President's Award; Honorary Doctor of Human Letters Degree by Lake Forest College of Illinois. Jarrett later served on the board of trustees at LakeForest College; Honorary Doctor of Human Letters Degree by Chicago State University on the occasion of the university's 125th Anniversary; 1984 chosen by DePauw University (Indiana) to deliver the annual Percy L. Julian Memorial Address at its $8 million Julian Science Building; keynote address at the 1989 National Science and Technology Conference, sponsored by the National Aeronautics and Space Administration (NASA) and Huston-Tillotson College, at the Johnson Space Center; the 1993 President's Award by the National Association of Black School Educators; and in 1976-77 Jarrett created the NAACP-sponsored national ACT-SO program. (ACT-SO is the acronym for Afro-Academic, Cultural, Technological and Scientific Olympics) The ACT-SO "Olympics of the Mind" grew from 19 cities in 1978 to over 900 cities and towns in 1997.

ACT-SO is designed to give young black academic achievers the public acclaim awarded to athletic stars. Through ACT-SO, over a million dollars in cash, computers, scholarships and bank stock, along with Gold, Silver and Bronze medals, have been awarded to thousands of young achievers, whose excellence is celebrated on national television.

Jarrett has been invited to dedicate the formal opening of five Chicago public schools named in memory of African Americans, including scientist Percy L. Julian, sports journalist Wendell Smith, author/poet Arna Bontemps, Olympic track star Jesse Owens, Chicago's first black mayor, Harold Washington, and Supreme Court Justice Thurgood Marshall, the latter of which declined only because of illness.

On February 2, 1993, the 125th anniversary of the birth of Dr. W.E.B. DuBois, Jarrett convened a group of black scholars and journalists at Fisk University (Nashville, Tennessee) to commemorate DuBois' birth with a memorial seminar. He later was moderator of a memorial seminar on DuBois at the 1993 Boston convention of the African Studies

Association. From 1975 through 1977, he was chairman of the board of Chicago's Jean Baptiste Point DuSable Museum of African American History.

The outspoken journalist is the youngest of two sons of two legendary Tennessee school teachers, the late William Robert and Annie Sybil Jarrett of Paris, Tennessee, children of Hardeman County ex-slaves. They devoted an aggregate 110 years to teaching in the public schools of western Tennessee.

Jarrett is married to the former Fernetta Hobbs, retired Chicago public school teacher. They have reared two sons, Thomas S. Jarrett, a cameraman and sound engineer at Chicago's Channel 7, WLS-TV, and the late Dr. William R. Jarrett, physician and surgeon. Vernon Jarrett is a graduate of Knoxville College and studied journalism at Northwestern University.

SAMUEL L. ADAMS (1926-)

Born January 25, in Waycross, Georgia, where he graduated from high school in 1944. Adams was one of the lucky ones in his community to pursue post-secondary education and eventually received the BA degree from Wayne Statellum in 1950, and the masters degree in journalism from the University of Minnesota in 1954. He also did additional graduate work at Atlanta University and was a Russell Sage Fellow in journalism and sociology at the University of Wisconsin, 1966-67.

The grandson of slaves and a pioneer among his peers, Adams has managed to excel in four related careers: an award-winning reporter, an educator at four major universities, a national political consultant, and a civil rights activist.

As an award-winning reporter, Adams' first job was at the *Atlanta Daily World*. This appointment led to a $1-million lawsuit for publishing that "police [were] investigating a red-headed white woman for the firebombing newly acquired black homes." Adams own house was also firebombed with an obscene KKK note thrown through his picture window (Sayers, 2001).

During the 1960's, Adams worked with Dr. Martin Luther King, Jr.. He had the distinction of being the only black reporter allowed on the campus during Alabama Governor George Wallace's school-door stand. Following the Civil Rights Act of 1964, Adams and his family were the first to test the admission of blacks to public accommodation in Klan country. Many incidents left indelible marks on Adams' mind. At a recent published interview by Karl Sayers (2001), "Black Journalist Shares moments of 1960's Civil Rights Movement", Adams recounted the famous gas station incident. While stopping for gas at a rural gas station, his 12 year-old daughter, Carol, had to use the restroom. But the sole restroom was marked "For Whites Only," and the attendant stopped her. Angrily, Adams ordered the attendant to stop fueling his car. The attendant put a gun in Adams's face. Emotions were high. Imagine a little girl watching her daddy being treated in this manner. The implementation of the Civil Rights Act of 1964 made a difference. A year later Adams went back and received better service. The lesson learned by Adams was, "True, you can't legislate love, but you can legislate behavior."

As a reporter for the *St. Petersburg Times* in the 1960's, Adams covered many other civil rights stories. He was the first to trace throughout the South the admittance of blacks in segregated public accommodations. In 1965, Adams' investigative stories covering thefts of national student loan funds led to indictments and the conviction of school officials. Two years later, as an undercover migrant farm worker, Adams broke stories in Mississippi and Florida that fueled a national campaign to investigate hunger in America. These stories and numerous anti-poverty research reports earned Adams an invitation to participate in the 1969 White House Conference on Hunger and Malnutrition. He was also a finalist for the Pulitzer Prize in 1964 and a nominee in 1965.

As a political consultant Adams served in the capacity of Director of the Atlanta-based Southern Regional Council and the Deputy Director of the Minorities Division of the Democratic National Committee. Adams wrote a grant proposal that attracted $1.5 million from the Ford Foundation to start a Voter Education Project.

As an educator, Adams worked tirelessly as professor and/or lecturer at the University of Wisconsin, 1969-70; University of South Florida, 1970-71; Distinguished visiting Professor at Hampton Institute, 1981-82; and the University of Kansas, 1973-1999. He also served as a Visiting Professor at the University of the Virgin Island where he directed a new journalism program, 1985-87. During his academic career, Adams increased tremendously the number of black journalist graduates by thousands. At the University of Kansas he founded Ida B. Wells Award in 1982, jointly sponsored by the National Conference of Editorial Writers. The awards were designed to honor people who have shown exemplary achievement in the advancement, hiring and promotion of people of color in the news media. He also created and directed the Gannett-AEJ Enrichment Project for Journalism Education for people of color, 1975-1980. Outside the classroom, Adams traveled throughout the nation to encourage students to pursue journalism as a career and to fund programs, internships and/or scholarships to help fund their education. He received several grant awards from the Newspaper Fund, Inc. for Urban Journalism Workshops and High School Visitation Programs, 1975-78.

Adams is the author of numerous publications and media productions. His media productions include: a talk show, WTVJ channel 4, Miami, Florida; Savannah affiliate CBS and ABC news show interviews; Public Affairs series on WREN radio, 1976-78. His research and publications include: *Race Related Deaths in the United States, 1955-66* (1965); *Rhetoric of Black Americans* (1976); and *Black Faculty Invisible at Most Journalism Schools* (1980). Adams continues to be active after his retirement from the University of Kansas in 1999. He maintains his membership in several professional and civic organizations: Sigma Delta Chi Professional Journalistic Society, Atlanta Press Club, the National Association of Black Journalism and the Omega Psi Phi Fraternity.

In a nearly 50-year career, Adams has not only achieved for himself but for his people and the country he loves so much. He is the recipient of dozens of awards. They include: The National Conference of Christians and Jews Regional Award, 1962; Brotherhood Award by the St. Petersburg Council on Human Relations, 1963; Sigma Delta Chi Green Eyeshade Sweepstakes Award for "Best in Journalism", 1969; Outstanding Leadership Award by the University of Kansas Center for Multicultural Leadership, 1999; the Distinguished Service in Journalism Education in 2001 by the Association for Education in Journalism. At his "Lifetime Achievement Award" by the National Association of Black Journalists in 1997, Adams commented, "It comes as a tremendous surprise, but the most marvelous of awards I've won. It just means somebody wishes to recognize good talent for somebody who has done it well for along time. It just means you're getting old, but gosh, it feels good." Adams' bluntness and sense of humor are probably his secret of success.

WILLIAM EDWARD BURGHARDT DUBOIS (1868-1963)

W.E.B. DuBois was born in Great Barrington, Massachusetts in 1868, the year of President Andrew Johnson's impeachment; he died in Ghana, West Africa, in 1963 as an African. He has been characterized by his biographers and numerous other writers as a poet, novelist, historian, sociologist, essayist, and a journalist. DuBois occupies a commanding position in African and American letters. He was an outstanding scholar, teacher, and a political activist, founding member of the NAACP, editor of its journal, *Crisis*, and in all of these roles, the champion of racial justice. As a scholar he published more than 2000 articles and 20 books, including *The Souls of Black Folk* in 1903. DuBois graduated from Fisk University in 1888, and received an M.A. in 1891 from Harvard University. He was the first black to receive the Ph.D. in history from Harvard University in 1896. He also studied sociology in Europe. The purpose of this case study is to examine DuBois as a journalist. DuBois' biographies and his works have been covered by many scholars: John Hope Franklin (1982); John White, (1985); W.E.B. DuBois (1968); Joy James (1997); David Levering Lewis (1995); and DuBois (1924).

DuBois was often regarded as one of the most profound scholars of his time, referred to as the Dean of Negro Intellectuals. In 1909, DuBois was one of the founders of the National Association for the Advancement of Colored People (NAACP). He became the editor of the NAACP's Crisis magazine, which became his voice to the nation to speak out against issues that beleaguered the African American community in the early 20th century until he died on August 27, 1963, on the eve of the March On Washington. He died in Accra, Ghana shortly after becoming a Ghanan citizen.

Under DuBois' editorship of the *Crisis*, 1910 to 1934, the magazine gained national and international recognition. The first issue of *Crisis* appeared in November 1910, with a circulation of 1,000 copies; within 12 months, it was selling 16,000 copies monthly. One of DuBois' biographers asserts: "As a writer, DuBois never surpassed the month-to-month prose of his editorials on social, political, and economic topics in *Crisis*. His reputation as a writer will rest more on *Crisis* than on his forays into belles letters" (Broderick, 1959). In the first issue of the magazine, DuBois declared that in *Crisis*, he intended to "set forth those facts and arguments that show the danger of race prejudice, particularly as manifested toward colored people." From the very beginning DuBois was determined that the magazine would reflect his own ideas, even when they ran counter to those of the NAACP leadership. He aimed his editorial shafts at the literate and middle class black public. Early issues of *Crisis* featured editorials and articles on "colored high schools, the colored college athletes and women clubs, and the repeated assertions that Blacks possessed a superior spiritual sense and beauty that made them a chosen people." He called for resistance against attempts being made outside the South to institute segregated schools, attacked the black churches for their racial conservationism and defended the rights of women.

The third issue carried DuBois' avowal, "I am resolved to be quiet and law-abiding, but refuse to cringe in body or soul, to resent deliberate insult, and to assert my just rights in the face of wanton aggression," and *Crisis* recommended black self-defense against white vigilante mobs. Employing a variety of techniques and literary devices, DuBois wrote in a clear, direct style, and used savage and sardonic humour to depict racial indignities and atrocities. In 1911, he dramatically described a lynching in Pennsylvania:

Ah, the splendour of that Sunday night dance. The flames beat and curled against the moonlight sky. The church bells chimed. The scorched and crooked thing, self-wounded and chained to his cot, crawled to the edge of the ash with a stifled groan, but the brave and sturdy farmers pricked him back with the bloody pitchforks until the deed was done. Let the eagle scream! Civilization is again safe!

In 1919, after an intensive investigation of lynching blacks, NAACP published *Thirty Years of Lynching in the United States. 1889-1914.* The publication estimated 3,224 black men and women who had been lynched during this period. Also during World War I, *Crisis* publicized the rising of lynch law, most dramatically in a 1916 account (published as an eight-page supplement) of the seizure and lynching of Jesse Washington, a mentally retarded adolescent, found guilty and sentenced to death for the murder of a white woman in Waco, Texas.

Between 1918 and 1928, DuBois who had earlier made three trips to Europe, visited Africa, France, England, Belgium, Switzerland, Portugal, Germany, and Russia. As he later wrote, these trips "gave me a depth of knowledge and breadth of view which was of incalculable value for realizing and judging modern conditions and, above all, the problem of race in America and the world." (Dubois, 1940). While the racial situation continued to engage most of his attention, DuBois increasingly came to realize that those conflicts must be set in the contest of the universal problem of the color line. He challenged black institutions including colleges, universities, and the NAACP not to be indifferent to the economic plight of the Black masses. He demonstrated that race was seriously underestimated in the theories and strategies proposed to bring racial change. To emphasize the larger social, economic, and political questions at the expense of racial considerations was, to him naive and dangerous. Like DuBois, most African-Americans believe today that racial classification and racism remain the heart of the American dilemma.

CHUCK STONE (1924-)

Chuck Stone was born on July 21, 1924 in Hartford, Connecticut, and later moved to St. Louis. He received the B.A. degree in 1948 from Wesleyan University, M.A. in 1951 from the University of Chicago, and attended the University of Connecticut Law School, 1954-1955 and Eastern Baptist Theological Seminary in Philadelphia, 1989-1991. He received several honorary degrees including the Doctor of Humane Letters from Winston Salem State University (1999), Wilberforce University (1977), Doctor of Letters from Wesleyan University (1995), and Rider College (1985).

Stone's career has been well documented by many authors. His career may be viewed from four related perspectives: reporter, editor, columnist and educator. In a recent volume on the achievements of African-Americans in journalism (Wolseley, 1995), Stone's story was told along with several other black journalists and writers, such as Frederick Douglass, T. Thomas Fortune, James Weldom Johnson, William Monroe Trotter, Susan L. Taylor and Martin R. Delany.

As an African American journalist, Chuck Stone began his first job in 1958 at the *New York Age,* a black-oriented weekly once edited by T. Thomas Fortune, sometimes called the dean of journalism of his time. The paper was owned by the Rev. Adam Clayton Powell, a former U.S. Congressman. In 1960, he became White House correspondent and editor of the

Washington edition of the *Afro-American*. Three years later he was named editor in chief of the *Chicago Defender*, another leading newspaper and now one of the few black dailies in the U.S. Between 1965 and 1972 Stone was engaged in other activities: first as a special assistant to Congressman Powell, 1965 to 1967, and he also took time out to complete three books. *Black Political Power in America* (1968), *Tell It Like It Is* (1967), *King Strut* (1970). He was also the author of numerous chapters and journal articles.

He returned to full-time journalism in 1972, becoming the first black columnist on the white-oriented general newspaper, the *Philadelphia Daily News*. He was also its first black senior editor until he resigned in 1991 when he became a professor of journalism at the University of North Carolina. He is currently the Walter Spearman Professor at the University of North Carolina, Chapel Hill. He also had several other teaching experiences: the University of Delaware, 1985-1991; Harvard, 1982; Syracuse University in 1975 as a visiting professor, Moscow State University, 2000; Asmara University in Eritrea. As a journalist, he was engaged in international reporting: Northern Ireland, 1981; Cairo, Egypt, Gaza and India, 1956-1958; and many African countries in 1985. His honors and numerous awards include: University of Delaware Medal of Distinction 2000; University of Chicago Public Service Citation, 2000; one of the 20th Century's Influential Black Journalists cited by the NABJ (one of the five still living); Distinguished Service in Journalism Award by the University of Missouri School of Journalism, 1996; Free Spirit Award by the Freedom Forum, 1992; and Panhellenic Faculty of the Year by the University of Delaware, 1989.

Stone is unique in that he was able to combine many career activities to accomplish his goal, including his military career as a Flight Officer Navigator in World War II, 1943-1945, and a Tuskegee Airman in the Army Air Corps. Everything he touched nearly turned to diamond as a journalist, professor and administrator and especially in his family life. Chuck is married to Louise Davis of Hampton, Virginia. They have three children, Krishna, Allegra, and Charles, III.

CARL THOMAS ROWAN (1925-2001)

Carl Thomas Rowan was born in Ravenscroft, Tennessee of a very poor family. He was a journalist, an author, former Ambassador, and former Director of the United States Information Agency. As a columnist, Rowan's column was circulated through many newspapers by Field Enterprise.

Rowan attended Tennessee Agricultural and Industrial State College in Nashville and graduated with a bachelor's degree in mathematics from Oberlin College in Ohio. He then went to the University of Minnesota, where he was awarded a master's degree in journalism. While he was attending the university, he was employed by the *Minneapolis Tribune*.

As a journalist, Rowan received many awards. In 1952, he received the Sidney Hillman award for the best newspaper reporting in the nation during 1951. In 1952, he was cited by Lincoln University in Jefferson City, Missouri, for his work. He is the only newspaperman to receive the Sigma Delta Chi award three years in a row for the best reporting. In 1951, he was selected Minneapolis Outstanding Man of the Year by the Junior Chamber of Commerce. In 1958, he was selected as one of America's Ten Outstanding Men of 1953, Distinguished Service Award by Capital Press Club, 1964, and National Brotherhood Award by the National Coalition of Christians and Jews, 1964. He also received a number of honorary degrees from many colleges and universities, including an LL.D. from Howard University. As an American diplomat, he was appointed Ambassador to Finland, 1963-1964, Director of USLA, 1964-1965,and Deputy Assistant Secretary of State for Public Affairs, 1961-1963. As an author, Rowan wrote many books, including: *South of Freedom* (1953), *The Pitiful and the Proud* (1956), *Go South in Sorrow* (1957), and the biography of Jackie Robinson called *Wait Till Next Year* (1960).

WILLIAM H. DILDAY. JR. (1937-)

William H. Dilday, Jr. was born in Boston, Massachusetts and was educated at Boston University, where he received the B.S. and B.A. degrees. Since 1984, Dilady has served as the President and Chief Executive Officer of Kerimax Communications, Incorporated. As a writer, he serves as a guest columnist for the *Jackson Clarion Ledger* daily newspaper in Mississippi. He was the first African-American to serve as the general manager of a network affiliate television station. This was during the period when there was no cable television. There were only three major networks: ABC, NBC, and CBS.

Dilday began his career with an appointment as an operations supervisor in 1964. In 1968 he became Personnel Administrator and Public Relations Director at Edgerton, Germehausen & Grier, Inc.; Director of Personnel at WHDH, Inc. between 1969-1972. His career in journalism as the General Manager of WLBT-TV came in 1972. He served in this capacity until 1984. As the Chief Operation Officer, he led the station to achieve the status of number one in both Nielson and Arbitron ratings from the period of November 1973 through February, 1984. He increased the gross revenue and profits every year during his tenure. He created and supervised an investigative reporting unit that received numerous awards including the Peabody Award for Documentary Reporting, the National Mental Health Association Media Award and two Iris Awards from the National Association of Television Program Executives (NATPE). He was also successful at increasing the enrollment of people of color and implemented awareness and sensitivity programs that improved morale and communications among all the 100 employees at WLBT and its satellite operation, WLBM.

In 1990, Dilday had a destined opportunity to serve another affiliate network - WJTV in Jackson, Mississippi as the General Manager and Executive Vice President. This was a CBS Affiliate. Here he implemented operational and programming plans that significantly improved profit and ratings, bringing the station from a distant second place to a virtual first place tie with the number one competitor. He left WJTV to become Corporate Vice President of News-Press and Gazette. He served in this capacity until 1993. During his tenure he had the overall responsibility for national sales at corporation's six television stations. He supervised General Managers and advertising agencies in creating, implementing and achieving short-term and long-range sales plans, and he was able to increase overall sales revenue each year.

Dilday has received numerous awards and citations for his unique role in American journalism. He has been listed in *Who's Who in America* several times: 1977 through 1995, and *Who's Who in Black America*, 1975-1976 through 1993-1995. He is a member of several national boards, including First American Bank, 1990-1993, 1994-2001. He was the founding Chairman and Member of the Board of Directors of Mississippi's first minority controlled commercial bank since Reconstruction; Founding Member of the National Association of

Black Journalists; Founding Member of the 100 Black Men in Jackson, Mississippi; National Broadcasting Company Television Affiliate Board, 1979-1983; National Association of Broadcasters Television Board of Directors, 1981-1984; Jackson Urban League President, 1978-1979, and a member of the Congressional Black Caucus' Communications Task Force. Dilday's story is not a personal success story but a succsss story of all men of color. Throughout his career in the business of journalism, Dilday has exemplified the scarce qualities of a true leader in American journalism. He was not only successful in his career. He is also happily married, a rather rare combination of accomplishments these days. He is married to Maxine and has two daughters, Erika Lynn and Kenya Aleafe.

REFERENCES

Bentz ValerieM.ed. (1993). *Women's Power and Roles as Portrayed in Visual Images of Women in the Arts and Mass Media*. Lewiston: The Edwin Mellen Press.

Broderick, F.L. (1959). *W.E.B. DuBois: Negro Leader in a Time of Crisis*. Stanford.

Cable News Network (2001). "Tribute to Longtime Anchor, CNN's Bernard Shaw: A Newsman's Career". Atlanta: http://www.cnn/SPECIALS.

Dates, Jannette L. and Barlow, William, eds. (1999). *Split Image: African Americans in the Mass Media*. Washington, D.C.: Howard University Press.

Dawkins,Wayne (1997). *Black Journalists: The NABJ Story*. Merrillville, Indiana: August Press.

deTocqueville, Alexis (1835). *Democracy in America*. Two volumes published in 1969. New York: Doubleday.

DuBois, W.E.B. (1924). *Dusk of Dawn*. New York:

DuBois, W.E.B. (1968). *The Autobiography of W.E.B. DuBois*. New York: International Publishers.

Franklin, John Hope and Meier, August (1982). *Black Leaders of the Twentieth Century*. Urbana: University of Illinois Press.

Gordon, Jacob (1993). *Narratives of African Americans in Kansas, 1870-1992: Beyond the Exodus Movement*. Lewiston, New York: Edwin Mellen Press, Ltd.

Jacobs, Ronald N. (2000). *Race. Media, and the Crisis of Civil Society*. Cambridge: Cambridge University Press.

James, Joy (1997). *Transcending the Talented Tenth: Black Leaders and American Intellectuals*. New York: Routledge.

Lewis, David Levering, ed. (1995). *W.E.B. DuBois: A Reader*. New York: Henry Holt and Company, Inc.

Myrdall, Gunnar (1944). *An American Dilemma: the Negro Problem and Modem Democracy*. New York: Harper and Row.

Parks, Gordon (1966). *A Choice of Weapons*.

White, John (1985). *Black Leadership in America, 1895-1968*. New York: Longman.

Wolseley, Roland F. (1995). *Black Achievers in American Journalism*. Nashville: James C. Winston Publishing Company, Inc.

Chapter 7

THE PRECARIOUS POVERTY SITUATION OF BLACK MALES IN THE UNITED STATES

Susan Williams McElroy
H. John Heinz III School of Public Policy and Management
Carnegie Mellon University
Leon T. Andrews, Jr.
University of Michigan
Ann Arbor, Michigan

ABSTRACT

Despite enormous gains in educational attainment and marked improvements in employment opportunities, black males continue to be overrepresented among the poor in the United States. That is, black males account for a larger percentage of the poor than they do of the overall population. The poverty situation of black males described in this paper is based on the poverty measure of the U.S. Census Bureau. The measure is based on pre-tax money income and does not include public assistance. Black males account for 6% of the total population of the United States, yet they account for 11% of the poor. Thus, their representation among the poor is twice what it is among the population as a whole. The overrepresentation of black male children among the poor is even more notable. Whereas black males account for 8% of the population under age 18, black male children account for 17% of the poor in this age group.

A second dimension of the precarious poverty situation of black males is that black males have high poverty rates as compared with the overall population. Also, black males have higher poverty rates than white males do, and this holds true across age groups. In 2000, 11% of the total U.S. population lived in poverty, as compared with 20% of black males. Why do black males have poverty rates that are higher than those of the overall population? Why are black males so likely to be poor and why are black males overrepresented among the poor? We explain the overrepresentation of black males among the poor in the following way. First, we demonstrate that black males are more likely than white males are to have no income at all. Further, the labor force participation rate of black males has declined in recent decades and continues to decline. Further, those black males who do have income are likely to fall into the lower income categories. In addition, employed black males are concentrated in the lower-paying occupations.

The black experience is unique in the history of the United States. The terms on which black males were incorporated into the U.S. economy were different from the terms on which males of any other race-gender group were incorporated into the economy. The history of slavery carries important ramifications for the present-day economic status of black males.

INTRODUCTION

The poverty situation of black males in the United States is precarious at best – precarious because millions of black children and black youth are growing up in poverty, in circumstances which negatively affect their life chances. At the other end of the age spectrum, many elderly black males face an uncertain future because the fixed incomes on which they survive are not large enough to lift them out of poverty. In the middle of the age spectrum are black males in their 20s, 30s, 40s, and 50s who either have low incomes or no income at all and therefore find themselves living in poverty.

This paper documents the poverty situation of black males in the United States, emphasizing the overrepresentation of black males among the poor. In many cases, we compare black males to white males in order to provide some comparative perspective and to assess how black males fare compared with others, especially their white male counterparts. In addition, we consider in detail a number of key factors that are relevant to poverty status, including age, educational attainment, employment status, and living arrangements. Our objective is to contribute to an explanation of why so many black males are poor and why black males of all ages are so likely to be among the poor.

COUNTING THE BLACK MALE POOR: A LOOK AT THE NUMBERS

In order to count the black male poor, we begin with a brief summary of how the Census Bureau defines and measures poverty. The Census Bureau's definition of poverty is based on annual pre-tax money income and does not include in-kind benefits or public assistance. Each year, the Census Bureau releases a set of income thresholds that vary by size of family unit and number of children. The official U.S. poverty standard grew out of a series of studies for the Social Security Administration in the mid-1960s. The poverty thresholds were originally developed by Mollie Orshanky of the Social Security Administration in 1964. The poverty thresholds do not vary geographically, but they are updated annually for inflation with the Consumer Price Index. Orshansky developed poverty measures by starting with a set of minimal adequate food budgets for families of various sizes and types that had been calculated by the Department of Agriculture. To obtain the poverty threshold, Orshansky multiplied these minimum food budgets by a factor of three, on the assumption that food typically represented about one-third of total family expenditures. According to the scale created from this study, any family whose income was less than three times the cost of the minimum food budgets of the Department of Agriculture was classified as poor. The poverty index has been revised twice by Federal Interagency Committees, once in 1969 and again in 1980. While the poverty scale developed from the study discussed above has been subject to considerable criticism, with relatively few minor changes, the poverty scale still forms the basis for measuring the U.S. official poverty rate. The thresholds are used mainly for statistical purposes – for instance, preparing estimates of the number of Americans in poverty each year. All official poverty population figures that the federal government releases are calculated using the poverty thresholds.

The official poverty measure thus consists of a set of dollar amounts that vary by family size. If a family of a given size has an income below the threshold for its size, the family is considered poor. This means that every person in the family is counted among the poor. Families with incomes above the threshold are counted among the nonpoor. The official poverty definition counts money income before taxes and excludes capital gains and noncash benefits such as public housing, Medicaid, and food stamps. To determine whether a person or family falls below the poverty threshold, one simply compares the person's or family's income with the poverty threshold. If the person's or family's income is below the poverty threshold, then that person or family is counted among the poor.

The Census Bureau defines poverty thresholds for family units according to the number of related children under age 18 -- the larger the family unit, the higher the poverty threshold. Figure 1 shows the poverty thresholds[1] by size of family unit for the year 2000. The poverty thresholds presented in the figure are for families with no related children under 18 years. In the year 2000, the poverty threshold for one person, an unrelated individual, that is, a person under age 65 who was not living with family members[2] was $8,959, while the poverty threshold for a two-person family with no related children under age 18 was $11,531. (U.S. Census Bureau 2001). The complete set of poverty thresholds for 2000, including the thresholds for families with related children under age 18 are shown in Table A1 in the appendix. For example, the poverty threshold for a family of four that includes two related children under age 18 was $17,463

Given the Census Bureau's definition of poverty as outlined above, one may raise the following straightforward question: how many black males in the United States are poor? As indicated in Table 1, in the year 2000, of the approximately 16.7 million black males in the United States, approximately 3.3 million, or 20%, were living in poverty. However, one should note that this figure of 20% is the poverty rate for black males of all age combined. Therefore, while a useful summary statistic, it does indeed mask the considerable variation in poverty rates of black males by age. When one reviews the poverty rates of black males by age, as depicted graphically in Figure 2, one observes that among black males, the age groups with the highest poverty rates are under 18 years (poverty rate of 30.5%) and 75 years and over (22.4%). These data reveal that it is the youngest and the oldest black males who are the most vulnerable from a poverty standpoint. The poverty rate of black male children (under age 18) is of particular concern given that growing up in poverty carries with it implications for a number of aspects of one's childhood – education, neighborhood safety and conditions, health care, and exposure to violence, just to name a few.

---

[1] The weighted averages based on size of family unit serve as a summary measure (U.S. Census Bureau 1999 *Poverty in the United States* report).

[2] The Census Bureau defines a family as "a group of two people or more (one of whom is the householder) related by birth, marriage, or adoption and residing together; all such people (including related subfamily members) are considered as members of one family."

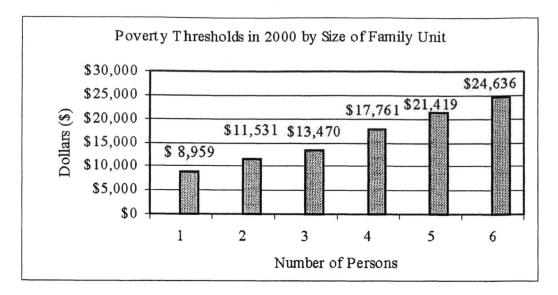

Figure 1. Poverty Thresholds in 2000 by Size of Family Unit

Source: U.S.Census Bureau, 2001. Poverty thresholds in 2000. Available at http://www.census.gov. Accessed on 30 January 2002. http://www.census.gov/hhes/poverty/threshld/thresh00.html

Figure 2 also shows the percentage of black males whose incomes are below twice the poverty level. The poverty level has been criticized on the grounds that it is too low. One response to such criticism is that the Census Bureau also reports the number and percent of persons whose incomes fall below various ratios of the poverty level, for example, twice the poverty level. Over half (57.8%) of all black males under age 18 had incomes below twice poverty, as did over half (56.9%) of all black males age 75 and over.

How do black males fare compared with white males in terms of poverty rates by age? Consider the under-18 age group first. As shown in Figure 3 and as noted above, the poverty rate of black males in this age group is 30.5%. The corresponding poverty rate for white males is 12.7%. Thus, black boys are more than twice as likely to be among the poor than are their white male counterparts. What about black elderly males? How do their poverty rates compare to those of white males of the same age group? The poverty rate of white males age 65 and over is 6.5%, as compared to a poverty rate of 17.1% for black males in this age group. Black males age 65 and over are more than twice as likely to be poor than are white males in that age bracket.

Table 1. Number and Percent of Persons below Poverty for Selected Race-Gender Groups by Age: United States, 2000 (numbers in thousands)

	Total (in population)	Number below poverty	Percent of Total
All Persons			
Total	275,924	31,054	11.3
under 18 years	71,936	11,553	16.1
18 to 24 years	26,965	3,890	14.4
25 to 34 years	37,440	3,892	10.4
35 to 44 years	44,780	3,678	8.2
45 to 54 years	38,040	2,441	6.4
55 to 64 years	23,785	2,241	9.4
65 years and over	32,978	3,359	10.2
Black Males			
Total	16,680	3,267	19.6
under 18 years	5,770	1,758	30.5
18 to 24 years	1,868	346	18.5
25 to 34 years	2,317	273	11.8
35 to 44 years	2,649	330	12.5
45 to 54 years	1,935	234	12.1
55 to 64 years	1,032	135	13.1
65 years and over	1,110	190	17.1
White Males			
Total	111,297	9,241	8.3
under 18 years	28,950	3,674	12.7
18 to 24 years	10,906	1,111	10.2
25 to 34 years	14,937	1,032	6.9
35 to 44 years	18,392	1,103	6.0
45 to 54 years	15,795	800	5.1
55 to 64 years	9,755	705	7.2
65 years and over	12,562	816	6.5
Hispanic Males			
Total	16,861	3,287	19.5
under 18 years	6,107	1,690	27.7
18 to 24 years	2,115	378	17.9
25 to 34 years	2,861	458	16.0
35 to 44 years	2,557	328	12.8
45 to 54 years	1,545	175	11.3
55 to 64 years	899	123	13.7
65 years and over	777	137	17.6

	Total (in population)	Number below poverty	Percent of Total
Black Females			
Total	19,072	4,595	24.1
under 18 years	5,637	1,728	30.7
18 to 24 years	2,127	595	28.0
25 to 34 years	2,829	609	21.5
35 to 44 years	3,090	566	18.3
45 to 54 years	2,342	348	14.9
55 to 64 years	1,367	316	23.1
65 years and over	1,680	434	25.8
White Females			
Total	114,700	12,001	10.5
under 18 years	27,462	3,608	13.1
18 to 24 years	10,626	1,597	15.0
25 to 34 years	14,930	1,706	11.4
35 to 44 years	18,299	1,466	8.0
45 to 54 years	16,169	862	5.3
55 to 64 years	10,654	976	9.2
65 years and over	16,560	1,785	10.8
Hispanic Females			
Total	16,855	3,866	22.9
under 18 years	5,776	1,639	28.4
18 to 24 years	2,063	519	25.2
25 to 34 years	2,780	622	22.4
35 to 44 years	2,481	454	18.3
45 to 54 years	1,667	220	13.2
55 to 64 years	984	196	19.9
65 years and over	1,104	216	19.6

Source: U.S. Census Bureau, Current Population Survey, March 2001.
Table 22. Age, Gender, Household Relationship, Race and Hispanic Origin - Poverty Status of People by Selected Characteristics in 2000; Based on a November 2001 weighting correction. Available at http://ferret.bls.census.gov/macro/032001/pov/new22_003.htm
Accessed 31 Jaunary 2002.

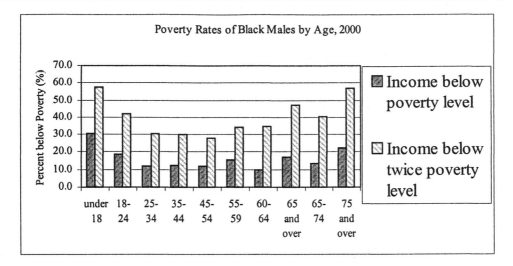

Figure 2. Poverty Rates of Black Males by Age, 2000

Source: U.S. Census Bureau, 2001.

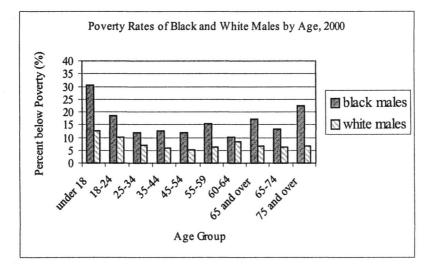

Figure 3. Poverty Rate of Black and White Males by Age, 2000

Source: U.S. Census Bureau.

Over half (54%) of all black males in poverty are under age 18 (Table 2). Persons under age 18 also account for a large percentage (40%), though less than half of all white males in poverty. Indeed poverty among both black and white males is concentrated among the younger ages. Persons ages 18 to 34 account for nearly one-fifth (19%) of all poor black males. Table 2 also shows corresponding statistics on the age distribution of persons in poverty for selected other race-gender groups (white males, black females, white females, Hispanic males, and Hispanic males).

THE OVERREPRESENTATION OF BLACK MALES AMONG THE POOR

Despite enormous gains in educational attainment and marked improvements in their employment opportunities, black males continue to be overrepresented among the poor in the United States. That is, black males account for a larger percentage of the poor than they do of the population as a whole. Black males accounted for 6% of the total population in the U.S., yet they account for 11% of the poor.[3] By contrast, white males account for 40% of the total population and 30% of the poor. These statistics reveal that while black males are overrepresented among the poor, white males are actually underrepresented among the poor. Table 3 shows detailed data on the representation of selected race-gender groups among the poor in 2000.

In order to understand why black males are overrepresented among the poor, one must understand why so many black males have either low income or no income at all. Let us consider first the case of no income. Figure 4 shows the percentage of black and white males age 15 and over who had no income from 1967 to 2000. In the year 2000, 15% of black males age 15 and over had no income at all, as compared with 6% of white males of the same age. During the period from 1967 to 2000, the percentage of black males with no income ranged between 11% (in 1968 and 1989 to 17% (in 1982). By contrast, the percentage of white males with no income was much lower, ranging between 4% (from 1979 through 1981 and from 1984 through 1991) and 8% (in 1971). Researchers have offered a number of explanations for why black men have low incomes. Most of these explanations can be categorized as supply-side explanations, which focus primarily on the educational attainment and skills of black males. However, researchers have paid less attention to the reality that a nontrivial percentage of adult black males have no income at all.

One crucial factor in proportion of black males with no income at all is the declining rates of labor force participation of black males. The labor force participation rate is the percentage of the population that is in the paid labor force.[4] In 1972, the labor force participation rate of black males 74%, and in the year 2000, it was 69% (Figure 5). Although there have been years since 1972 when the black male labor force participation rate did increase, in general the labor force participation rate of black males has been steadily drifting downward. While some persons who are not in the paid labor force have incomes, declining rates of labor force participation are certainly related to the percentage of black males with no income at all and in turn related to the poverty rates of black males.

---

[3] Data are for the year 2000 and are taken from the March 2001 Current Population Survey conducted by the U.S. Census Bureau.

[4] Unemployed persons are counted among the labor force. At any given point in time, an individual person is either employed, unemployed, or not in the paid labor force. The number of persons in the labor force is the sum of the employed plus the unemployed.

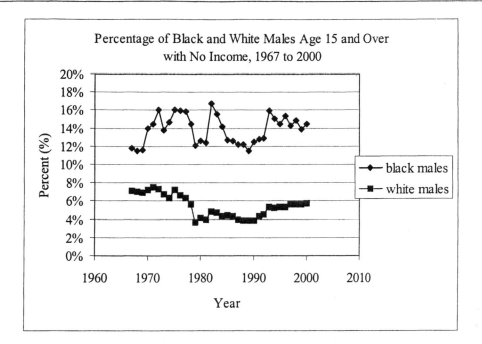

Figure 4. Percentage of Black and White Males Age 15 and Over with No Income, 1967 to 2000

Source: U.S. Census Bureau, 2001.

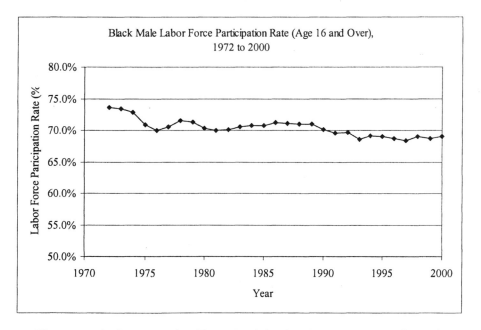

Figure 5. Black Male Labor Force Participation Rate (Age 16 and Over), 1972 to 2000

Source: U.S. Bureau of Labor Statistics, various years.

We explain the overrepresentation of black males among the poor in the following way. First, we demonstrate that black males are more likely than white males are to have no income at all. Further, those black males who do have income are likely to fall into the lower income categories for a variety of reasons. Also, and as important, a nontrivial percentage of black males who are employed work part-time rather than full-time. In addition, employed black males are concentrated in the lower-paying occupations (McElroy and Darity 1999).

LOW INCOME AND NO INCOME: TWO SIDES OF THE ECONOMIC STATUS OF BLACK MALES IN WHITE AMERICA

Because poverty as defined by the Census Bureau is based on money income, the number and proportion of black men living in poverty is determined by the number of black males with incomes below the poverty threshold. It is also the case that persons with no income at all are also considered poor. The percentage of black males who have no income at all is nothing short of startling. For example, in 1999, of the 11,687,0900 million black males age 15 and over, 31.5% (3,680,000) or nearly one-third of them had no income at all. This act is important because it points to the precarious position of black males in the United States economy. While it is true that there is an earnings gap between black males and white males, perhaps even more startling is the considerable percentage of black males who have no income at all.

Among those black males who are in the paid labor force and employed, the number of hours worked has a profound influence on earnings and hence on the likelihood of being in poverty. Table 4 details the median earnings (dollars) of black and white males age 15 and over and earnings relative to poverty threshold in 1999 by work experience in 1999. In addition to reporting median earnings, we also report how the median earnings compare relative to the poverty threshold of $8,959 for 2000.[5] Black males who worked full-time, that is 35 or more hours per week, had a median income of $26,416 in the year 2000. This means that they earned on average nearly 3 times the poverty threshold (for an unrelated individual).[6] By contrast, black males who worked at part-time earned an average[7] of $4,551 per year, or roughly half (51%) of the poverty threshold. The upshot of the information presented here is that whether black male are working full-time or part-time has important implications for income and hence for poverty status.

---

[5] The poverty threshold of $8,959 is defined for an unrelated individual, that is a person who is not living with relatives.

[6] We use the poverty threshold for unrelated individuals here, but of course many black males are living in families and so for them the relevant poverty threshold would be higher.

[7] Here we use the median for the average.

Table 2. Age Distribution of Persons below Poverty by Race–Gender Group, 2000 (Numbers in thousands)

	black males		white males		black females		white females		Hispanic males		Hispanic females	
	number	%	number	%	number	%	number	%	number	%	number	%
Total	3,267	100%	9,241	100%	4,595	100%	12,001	100%	6,148	100%	8,384	100%
Under 18 years	1,758	54%	3,674	40%	1,728	38%	3,608	30%	2,106	34%	2,079	25%
18 to 24 years	346	11%	1,111	12%	595	13%	1,597	13%	754	12%	1,108	13%
25 to 34 years	273	8%	1,032	11%	609	13%	1,706	14%	591	10%	1,124	13%
35 to 44 years	330	10%	1,103	12%	566	12%	1,466	12%	795	13%	1,044	12%
45 to 54 years	234	7%	800	9%	348	8%	862	7%	632	10%	652	8%
55 to 59 years	90	3%	357	4%	163	4%	497	4%	314	5%	416	5%
60 to 64 years	45	1%	348	4%	153	3%	479	4%	275	4%	378	5%
65 years and over	190	6%	816	9%	434	9%	1,785	15%	681	11%	1,582	19%
65 to 74 years	87	3%	459	5%	230	5%	731	6%	361	6%	621	7%
75 years and over	103	3%	357	4%	204	4%	1,055	9%	320	5%	961	11%

Source: U.S. Bureau of the Census, 2001.

CPS Annual Demographic Survey, March 2001, Table 22.

Available at http://ferret.bls.census.gov/macro/032001/pov/new22_003.htm Table 22.

Table 3. Representation of Selected Race–Gender Groups among the Poor, 2000 (Numbers in thousands)

	All races male + female	black males		white males		black females		white females		Hispanic males		Hispanic females	
		number	%	number	%	number	%	number	%	number	%	number	%
Total	31,054	3,267	11%	9,241	30%	4,595	15%	12,001	39%	6,148	20%	8,384	27%
Under 18 years	11,553	1,758	15%	3,674	32%	1,728	15%	3,608	31%	2,106	18%	2,079	18%
18 to 24 years	3,890	346	9%	1,111	29%	595	15%	1,597	41%	754	19%	1,108	28%
25 to 34 years	3,892	273	7%	1,032	27%	609	16%	1,706	44%	591	15%	1,124	29%
35 to 44 years	3,678	330	9%	1,103	30%	566	15%	1,466	40%	795	22%	1,044	28%
45 to 54 years	2,441	234	10%	800	33%	348	14%	862	35%	632	26%	652	27%
55 to 59 years	1,175	90	8%	357	30%	163	14%	497	42%	314	27%	416	35%
60 to 64 years	1,066	45	4%	348	33%	153	14%	479	45%	275	26%	378	35%
65 years and over	3,359	190	6%	816	24%	434	13%	1,785	53%	681	20%	1,582	47%
65 to 74 years	1,592	87	5%	459	29%	230	14%	731	46%	361	23%	621	39%
75 years and over	1,767	103	6%	357	20%	204	12%	1,055	60%	320	18%	961	54%

Source: U.S. Bureau of the Census, 2000.

CPS Annual Demographic Survey, March 2001, Table 22.

Available at http://ferret.bls.census.gov/macro/032001/pov/new22_003.htm Table 22.

Table 4. Median Earnings (Dollars) of Black and White Males Age 15 and Over* and Earnings Relative to Poverty Threshold in 1999 by Work Experience in 1999 (population numbers in thousands)

	Black males				White males				White/black ratio earnings ratio
	Median earnings ($)	% of poverty	Number of persons	Percent dist.	Median earnings ($)	% of poverty	Number of persons	Percent dist.	
Total (all levels of work experience)	$23,060	2.57	8,007	100%	$30,793	3.44	66,800	100%	1.34
worked at full-time** jobs									
total	$26,416	2.95	6,911	86%	$34,612	3.86	58,237	87%	1.31
worked 50 weeks or more per year	$30,026	3.35	5,642	70%	$37,248	4.16	49,160	74%	1.24
worked 27 to 49 weeks per year	$17,046	1.90	651	8%	$20,876	2.33	5,468	8%	1.22
worked 26 weeks or less per year	$5,564	0.62	618	8%	$5,972	0.67	3,609	5%	1.07
worked at part-time jobs									
total	$4,551	0.51	1,097	14%	$5,267	0.59	8,563	13%	1.16
worked 50 weeks or more per year	$8,632	0.96	452	6%	$9,349	1.04	3,685	6%	1.08
worked 27 to 49 weeks per year	$5,146	0.57	181	2%	$6,219	0.69	1,837	3%	1.21
worked 26 weeks or less per year	$1,968	0.22	463	6%	$1,921	0.21	3,041	5%	0.98

Poverty threshold in 1999 $8,959

* Numbers of black and white males are in thousands.

** Full-time is defined as 35 or more hours per week.

Sources: U.S. Bureau of the Census, 2000, *Money Income in the United States 1999*, Available at http://www.census.gov/prod/2000pubs/p60-209.pdf, U.S. Bureau of the Census, 2001,
Poverty Thresholds in 1999, by Size of Family and Number of Related Children Under 18 Years,
Available at http://www.census.gov/hhes/poverty/threshld/thresh99.html, Date accessed 22 January 2002.

WHAT DIFFERENCE DOES EDUCATIONAL ATTAINMENT MAKE?

Table 5. Poverty Rates of Black and White Males by Age and Education Level, 2000

	Black Males	White Males	Black-White ratio
All Education Levels			
Total	12.9	6.2	2.1
25 to 34 years	11.8	6.9	1.7
35 to 54 years	12.3	5.6	2.2
55 to 64 years	13.0	7.2	1.8
65 years and over	17.1	6.5	2.6
65 to 74 years	13.3	6.3	2.1
75 years and over	22.4	6.7	3.3
No High School Diploma			
Total	25.1	16.9	1.5
25 to 34 years	34.4	22.1	1.6
35 to 54 years	26.3	16.9	1.6
55 to 64 years	16.3	17.4	0.9
65 years and over	24.8	13.9	1.8
65 to 74 years	23.7	14.9	1.6
75 years and over	25.9	12.8	2.0
High School Diploma, No College			
Total	13.7	6.0	2.3
25 to 34 years	11.1	6.0	1.9
35 to 54 years	15.0	5.9	2.5
55 to 64 years	17.5	7.3	2.4
65 years and over	9.9	5.0	2.0
65 to 74 years	7.2	4.7	1.5
75 years and over	15.1	5.5	2.7
Some College, No Bachelor's Degree			
Total	7.3	4.4	1.7
25 to 34 years	8.7	4.4	2.0
35 to 54 years	6.5	4.4	1.5
55 to 64 years	8.4	5.9	1.4
65 years and over	7.1	2.6	2.7
	Black Males	**White Males**	**Black-White ratio**
65 to 74 years	1.9	3.0	0.6
75 years and over	(B)	2.0	(B)
Bachelor's Degree or More			
Total	4.1	2.5	1.6
25 to 34 years	4.6	3.3	1.4
35 to 54 years	3.7	2.1	1.8
55 to 64 years	3.1	2.9	1.1
65 years and over	6.3	2.2	2.9
65 to 74 years	0.5	2.0	0.3
75 years and over	(B)	2.6	(B)

Source: U.S. Census Bureau, Current Population Survey,
Annual Demogrpahic Survey, March 2001, Detailed Poverty
(P60 Package), Available at
http://ferret.bls.census.gov/macro/032001/pov/toc.htm Accessed 1 Febuary 2002.

The data presented in Table 5 demonstrate how poverty rates of black and white males vary with education level. In 2000, 35% of all black males age 25 and over were living below poverty, as compared with 16.9% of white males. Poverty rates were lowest for black males who had completed a bachelor's degree or higher (poverty rate of 4.1%). Black males with less education were noticeably more likely to be in poverty. Specifically, the poverty rate of black males who had completed high school but not attended college was 13.7%, while the rate for white male high school graduates was 6.0%. We consider next the 25 to 54 age group in detail, emphasizing black-white differences in poverty rates.

Figure 6 shows the poverty rates of black and white males age 35 to 54 by education level in 2000. Among black males in this age group, those who had completed high school but not attended college had the highest poverty rate, 15.0%. Note that only 5.9% of white males with the same education were in poverty. Completing even some college, that is, without receiving a bachelor's degree, has a noticeable effect on poverty rates, and the effect of completing college is even more dramatic.

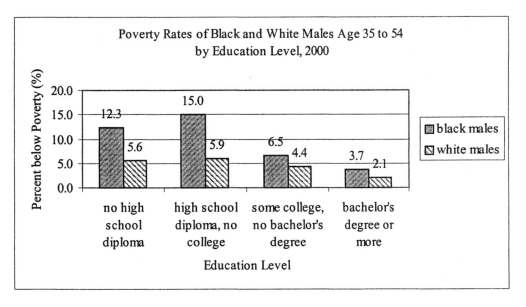

Figure 6. Poverty Rates of Black and White Males Age 35 to 54 by Education Level, 2000

Source: U.S. Census Bureau, Current Population Survey, March 2001.

Black men age 35 to 54 who had completed some college but not received a bachelor's degree had a poverty rate of 6.5%, as compared to a poverty rate of 4.4% among their white male counterparts. Black male college graduates (bachelor's degree or higher) had a poverty rate of 3.7%, while those white males in the same educational attainment group had a poverty rate of 2.1%. Clearly, educational attainment matters as a key factor that influences the likelihood that black males are in poverty -- the higher the educational attainment level, the lower the poverty rate. Nevertheless, even at higher levels of education, black males have higher poverty rates than white males do. Therefore, higher education does not close the black-white gap in male poverty rates.

THE CRUCIAL ROLE OF FAMILY STATUS

The connection between family status and economic status has been often been made for Black women. That is, the prevalence of poverty among families headed by Black females with no spouse present is frequently highlighted. While there is also a connection between family status and economic status for Black males, this connection has received much less attention in the scholarly literature. We document the connection between family status and poverty status of Black males while acknowledging that we can not prove causality, nor do we intend to do so. Black males who live as unrelated individuals are more likely to be in poverty as compared with black males who live in families.

An important, though often overlooked, aspect of black men when discussing their disproportionate overrepresentation among the poor is the family. Black men who are in married-couple families have much lower poverty rates than do black men who are living as unrelated individuals (Table 6). The Census Bureau defines unrelated individuals as people of any age who are not members of families (U.S. Bureau of the Census 2001). In 2000, 6.5% of black men living in married-couple families were living below the poverty level, compared to 24.6% of black who lived as unrelated individuals. The disparity in poverty rates of black men who are married and black men who live as unrelated individuals exists across age groups. These findings are startling and raise the question of whether marriage is important to moving black men out of poverty.

Although the data show that black men who are in married couples are less likely to be poor, the data also show that black men are less likely to live in a married couple family, as compared to white males. The data do not suggest a causal relationship between black males who marry and lower poverty rates. However, the data do provide a context for understanding the importance of black families to the poverty status of black males.

The percentage of black family households headed by a male with no spouse present doubled between 1980 and 2000, increasing from 4% of all black family households in 1980 to 8% in 2000 (U.S. Census Bureau 1998). In absolute numbers, the number of such black family households more than doubled during this period, growing from 256,000 in 1980 to 706,000 in 2000. Thus, while such black families still account for a small percentage of all black families, particularly relative to the percentage of black families that are headed by a woman with no spouse present, it is important to note that such black families constitute a growing segment of all black family households.

Table 6. Poverty Status of Black Males by Living Arrangements and Age, 2000

	Total	Below poverty level	
		Number	Percent
All Living Arrangements			
Total	16,680	3,267	19.6
Under 18 years	5,770	1,758	30.5
18 to 24 years	1,868	346	18.5
25 to 34 years	2,317	273	11.8
35 to 44 years	2,649	330	12.5
45 to 54 years	1,935	234	12.1
55 to 59 years	590	90	15.3
60 to 64 years	442	45	10.1
65 years and over	1,110	190	17.1
65 to 74 years	652	87	13.3
75 years and over	458	103	22.4
Black Males Living in Families			
Total	13,602	2,497	18.4
Under 18 years	5,704	1,725	30.2
18 to 24 years	1,546	229	14.8
25 to 34 years	1,578	145	9.2
35 to 44 years	1,881	157	8.3
45 to 54 years	1,364	106	7.8
55 to 59 years	415	48	11.4
60 to 64 years	309	13	4.3
65 years and over	804	75	9.3
65 to 74 years	492	32	6.4
75 years and over	312	43	13.8
Black Males In Married-Couple Families			
Total	7,823	507	6.5
Under 18 years	2,442	192	7.9
18 to 24 years	691	34	4.9
25 to 34 years	1,007	72	7.2
35 to 44 years	1,384	64	4.6
45 to 54 years	1,015	58	5.7
55 to 59 years	336	19	5.6
60 to 64 years	265	13	5.1
65 years and over	684	55	8.0
65 to 74 years	429	24	5.6
75 years and over	255	31	12.1
Black Males Living as Unrelated Individuals			
Total	3,013	742	24.6
Under 18 years	16	13	(B)
18 to 24 years	319	118	36.9
25 to 34 years	736	125	17.0

35 to 44 years	759	168	22.2
45 to 54 years	571	129	22.5
55 to 59 years	175	43	24.4
60 to 64 years	133	31	23.4
65 years and over	305	115	37.7
65 to 74 years	160	55	34.7
75 years and over	146	60	40.9

Source: U.S. Census Bureau, 2001. Available at
http://ferret.bls.census.gov/macro/032001/pov/toc.htm
Accessed 31 January 2002.

BLACK MALE LEADERS CONFRONT POVERTY

Throughout this chapter, we have spent discussed the overrepresentation of black males among the poor. As the data suggests, black men demonstrate a population at risk. Most social and economic indicators for black men depict individuals whose development and quality of life are in serious jeopardy. That is not to say that there are not many successful black men. Black males have made significant contributions. A significant number of black males have received a bachelor's degree or higher in recent decades. Black males have made inroads in professional occupations in increasing numbers. Also, a significant number of black males are supporting themselves and their families. Although there is strong evidence of successful strides black men have made over the recent decades, it is difficult to ignore the overwhelming problems black men confront. Black men continue to be overrepresented among the poor and among many, if not all, of the other indicators that represent elements needed to reach a decent standard of living, i.e., educational attainment, employment, and income.

We consider the role of black male leadership in addressing the problems confronting the overrepresentation of black men among the poor. Many black males play vital roles in their neighborhoods and communities. There is also strong evidence of black males taking leadership roles to fight the problems confronting the overrepresentation of black males among the poor. Black male leadership takes the form of involvement in community, social organizations, and churches.

There are several organizations where black males assume leadership roles and are working diligently to address the myriad of problems affecting black men and their families. When one discusses black leaders in America, there is a tendency to highlight the typical core of black male leaders – Jesse Jackson, Sr., Kweisi Mfume, Dick Gregory, Colin Powell, and Louis Farrakhan. The tendency to focus on the same national core of black male leaders overlooks several other efforts at the local level where black males assume leadership roles in their city and their community. There are three examples of local black male leadership reviewed in this paper that demonstrate their impact in their respective city, neighborhood, and black men:

1. Ajuma Muhammad of the Association of African-American Role Models (AAARM)
2. David Cheek of the African American Men of Winchester, and

3. Lyman Rhodes of the Indianapolis Commission On African-American Males (ICAAM)

The Association of African-American Role Models is a community-based organization in St Louis, Missouri whose mission is to empower African-American male youth to become productive members of society through education and motivation. AAARM has made significant contributions to the communities across St. Louis by identifying minority and disadvantage black male youth. The members of this organization are primarily black men that serve as role models for these minority and disadvantage youth. This organization emphasizes the importance of academic development relative to career opportunities. AAARM believes in the importance of empowering black male youth through information and cultural awareness.

The African-American Men of Winchester is an organization of black men that have distinguished themselves in the fields of finance, politics, government operation and management, telecommunication, education, social services, business organizations and management, engineering and a wealth of other civic and community activities. Since 1987, this New York-based organization is focused on developing strategies for the advancement of African American men and their families in the areas of economic development, cultural and social impact. The African-American Men of Winchester also seek to strengthen the family institution and to focus their attention on social issues such as employment, housing, crime, health care, and education, which have a disproportionately negative impact on the black community.

Finally, the Indianapolis Commission on African-American Males is a community-based organization established in 1992 by former mayors Stephen Goldsmith. ICAAM is a black male-led organization that has been recognized in the city for it leadership in examining the conditions facing young black men. Their goal is to ensure that black men are able to more proportionately participate in all aspects of their community. The role of ICAAM is to act as a catalyst in identifying issues affecting black males, organizations currently providing services to black males, as well as organizations that should be, and facilitating the coordination of services and resources to collectively provide remedies to problems affecting black males in Indianapolis. ICAAM has become an organization of important influence for black males and their families in the city of Indianapolis.

It is difficult to evaluate and assess the success of the black male-led organizations that have dedicated their efforts to empowering and supporting black men in recent decades. There are many intangibles that come from these efforts that can never be quantified. It is clear, however, that either the efforts made by the black male leaders have not been successful or there are certain obstacles that intervene to restrict efforts made by these black male-led organizations.

Although the cases cited above exemplify the continuous efforts of black male-led organizations to target black men in recent decades, black men still are overrepresented among the poor. Black men continue to be disproportionately represented in the lower echelons of the social and economic indicators needed for a basic standard of living despite the efforts made at the national level and local level by black male leaders and other organizations.

It is evident that despite the efforts of the black male-led organizations to address the problems of black men, there are many stumbling blocks that have minimized their efforts.

The proliferation of drugs, gun-related violence in the black community, the escalation of black male fratricide, and the reconstruction of the black family has diminished the positive role and attributes of these black male-led organizations. These obstacles that confront organizations do not suggest that the efforts of black male leaders and others have been in vain. Rather, the evidence should serve to strengthen the convictions of black male leaders and others that continue to empower black men and their families. The evidence should also serve to encourage others to become more involved in their communities. There is power in numbers who are dedicated and committed to ensuring that black men and their families are no longer disproportionately represented among the poor.

REFERENCES

Blank, Rebecca M. 1997. *It takes a nation: a new agenda for fighting poverty*. New York: Russell Sage Foundation; Princeton, N.J: Princeton University Press.

Carrington, William J. and Bruce C. Fallick. 2001. Do some workers have minimum wage careers? *Monthly Labor Review* vol. 124, no. 5 (May).

Dalaker, Joseph, and Bernadette D. Proctor, U.S. Census Bureau. 2000. Current Population Reports, Series P60-210. *Poverty in the United States: 1999*. U.S. Government Printing Office. Available at http://www.census.gov/prod/www/statistical-abstract-us.html. Accessed on 18 April 2001.

McElroy, Susan Williams and William A. Darity, Jr. 1999. Labor Market Discrimination by Race. In *Readings in Black Political Economy*, ed. John Whitehead. Co-authored with Dubuque, Iowa: Kendall/Hunt Publishing Company.

U.S. Census Bureau. 1998. *Statistical abstract of the United States 1998*. Washington, D.C.: U.S. Government Printing Office.

2000. *Educational Attainment in the United States: March 1999*. Current Population Reports. P20-536. Detailed tables. Washington, D.C.: U.S. Government Printing Office. Available at http://www.census.gov/population/www/socdemo/education/p20-536.html. Accessed on 18 April 2001.

_____. 2000. *Money income in the United States*. Current Population Reports. P60-209. Washington, D.C.: U.S. Government Printing Office. Available at http://www.census.gov/prod/2000pubs/p60-209.pdf. Accessed on 18 April 2001.

_____. 2000. *Statistical abstract of the United States 2000*. Washington, D.C.: U.S. Government Printing Office. http://www.census.gov/prod/www/statistical-abstract-us.html. Accessed on 18 April 2001.

_____. Various years. Unpublished tabulations from the Current Population Survey.

_____. Current Population Survey. 2001. *America's Families and Living Arrangements: March 2000*. By Jason Fields and Lynne M. Casper. Series P-20-537. Available at http://www.census.gov/population/socdemo/hh-fam/p20-537/2000/tabH1.pdf Accessed on 30 January 2002.

_____. Current Population Survey. 2002. *Poverty Thresholds*. Available at http://www.census.gov/hhes/poverty/threshld.html. Accessed on 30 January 2002.

U.S. Department of Labor. Bureau of Labor Statistics. 2001. *Employment and Earnings*. January issue. Available at http://stats.bls.gov/cpsaatab.htm. Accessed on 18 April 2001.

Chapter 8

AFRICAN-AMERICAN MALES IN THE CLINTON ADMINISTRATION

Reginald E. Vance

Nelson Mandela School of Public Policy and Urban Affairs
Southern University and A&M College

ABSTRACT

This chapter focuses on the role of African-Americans in the Clinton administration with emphasis on the African-American male. The author examines the role of Blacks in the election and re-election of Bill Clinton and the positions they held within his administration. This chapter also examines the influence of African-Americans on policy-making in America. Finally, this chapter presents a case study of diversity in the United States National Park Service.

The political process in the United States is steeped in a history of whimsical gamesmanship and partisan policy-making. Far into the Twenty-first Century and beyond, political scientists and scholars of public policy—in an attempt to understand the American political process— will continue to examine interest groups and their effect on policy-making in America. One of the interest groups that will warrant examination is African-Americans. Many of the significant findings will be entrenched in the forward progress gained and battles lost by Blacks, particularly the African-American male during the various presidential administrations.

Further compounding the perplexity faced by public policy students will be the fact that many times in American history, African-Americans sacrificed and served their beloved country— only to be denied proper recognition and equal justice. The shift in political ideology that led to inclusive policy-making will be addressed at many levels. Scholars will focus special attention on the presidential administration of William Jefferson Clinton when explaining the advances made by African-American males in the political process.

As early as the Eighteenth Century, African-Americans' participation in federal government existed with minimal formal recognition. Prominent Blacks served as subject matter experts for many of the domestic policies of earlier presidential administrations and provided our nation's leaders with critical insight on issues pertaining to but not limited to civil rights. While many of these Blacks never received formal recognition for their services, some former presidents made legitimate efforts to include African-Americans in the decision-making process. The utility of African-Americans as national decision-makers however was not earnestly pursued until the Clinton presidency; he rewarded Blacks with representative policies and key executive positions within his administration. Those appointments lead to further policy considerations, which reflected the concerns and choices of diverse groups within the American polis.

The purpose of this chapter is to expand on the limited dialogue of African-Americans in federal government decision-making roles. This chapter contributes to the body of work on the doctrines, policies, and laws that affect African-Americans' participation in policy-making. Also, a portion of this chapter examines the role of African-Americans during Clinton's election and reelection and focuses on the many contributions of African-American males. Finally, this chapter presents a specific case study about one of America's most revered institutions and the effects of representative policy-making.

This chapter should contribute to the readers understanding of:

1. The history of African-Americans in federal government.
2. The overwhelming support Bill Clinton received from African-Americans in his campaigns for election and re-election
3. The contributions made by African-Americans and African-American males during the Clinton administration.
4. The extent that Blacks influenced Clinton's public policy agenda.

REJUVENATED: BILL CLINTON AND THE AFRICAN-AMERICAN

Many former presidents have made legitimate efforts to include African-Americans in the federal decision-making process. However, William Jefferson Clinton is the first United States President to fully utilize the talents of African-Americans to shape and direct national and international policy. Of the fourteen Cabinet Secretary positions, Clinton by far appointed more African-Americans to these posts than any other president in the history of the United States. A White House Fact Sheet dated 6/12/97 proclaimed "President Clinton has appointed the most diverse Cabinet and White House staff in history, presiding over an administration that looks like America." The White House Office of the Press Secretary released the same statement on February 5, 1999. This section chronicles the roles of African-Americans in the Clinton Administration.

In order to gain a clearer perspective of why African-Americans supported Bill Clinton through his initial election in 1992 and his re-election in 1996, it is important to reflect on the prior condition of African-Americans (politically and economically), their hope for a brighter future, and their fervor for social justice. Many Blacks made strides to reach middle class status during the protests of the 1960s and 1970s; some even reaped the benefits of the economic booms of the 1980s. However, by 1992, most blacks had had the "economic rug" pulled from beneath their feet during a twelve-year Republican reign highlighted by Reagonomic policies. What African-Americans wanted was similar to the wants and desires of any other group. They wanted equal access, economic stability, and fewer taxes. With the help of many Black leaders, Bill Clinton campaigned on a promise of diversity and economic reform that captured the attention and support of the African-American community. Ron Brown, former chairman of the Democratic National committee and Vernon Jordan, former Urban League CEO and civil rights activist continued to be two of Clinton's top advisors and personal friends. Both men helped shape Clinton's campaign strategy during his bid for the presidency and his policy agenda once elected.

Motivated by three terms of exclusionary Republican policies that consistently ignored their concerns, African-Americans as a group rallied their forces and helped to elect a president who would include them in the political process. "Because black people have not been able to control American economic policy, they have had to use whatever leverage they could to bend policy decisions to their advantage: demonstrations, lobbying, group pressure, court action, electoral politics, and any other weapon at their command" (Newman et. al, 1978). African-American's weapon of choice in 1992 was the Black vote. The unification of African-Americans for a common concern was evident during the Clinton Administration. Approximately one million more Blacks voted in 1992 than in 1988, and Clinton received 82 percent of the Black vote (Perry and Parent, 1995). Similar support of Blacks was garnered in the 1996 election. By supporting Clinton, African-Americans were able to mobilize as a group and demand a stake in the decision-making process. Clinton reclaimed the White House for the Democrats and announced that he would build a White House administration that "looks like America", which had been at the center of his Cabinet selection strategy (Warshaw, 1996). Shortly after his election in 1992, Clinton began work on bringing his promises to fruition.

Incumbent with the newly elected president's plethora of responsibilities is the daunting task of assembling a bureaucratic team capable of transforming dreams, hopes, and agendas into effective policies that can be carried over into re-election. In order to accomplish this, president-elects rely on the competencies of a group of constituents and proven allies known as the "transition team". The transition team is responsible for ferretting out the most qualified, loyal, scandal-free potential candidates to fill positions on the soon-to-be president's staff and in his cabinet. One of the key people on Clinton's transition team was long-time friend and confidant, Vernon Jordan. Jordan, a Washington insider and notable lawyer served as co-Chairman of the Clinton-Gore transition team (Perry and Parent, 1995, Gergen, 2000). Such influential political gurus as Mickey Kantor, and Warren Christopher also aided Clinton. However, he entrusted Jordan with the chairmanship of his transition efforts. This marked the fisrt time in American history that an African-American was selected to advise the President on nearly every appointment to the Executive Office of the President (EOP). Though he eventually declined, Clinton offered Jordan the position of Attorney General in his first administration.

CONTRIBUTIONS OF AFRICAN-AMERICANS

Clinton continued to reward the support of African-Americans by appointing several Blacks to Cabinet, sub-Cabinet, and other executive level positions and in essence giving them the authority to initiate and formulate policy. The Black power base support that Clinton received from African-Americans and the trade off of policy-making positions is consistent with the pluralist theory. Through a series of bargaining and negotiation Blacks were able to gain access to the public policy formulation and implementation process as well as key positions in federal government. The record number of African-American appointments to Cabinet level positions reaffirmed their entitlement to participation in the decision-making process. Many of the policies enforced by public servants in the federal branch of government during the Clinton administration were consistent with the president's commitment to diversifying the federal workforce.

In 1993, Albert Michael "Mike" Espy became the first African-American appointed to a Cabinet level position in the Clinton administration. Espy joined the Clinton administration after serving as a United States Congressman. The first Department of Agriculture Secretary during the Clinton administration, Espy was also the first African American from the state of Mississippi to serve in the House since the first Reconstruction. In 1986, as a native of Yazoo, Mississippi, Espy capitalized on the poor economic conditions and a slight Black Majority in his Congressional District to secure a seat in the United States House of Representatives. By appointing Espy as Secretary of the Department of Agriculture, President Clinton relied on him to shape policy and administer all federal programs related to food production and rural life. Espy served as Chief Administrator for the Food Stamps Program, which affects many poor Whites, African-Americans, and other minorities in America. He also advised the President on matters regarding the Forest Service and Soil Conservation Service. Not only were decision-making opportunities granted; Espy's appointment to the Department of Agriculture opened the door for constituents from the African-American community and other underrepresented groups to assert some level of influence in policy matters that directly affected their groups.

The Department of Commerce plays an important role in the executive branch of government by promoting economic stability in the country. By definition, the Department of Commerce promotes job creation, economic growth, sustainable development, and improved living standards for all Americans. Clinton appointed Ron Brown to head the Department of Commerce. One of the most important functions of the Department of Commerce in terms of policy implications is the constitutionally mandated decennial census. Federal programs and policies are formulated based on the number of people demographically represented in that count. The importance of the census count is illuminated by the fact that Herbert Hoover was met with contention from southern congressmen for his efforts to desegregate the Census Bureau and enforce non-discrimination practices in government (Krislov, 1967). White Southerners were skeptical to allow an accurate count of Blacks for fear of its potential to impact policy, which would not be favorable in the segregated South.

Ron Brown was also responsible for overseeing the Economic Development Administration, the Minority Business Development Agency, the Telecommunications and Information Administration as well as many other significant federal agencies. Of great importance to African-Americans is Brown's authority over the Minority Business Development Agency and the policies that guide the agency. Under his administration, more Small Business loans were granted to Africa-Americans than at any other time during the existence of that agency. This was accomplished without any decreases in loans to non-Blacks. Brown also supported efforts to expand American involvement in African economies. According to a Whitehouse fact sheet dated March 28, 1998, the Ron Brown Commercial Center, operated and funded by the department of Commerce and located in Johannesburg, South Africa is one of only four Commercial Centers worldwide. Brown served as Secretary from January of 1993 until his untimely death in April of 1994. There are many corporate and federal government awards, foundations, and buildings named in honor of Ronald Brown.

Established in 1977, The United States Department of Energy is responsible for coordinating all national activities relating to the production, regulation, marketing, and conservation of energy. In 1993, President Clinton selected Hazel O'Leary to head this department. As the seventeenth Secretary of Energy, Ms. O'Leary was also responsible for overseeing the federal nuclear weapons program. Secretary O'Leary earned a Bachelor's degree at Fisk University—one of the nation's Historically Black Colleges and Universities (HBCU) and a law degree from Rutgers University. She joined the Clinton administration with a wealth of knowledge and experience in federal government. O'Leary worked as a presidential appointee in the U.S. Department of Energy during the Carter administration and the Federal Energy Administration under President Ford. Working as the Secretary of Energy, O'Leary was responsible for overseeing a work force, which numbered well over 150,00 people. She was applauded for her knowledge of the budgetary process and consistent reduction of excessive spending in her agencies. After one full term, Hazel O'Leary did not seek reappointment to her position.

Jesse Brown was the fourth African-American appointment in the first Clinton Cabinet. Clinton nominated and congress confirmed Brown to head The Department of Veterans Affairs. The department began as the Veterans Administration in 1930 and was later established as a Cabinet department in 1989. The Department of Veterans Affairs is the federal government's second largest department. The department administers a nationwide system of health care services including medical and rehabilitation services, educational assistance, loan guarantees, insurance, burial costs, and other benefits to qualifying veterans and their dependents. The department is also responsible for administering several other programs and developing policies that are consistent with federal laws and regulations to serve American service men and women. Under his leadership, the Department of Veterans affairs developed and implemented policies expanding services to a wider group of veterans.

In addition to the four African-Americans appointed to the first Clinton Cabinet, there were many others who played key roles in the Clinton administration. Vernon Jordan continued to be a life long friend, confidant, and close advisor to Bill Clinton. Joycelyn Elders was born in Arkansas and had worked as the Director of the Arkansas Department of Health while Clinton served as governor of Arkansas. Clinton selected Elders as the United States Surgeon General. She became the first African-American ever to serve as Chief Medical Officer for the United States. David Satcher later became the first African-American male to hold that post and continues to serve in that capacity under the leadership of George W. Bush. Robert L. Mallett served as the Deputy Secretary of the Department of Commerce. Alexis Herman was appointed Assistant to the President and Director of the White House Liaison Office. Herman was the youngest Director of the Women's Bureau during the Carter administration. During Clinton's second term as president, she became the first African-American to head the Department of Labor. Among the many other Black appointees, Rodney Slater was appointed Secretary of the Department of Transportation during Clinton's second term. Summarily, Clinton advanced the formal recognition of African-Americans and other minority groups as well as their ability to formulate and direct public policy. It should be noted that many of the African-Americans appointed during the Clinton administration held positions that allowed them to influence economic policy. President Clinton's endorsement of African-American as policy makers enhanced Blacks' opportunities to serve in executive position for future presidential administrations.

CONCLUSION

Throughout his two terms as president, Bill Clinton continued his commitment to diversifying the federal government. All of the African-American appointments to sub-Cabinet and White House level positions were too numerous to name in this chapter. These appointments reaffirmed African-Americans worth as policy makers and gradually gave Blacks authority to affect public policies in areas where they previously held no influence. Craig Allen Smith credits Bill Clinton with being the master of institutionalized pluralism (Denton and Holloway, 1996). This lends explanation to why Clinton embraced the African-American community and why he entrusted Blacks in his Cabinet. William Jefferson Clinton grew up around Blacks and understood their concerns and political issues. Blacks in America were disenfranchised during the reign of the republican presidents who preceded Clinton and they deeply resented the exclusionary policies that were promulgated during that period. His association with African-Americans, as friends and political allies, gave Bill Clinton a genuine sense of compassion for their human, civil, and social rights.

President Clinton committed himself to strengthening the Democratic Party and diversifying the American political process. Naturally, he approached a power base that he was extremely familiar with from his political days in Arkansas. Blacks were a major part of his success on the state level and he relied on their support while seeking the presidency. As expected, Blacks voted overwhelmingly for Clinton and propelled him into the White House. In return, Clinton selected many of the people with whom he shared a working relationship and could trust. The representation of African-Americans in Cabinet level and other executive level positions reaffirmed Clinton's campaign promises of diversity. What Clinton ultimately delivered was the lowest rates of unemployment in recent years, lower inflation, greater reasons for Blacks to have feelings of efficacy about the federal government, and a rejuvenated hope for social justice.

Hiring practices in the federal government evolved from an ideology that excluded Negroes from federal government, public policy formulation, and decision-making. Since that time African-Americans have gained wealth, prestige, professional status and political influence. This influence has assailed Blacks into positions of authority and political inclusion. Inclusive status has allowed Black power groups to form and work to advance national policy that directly affects similar interest groups. Meritoriously, Blacks have responded with due diligence to shape policy that reflects a diverse cadre of political and economic concerns. By appointing a record number of African-Americans and other minorities to Cabinet level positions, Bill Clinton successfully upheld a campaign promise to build a government that looks like America. In doing so, he reassured the public of his commitment to affirmative action programs and greater levels of efficacy in federal government. The Clinton Administration marks the first time in American history that African-Americans have been afforded such a significant presence in the policy-making arena at the federal level. He also brought a greater balance to his administration through racial, ethnic, and gender diversity. Public Policy students will continue to compare inclusive policy making and the advances of African-American males to the presidential administration of William Jefferson Clinton.

INFLUENCING POLICY

A Case Study in Employment Diversity in the National Park Service

The policies promulgated by decision-makers are predicated on the policy agenda of the President and tend to trickle down to administrators appointed directly or indirectly by the President. Although there is a common argument that Cabinet level administrators are reduced in power by reigning Presidents' agendas to control policy and decisions at the highest level of government, it can also be argued that the policies set forth by Cabinet Secretaries and their subordinates are effective means of power sharing among otherwise neglected groups (Cabinets and Counselors, 1997). One example of inclusive policy-making is the National Park Service and its Diversity Action Plan.

One of America's most cherished institutions; the National Park Service remained virtually inaccessible to African-Americans, women, and other groups of minorities for more than one hundred years. The slow movement toward balance and diversity in workforce composition continues to stain a most pure concept of preservation and enjoyment for the American people. However, there are efforts at the national, regional, and park levels to build an agency that reflects the overall diversity of America. This case study examines the diversity efforts and policy initiatives of the National Park Service during the Clinton administration and includes a case study of diversity in Alaska.

The National Park Service began as an undertaking to preserve pristine places in America as summertime pleasuring grounds. The shear beauty and majesty of lands located in the undeveloped west coupled with economic opportunities, motivated a preservation movement among citizens, federal government, and private industry. Established in 1872, Yellowstone Park was the first national park in the world. The park contained more than two million acres located mostly in the northwest corner of present-day Wyoming, to be preserved and managed by the federal government for the enjoyment and benefit of the people (Sellars, 1997). Western explorations led to the discovery of untapped resources and economic opportunities for the government as well as private interests.

At the conception of national parks in America, the country had recently concluded a brutal civil war and was engaged in battles with American Indians resistant to America's westward expansion. Although the language of the enabling legislation that created Yellow Stone National Park and others like it reference "the People", the remoteness of the original parks coupled with limited mobility of lower classes of Americans during that period precluded visitation for the non-wealthy and non-elite. The relegation of the nation's treasures would be reserved for the enjoyment of the wealthy for many years following the original ideal of a national park. More consequential, white males controlled the management, employment and economic opportunities inherent with such an undertaking. The fact that white males controlled the resources located in the parks and the policies which guided them limited opportunities for other groups (women, Naitive Americans, African-Americans, and Hispanics) to enter into the Service.

With a history of employing only white males, it has only been in recent years that policies have directed the NPS to diversify the employment arena to be more representative of the American public. Kaufman and Stellar concur that before the social revolution of the 1960s and 1970s, all Park Service Leaders were white males. In the 1970s, women and minorities began to attain leadership roles, which led to a diversified composition of the decision-making cadres (Kaufman, 1966). For the first time in National Park Service History persons other than white males were making resource preservation, employment, financial and management decisions.

During the Clinton Administration, the National Park Service was charged with the same universal presidential mandate facing all other federal government agencies: to diversify and build an organization that looks like America. During Clinton's second administration an African-American male was selected to head the National Park Service. Department of the Interior Secretary Bruce Babbitt selected one of the National Park Service's own to lead the fundamentally sound campaign to diversify the work force in our national parks. Robert Stanton was appointed as Director of the National Park Service in 1998. This marked the first time that an African-American would hold the highest post in the Park Service. Under the leadership of Director Stanton, the National Park Service developed a Diversity Action Plan to serve as a formal framework for implementing constructive changes in the workforce and enhancing the quality of worklife for employees in order to retain a diverse workforce.

A National Leadership Council (NLC) memorandum dated July 20, 1998 stated the following: "In order to carry out our mission and vision, we are committed to recruiting, hiring, developing, promoting and retaining a highly qualified diverse workforce." The Council delineated the meaning of diversity to encompass more than differences in race, national origin, disabilities, age, gender, religion or sexual orientation. According to the NLC, diversity includes the different values cultures and perspectives possessed by individuals from different backgrounds. This marked the first comprehensive effort for the Park Service to begin correcting past hiring practices and reporting on new initiatives to improve diversity in the workplace.

The National Park Service has long been recognized for its tradition of preserving and protecting national treasures and serving a wide range of visitors who represent all segments of society and beyond. And yet, full diversity as a sound business practice had not been fully achieved throughout the Service. In 1998, The Park Service developed the Service Diversity Action Plan as a five-year strategic plan for increasing diversity within the work force and integrating diversity into the daily operations of the National Park Service. The five-year plan laid the foundation for recruitment and diversity in the National Park Service; and each region was tasked with putting a plan into action that would promote positive results in all areas of concern delineated in the Service Diversity Action Plan. The plan opened the door of opportunity for regional and park level operations to develop diversity outreach programs that would attract highly qualified diverse candidates with wide ranges of backgrounds and experiences.

The Alaska Region – Diversity Recruitment Outreach Program

The Alaska Region of the National Park Service responded to the Service Diversity Action Plan with an aggressive action plan of its own. Recognizing the need to address the problems inherent with the lack of underrepresented populations in the National Park Service (NPS) and in the Alaska Region; the Regional Directorate along with park management made a concerted effort to diversify the workforce throughout the Alaska Region. In 1999, The Alaska Region implemented a comprehensive Recruitment Outreach Program. A significant component of the program is its relationship with seven scholastic entities to recruit students from across the country to work in Alaska during the summer seasons. One problem plaguing the National Park Service at all levels is the under representation of African-Americans, Hispanics, Native-Americans, and other minorities. To address this problem, the Alaska Region established partnerships with specific academic institutions based on the pools of diverse human resources at those institutions. A huge benefit for students working in National Parks, as Summer Seasonal Employees is the potential for them to be selected for permanent employment upon graduation.

Each of the seven partnership institutions provides opportunities for the Alaska Region to improve workforce diversity. One of the academic institutions partnered with the Alaska Region administers a program that helps transition handicapped high school students from the classroom to a productive career path. Most of the students are learning disabled and attended high schools that have an eighty-percent Hispanic population. Students who graduate from the program are interested in careers that involve working with their hands such as cooks, automotive mechanics, and heavy equipment operators. Two of the academic institutions are predominantly White, but are attended by a large population of Naitive Alaskans. Also, two of the seven institutions involved in the Alaska Region partnership program are Historically Black Colleges and Universities (HBCU); Southern University and A&M College (SU) located in Baton Rouge, Louisiana and Tuskegee University (Tuskegee) located in Tuskegee, Alabama. All National Park Service sites in the Alaska Region were offered the opportunity to consider students matriculating at partnership entities for employment.

This section details the results of the diversity recruitment efforts at the regional level and in the largest park in Alaska (based on employees and funding). In 1998 Denali National Park and Preserve hired a total of 163 people through its Summer Seasonal Employment Program. Of the 163 summer hires, approximately twelve percent (12.2%) were minorities and less than three percent (2.4%) African-American. In 1999, the year prior to the placement of Southern University and Tuskegee students, the percentage of minorities and African-American hires reached the lowest it had been between 1998 and 2001. Summer Seasonal Employment Program hires decreased to 136 total summer/seasonal hires. Of the 136 hires, less than five percent (4.4%) were minorities and less than one percent (0.7%) were African-Americans. See Table 1. The trend of diversity at the regional level followed a similar pattern; however the numbers were not as disproportionate. See Table 2.

Table 1. Denali National Park and Preserve Summer Seasonal Hires

Year	White Hires	Black Hires	Hispanic Hires	AA/PI Hires	AI/AN Hires	Total Hires	Total Minority Hires	% Minority Hires
1998	143	4	5	6	5	163	20	12.3%
1999	130	1	1	1	3	136	6	4.4%
2000	156	8	1	1	3	169	13	7.7%
2001	145	7	3	3	5	163	18	11.0%

Source: Denali National Park and Preserve Summer Seasonal Workforce Report 2001.

Beginning in the summer of 2000 the Alaska Region made a long-term commitment to recruit and hire students from SU and Tuskegee to work at National Park sites in Alaska during the summer season. Students who are hired have the opportunity to gain valuable work and life experiences. Many of the students have never been to Alaska and would not otherwise have the opportunity to work in Alaska or in a federal branch of government. The program is intended to develop students and prepare them for future careers in the Park Service or other federal agencies. Recruitment efforts in the year 2000 resulted in the hiring of sixteen students from Southern University A&M College (SU) and Tuskegee University to work in park sites throughout the Alaska Region. Three students from SU worked in the Regional Office and five others worked in various park sites throughout Alaska. The eight Tuskegee University students all worked in Denali National Park and Preserve (Mt. McKinley). In 2000, the Summer Seasonal Employment Program at Denali hired a total of 169 summer hires. Of the 169 summer/seasonal hires, nearly eight percent (7.7%) were minorities and African-Americans represented nearly five percent (4.7%) of the total population. Based on a survey conducted by the Alaska Region in the summer o f 2000, students from Southern University and Tuskegee University experienced various levels of enjoyment and job satisfaction. Depending on their location and work environment, students realized varying levels of acceptance on the job and responsibility allocations. However, without exception, each student expressed a need for such a program to continue and their willingness to support the program in the future. In 2001, the Summer Seasonal Employment Program hired a total of 163 summer hires. Of the 163 summer hires, 18 were minorities (11%), seven were African-American (5%), three were Hispanic (2%), three were Asian American/Pacific Islanders, and five were American Indian/Alaska Naitives (4%). See Table 2.

Table 2. Alaska Region Seasonal Hires

Year	White Hires	Black Hires	Hispanic Hires	AA/PI Hires	AI/AN Hires	Total Hires	Total Minority Hires	% Minority Hires
1998	461	11	11	16	43	542	81	14.9%
1999	432	8	7	7	28	482	50	10.4%
2000	441	12	5	4	25	489	47	9.6%
2001	482	23	9	5	23	482	71	14.7%

Source: Alaska Region Summer Seasonal Workforce Report 2001.

CONCLUSION

The appointment of Robert Stanton as National Park Service Director initiated efforts to study and address the problem of diversity within a national agency. By implementing the Service Diversity Action Plan, the Park Service was provided with directives that would bring it in line with forward thinking and inclusive policy making. That initiative directed regional policy makers to act in the best interest of the National Park Service.

Since its inception, the Alaska Region Minority Recruitment Outreach Program has created opportunities for African-Americans and other underrepresented groups to work in federal government positions that were previously unavailable to them. As a result, diversity in the National Park Service-Alaska Region has a chance to improve and the Mission and message of the National Park Service is reaching groups that would not otherwise be reached. Based on current trends, the Minority Recruitment Outreach Program has the opportunity to create a Regionwide organization the "looks like America." The efforts of the Alaska Region-National Park Service are an example of policy-making impacting workforce diversity.

REFERENCES

Denton, Robert E. *The Clinton Presidency: Images, Issues, and Communication Strategies.* Westport, CT: Praeger Publishers, 1996.

Gergen, David *Eyewitness to Power.* New York, NY: Simon and Schuster, 2000.

Kaufman, Polly W. *National Parks and the Woman's Voice.* Albuquerque, NM: University of New Mexico Press, 1998.

Krislov, Samuel. *The Negro in Federal Employment: The Quest for Equal Opportunity.* Minneapolis, MN: University of Minnesota Press, 1967.

Newman, Dorothy K., Amidei, Nancy J., Carter, Barbara L., Day, Dawn, Kruvant, William J. and Russell, Jack S. *Protest, Politics and Prosperity: Black Americans and White Institutions, 1940-75.* New York, NY: Pantheon Books, 1978.

Perry, Huey L. and Parent, Wayne (Eds.) *Blacks and the American Political System.* Gainesville, FL.: University of Florida Press, 1995.

Sellars, Richard W. *Preserving Nature in the National Parks: A History.* Yale University: Yale University Press, 1997.

Warshaw, Shirley A. *Powersharing: White House-Cabinet Relations in the Modern Presidency.* Albany, NY: State University of New York Press, 1996.

Chapter 9

TRANSITIONING AFRICAN AMERICAN MEN FROM PRISON BACK TO THE AFRICAN-AMERICAN COMMUNITY

Garry A. Mendez, Jr.
International Health Fellow,
University of Illinois, Chicago

ABSTRACT

The mass incarceration of African-American men has not made African-American communities safer and there is an indication that in fact, communities may be unstable as a result of incarceration policies and practices. According to the U.S. Justice Department 95% of those incarcerated return to the community and upwards of 60% of those recidivate as a result of either a new crime or violation of parole.

It is estimated that over 500,000 ex-offenders will re-enter society each year for at least the next decade. What preparations have been made to assure that these individuals become productive crime free citizens? What role can the community play in the transition process? This paper examines this issue and proposes a plan for the community to provide for its own safety and development.

Vivien Stern notes, "a most striking feature of the United States prison system is the racial mix of the prison population" (Stern, 1998). Six percent of the population of the United States is African-American and male, yet they make up half of the incarcerated population (Stern, 1998). African-Americans are imprisoned at a rate six times higher than the rate of white American males (Stern, 1998). Out of every 100,000 white males 306 are incarcerated, out of every 100,000 African-American males 1947 are incarcerated (Stern, 1998).

According to the Sentencing Project, on an average day in America, one out of every three African-American men aged twenty to twenty-nine is in prison or jail, on probation or on parole. In their study conducted in 1992, in Washington DC, they found that more than four out of every ten African-American men aged eighteen to thirty-five were in prison, on probation, on parole, on bail or being sought by the police with a warrant (Mauer, 1999).

Official statistics suggest that nearly three out of ten African-American men face the prospects of going to prison during their lifetime, a figure that does not include going to jail, which would constitute those who have been sentenced for a period less than one year (Mauer, 1999).

The so-called "war on drugs" and mandatory sentencing policies that accompany it have accounted for the huge increase in the number of African-American men who are currently incarcerated. Although data indicated that African-American men constitute only about ten percent of the drug users, they represent nearly eighty percent of the people who are incarcerated for drugs. On the other hand, white American men account for nearly eighty percent of the drug users and only about ten percent of the persons incarcerated for drugs (Mauer, 1999). In other words, the "war on drugs" has been a limited war and if "won" would only solve ten percent of the problem. This puts into question how serious the "war" is and furthermore might suggest that the strategy of the general in this "war" needs to be examined. Such inept leadership seems to shed light on why the "war" has failed and will continue to fail.

It has been estimated that drugs are a fifty billion dollar a year enterprise. In a quick examination of the communities from which the incarcerated African-American population comes one notes that for the most part they all reside in poor inner-city communities. They do not own homes, boats, or airplanes, do not have political connections and when they are arrested they will be represented by a public defender who will urge them to plead guilty and hope for a lesser sentence.

The media paints a distorted image of these young men while they sanitize the image of organized crime and suggests that the individuals who participate in this type of crime are just common non-violent business people. This mass incarceration and criminalizing of African-American men has had a devastating impact upon the African-American family and communities nationwide. Never before has the need for strong families and communities in the inner city been so apparent. It is the theme that threads its way through most discussions about the problems and issues facing African-Americans. The single most mentioned contributor to the deterioration of the African-American community has been the absence of the men particularly fathers.

Yet little if any attention has been directed towards the effects of the incarceration of African-American men. It has been suggested that incarceration will make the community safe; however given the rate at which African-American men are incarcerated one would think that the safest communities in the world would be African-American.

"In a system that removes individuals from their neighborhoods, incarceration may improve the quality of community life when only a few residents are removed. In neighborhoods that have many more offenders, however, removing these residents may disrupt the social networks that are the foundation of social control. Because high-incarceration neighborhoods are socially disorganized, their capacity to absorb these disruptions is limited. Thus, high levels in incarceration in some communities may leave them in worse condition than before because of the resulting disruptions in social organization (Clear and Rose, 1999)."

The victimization records clearly demonstrate that African-American communities are not the safest and in fact victimization is frequent in those communities. The greatest victims of violent crime are young African-American men. Furthermore, African-Americans are more likely to be the victims of murder, rape, sexual assault, robbery and aggravated assault (BJS, 2000).

These incarceration policies have resulted in single-parent households, poverty-stricken children, fatherless communities, reduced voting strength and untold social and emotional stress within African-American communities nationwide. For example, it is estimated that at least sixty percent of incarcerated men have at least one child. In a recent study conducted by The National Trust for the Development of African-American Men, it was found that seventy-five percent of the men had one child and over fifty percent had two or more (Mendez, 2000). This means that at least two million children are currently being raised in a single-parent household. The absence of the man creates a financial strain on the family and often leads to children growing up in poverty. Fatherless communities often are less safe because the men are not present to protect and secure the neighborhoods, which make them subject to anti-social behavior on the part of the younger male children.

In a democratic society it is critical for the citizens to vote in order to have their needs met; however, incarceration has seriously reduced the number of eligible voters in the African-American community. This reduction of voters seriously impedes the ability of the community to have its views considered by policymakers in the government at the local, state and national level.

Reduced services due to the redistribution of tax money due to the census count are another result. When a man is placed in prison he goes off the census roll in his home community and goes on the roll of the community in which the prison is located. In effect this movement functions as a voucher in that the tax credit moves with the incarcerated individuals. The community of the prison gains and in most cases the inner-city community, which is the person's real home, loses, although it is perfectly clear that the inmate is not a true resident of the community in which the prison is housed.

Clearly one could argue that social and emotional stress is created by the behavior of the men and the blame should be placed there but should the nation's leaders further exacerbate the problem by severely cutting the financial base from their home communities?

As negative as this is, it is only the beginning of the story. The African-American community is faced with yet another attack. The incarceration rate and the sentencing patterns for African-Americans has come back to haunt African-American communities in what is euphemistically referred to as re-entry. In the past it was called parole.

Ninety-five percent of the men who are incarcerated will return to the community (Travis, 2000). Before the period of mass incarceration of African-Americans, this might not have been a concern to the community but with the density of incarceration the entire young male population might be returning from the penitentiary.

It is estimated that, for the next decade, more than half a million inmates will be released from prison annually – re-entering their communities (Travis, 2000). The majority of these men will return to communities that are already besieged by a myriad of social problems, an absent economic base, poor schools, single-parent households, teen pregnancy, substance abuse and a sense of hopelessness. The decision on the part of correction departments to give up on rehabilitation and focus strictly upon punishment seems to raise questions and concerns for the African-American community.

Is it a good idea to eliminate college education in prisons when education is viewed as the best predictor of success in the American society? Is it a good idea to restrict access to the Internet if the economy and society is moving at warp speed in that direction?

Is it a good idea to locate inmates hundreds of miles from their families if we know that family support is one of the best predictor of reduced recidivism?

These and other practices and policies have led to the men returning to their communities lacking skills and the necessary tools to become productive community members. Furthermore the long separations from the family often leave them unable to function as a responsible member of the family unit as a father, sibling or son.

The men return to the same physical communities from which they came but the community has changed and they are totally unprepared for this new community that has moved on without him while he was in a time capsule.

If under the pressure they revert to their former behavior patterns, they will do so in the same inner-city neighborhood – the African-American neighborhood. It should be noted that these behavior patterns do not always surface in the form of major crime, but in lesser acts that reduce the quality of life for the total community such as drinking and using profanity on the street.

WHAT CAN AND NEEDS TO BE DONE

President Bush and others have indicated that faith-based and community organizations are best suited to address this issue and has created a faith-based office and initiative to take on the task. In some ways this is consistent with the belief of progressive criminal justice experts who have indicated that the best predictor of success for an ex-offender is the strength of family and community support.

It should be noted however; that the criminal justice system in general still operates within itself and does not make an effort to involve the community. When they do involve the community it is after they have decided how they are going to function and they make an announcement at a community meeting.

The most recent example of this approach is the much heralded "community policing" movement. Community policing is strictly a creation of the police and in most cities is little more than a community relations operation. If a department is practicing "community policing" it is confined to a small group of officers who head up the unit, it is not a total department movement.

Furthermore, the community was never considered an equal partner in the relationship and no one ever checked to see if they wanted to be "community policed."

A well-known former Police Chief in a major United States city when questioned about "community policing" said his department practiced "community-policing but there was a place for it and at other times you just had to kick butts. He went on to say that the police would make the decision when to do which. Finally, he said that the Black community was very happy with this arrangement.

In order to avoid a similar fate with corrections and faith-based and community organizations, there must be a conscious effort on all sides to establish partnerships and working relationships that demonstrate mutual respect and equality for all parties.

It should be further noted that most communities and families lack the mechanisms and programs to support the returning men in their efforts to re-acclimate to life in the community. Because of this, these men are unable to connect to the educational, employment, health and other services they need to be successful and avoid a returning to jail or prison.

The re-entry process must begin when the individual enters the system. In conjunction with the sentence given to the convicted person there must also be a plan for how the time will be most productively spent.

The partnership between the community, corrections, parole, parole authority and the inmate begins immediately. All concerned partners must understand that 95% of the individuals will be returning to their community and that it is the responsibility of all to assure that the individual returns a better person than when he entered the prison.

It should also be understood that once the individual has been incarcerated, the incarcerators have complete power over the person. Attached to that power is responsibility for the person. This responsibility means that the formal system (corrections and parole) must provide the individual with the resources to make a successful change into a positive citizen. The formal system cannot take responsibility for the individual utilizing the resources but they must make sure that the resources are available.

Motivation experts have stated that people respond to rewards as opposed to punishment and in this case the parole authority is the reward system. Individuals who demonstrate change must be rewarded through release when they appear before the parole board.

Currently parole authorities across the country have taken a very hard-line regarding parole, especially if the person appearing before them committed a "violent crime". When individuals have demonstrated a change in their behavior over a long period of incarceration, they must be rewarded with parole. If this does not occur then there is no incentive for others to change because they feel they will not be released, they merely wait for their time to expire and return to the community angry, frustrated, lacking skills and basically dysfunctional.

Dysfunctional men returning to families and communities that are often dysfunctional result in the further deterioration of all three components.

The key new player in this model is the African-American community. Except as inmates and visitors, the African-American community has been virtually absent from corrections, parole and the parole authority process. This despite the fact that the African-American community has been much more affected by the system than any other group of people in the country. The African-American community, for its own survival, must assume a leadership role in preparing the incarcerated men to return to the community. This is too critical a situation to be left to the system or any outside entity to handle.

It should be understood that, values drive all behavior and the value system of the prison is not the value system that is needed in the African-American community. With the large numbers of African-American men who have been, currently and are projected to become incarcerated in the future, the prison value system could become the dominate system in the community.

The traditional African-American value system that is dominated by attributes such as: cooperative and collective behavior, respect for family, respect for elders, and non-violence, is replaced by a prison value system that is violent, individualistic, trust no one, and only respect money and power. If the community does not check such decay it will poison all of the people and destroy the foundation of the African-American community.

The primary task of the community is to convert the incarcerated population into *assets* as opposed to the *liabilities* that they currently represent.

The conversion/re-entry process begins when the individual enters the prison system and the community becomes a partner with the formal system at that point.

The National Trust suggests the following program to address the transition of men back into the African-American community.

RE-ENTRY: THE NATIONAL OPERATIONAL PLAN FOR THE COMMUNITY

The focus of the National Trust's plan for inmates returning to the community is their need for "re-socialization". They must unlearn their prison culture and norms and learn a set of norms that will assure their success in the community.

The re-socialization process is divided into three major components:

I.   Purging
II. Trust Values.
III. Release Plan.

In addition to these components each community should establish two support services:

I.   A Crisis Management Desk
II. A Computer Center
III. Aftercare Services

Description of the components:

Purging

During their period of incarceration the participants assumed a culture and a value system that conformed to the value system of incarcerated people. This value system is distorted and totally inappropriate for individuals living in the free community yet it is the foundation of the incarcerated population. The longer they have been incarcerated the more entrenched the prison culture and value system is within their psyche.

Before they can function in a normal manner they must rid themselves of this value system which effects such critical areas as:

1. **Male/female relationships.**
2. **Work ethic.**
3. **Health.**
4. **Money.**
5. **Family.**
6. **Associations.**
7. **Hustling/Crime.**
8. **Partying.**
9. **Housing.**

The participants are expected to become aware of these negative distorted attitudes, confront them and begin the purging process. Absent the purging process communities would be attempting to instill a positive value system on top of the current negative system. It is necessary to clean out as much of the negative value system as possible so that we would have a more secure foundation upon which to build the new positive value system.

Trust Value System

After the purging process the participants then go through the process of taking on another value system that allows them to function in the community as a positive contributing citizen.

New Awaking Sessions:

1. **Cultural Equation.**
2. **Pyramid Leadership.**
3. **Traditional Family Values vs. Drug Culture Values.**
4. **Manhood/Womanhood.**
5. **Independence/responsibility.**
6. **Fundamental Management.**
7. **Preventive Healthcare/HIV/AIDS.**
8. **Communication.**
9. **Conflict Management.**
10. **Group Dynamics.**
11. **Decision Making.**
12. **Human Development.**
13. **Asset Mapping.**

Release Plan

When a man is released from prison it is necessary for him to have a sound realistic plan to assure a successful transition.

Release Plan Components:

1. **Assessment of Individual Capacity/skill level and community marketability.**
2. **Realistic Goals.**
3. **Individual Asset Mapping.**
4. **Time Management.**
5. **Conflict Management.**
6. **Financial Management.**
7. **Family Management.**

Aftercare

During the aftercare period is the immediate time after the person is released from prison. Under the current system, the parole officers who are often overloaded with cases handle this aspect of the person's re-entry, which makes it virtually impossible for the officers to truly assist the men in their transition period. Hence, the transitioning individuals are left to their own devises. Unfortunately, the individual finds himself in a situation of trying to manage this new experience on his own in a society that has little remorse for an ex-offender.

The transitioning individual needs a "landing pad". A place where they can talk with someone who has some understanding of their situation. This location should have successful ex-offenders from the community available to counsel and confer with the new arrivals. In addition the successful men serve as role models and examples to the men of what can actually occur if they avail themselves of the community resources. The aftercare services should also include assistance in housing, education, health, family counseling, money management and other basis needs of the men.

Special attention will be given to review and reinforced learning of the areas addressed in the purging and new values training sessions conducted while the men were incarcerated. These meetings will also be used to provide the participants an opportunity to reflect and discuss amongst themselves their progress. It will give them a chance to share ideas and provide support to one another.

Computer Center

For several years the National Trust operated a computer center in Green Haven Prison, in New York State that was managed by the men themselves. Although the center is no longer in operation it was found that it served several needs of the men; it gave them basic computer literacy skills, it allowed inmates to teach one another and during the periods that the center was open the Trust value system teaching were reinforced. Centers of this nature should be established for the transitioning men and their families to attend when they are released to the community. The objectives of the center will be to:

1. Provide the participants with basic computer and Internet literacy, closing the digital divide.
2. Serve as a safe meeting place for the participants to discuss their progress.
3. Provide ex-offenders an opportunity to teach basic classes.
4. Provide the participants a place to bring their family to give them the opportunity to have access to the Internet.
5. Reinforce the learning objectives from the sessions the participants attended while still incarcerated.

Crisis Management Desk

It is recognized that the value system that the re-entering men assumed in the prison was begun on the street and is still present in the community. Therefore, in order to help the transitioning men address the very real pull of the negative community a Crisis Management Desk should be established in the community that would be managed by successful ex-offenders from the community. These men and women have successfully negotiated their return to the community and fully understand the issues with which the participants are struggling.

The desk should be one of strict confidentiality and would function as a support for the participants. The desk should be managed on a twenty-four hour basis and as the community discovers successful participants they would expect them to assist with the desk.

Asset Mapping the Target Community

Often African-American communities are seen as devoid of resources and it is assumed that all assistance must come from outside the community. Each community should conduct a mapping of the community to ascertain what resources are available to the transitioning men and their families.

These maps combined with the individual self-mapping will give the participants a fuller picture of what they have at their disposal for making a successful return to the community.

Concluding Statement

By designing and building a base of this nature, starting when the person enters the system, the transition process becomes seamless and natural and represents the community reclaiming its men.

This reclamation process will help restore stability to communities and allow for true community development and growth.

REFERENCES

Clear, T., Rose, D.R. (1999). *When Neighbors go to Jail*: Impact on Attitudes about Formal and Informal Social Control. *Research Review* National Institute of Justice, U. S. Department of Justice, Washington, DC.

Mauer, Marc (1999). *Race to Incarcerate*. The Sentencing Project, New York: The New Press

Mendez, Garry A. Jr., (2000). *Incarcerated African-American Men and their Children*: A Case Study. Annals Volume 569. Sage Publications.

National Crime Victimization Survey. (1999). Victim Characteristics. Bureau of Justice Statistics. U. S. Department of Justice, Washington, DC

Stern, Vivien (1998). *A Sin Against The Future Imprisonment In the World*, Boston, MA Northeastern University Press

Travis, J. (2000). *But They All Come Back: Rethinking Prisoner Re-Entry*. National Institute of Justice, U.S. Department of Justice, Washington, DC.

Chapter 10

Unfulfilled But Urgent Needs: HIV Prevention and Intervention for African American MSM

Dominicus W. So[1]

Howard University

Abstract

HIV/AIDS among ethnic minorities has become a public health crisis in the United States. The HIV/AIDS subgroup within the African American gay and bisexual male population has a unique set of problems, including multiple stigma, racism, and discrimination, besides coming out, homophobia, discrimination, oppression, and hate crime. Responses to that group's unfulfilled need are urgently called for. We critiqued on the current models of health services for African American gay and bisexual men living with HIV/AIDS. Public clinics are often too bureaucratic and impersonal while smaller private health centers for the gay community may not cater to the African-American clientele. Suggestions are made to develop culture-specific programs for gay and bisexual African American men.

Keywords: African American men; minorities; gay and bisexual; men who have sex with men (MSM); HIV/AIDS; HIV prevention and intervention; risk reduction; community-based prevention;

[1] Author Note: Correspondence should be addressed to Dominicus W. So, Ph.D., Howard University, Department of Psychology, CB Powell Building, 525 Bryant Street, NW, Washington, DC 20059. Telephone: (202)806-9462. Fax: (202)806-4873. E-mail: <dso@fac.howard.edu>

INTRODUCTION

A Public Health Crisis

HIV prevention and intervention efforts for African American gay and bisexual men[2] are urgently needed. Among AIDS cases, gay and bisexual men remain the largest group in the United States (Centers for Disease Control and Prevention [CDC], 1995). In examining trends in HIV incidence among adolescents and young adults, Rosenberg and Biggar (1998) found that homosexual contact was the leading cause of infection among young men between 18 and 22. According to the authors, from 1988 to 1993, while HIV prevalence in white men reduced by half, HIV prevalence among black and Hispanic men remained stable over those years. From 1996 to 1998, black men and Hispanic men accounted for a raising proportion of full-blown AIDS cases and had smaller proportionate declines in AIDS incidence and deaths (Center for Disease Control and Prevention, 2000). As a public health emergency in the African American community, HIV/AIDS becomes one of the three leading causes of death among African American males and the death rate from AIDS is disproportionately higher for this population than for white Americans (Feldman & Fulwood, 1999).

Unfortunately, the African American community's responses to HIV/AIDS overall have not relieved its members from such an epidemic. African American churches, the source of emotional and social support and traditional gatekeepers of material help and social assistance, are slow to deal with the HIV/AIDS epidemic in their community. Many HIV-positive African Americans continue to deny their infection and the source of infection. Peterson, Catania, Dolcini, and Faigeles (1993) note that many African American men report low rates of condom use, but multiple risk factors. Many other barriers to reducing the black-white disparity of HIV/AIDS infection continue to hinder the fight against AIDS in the African American community (Feldman & Fulwood, 1999).

In fact, HIV-positive African American gay men are less likely than the white counterparts to use conventional medical treatments even if their CD4 cell counts are high. In comparing between white and black gay men who are HIV positive, Kass, Flynn, Jacobson, Chmiel, and Bing (1999) found that black gay men were less likely than their white counterparts to use outpatient and dental services even though they are more likely to have dental insurance than whites. However, among these two groups, no difference was found in their likelihood of having private health insurance or using inpatient or emergency department services or antiretroviral medications (Kass, Flynn, Jacobson, Chmiel, & Bing, 1999). It appears that the African American gay men tend to delay treatment until symptoms drastically deteriorate requiring immediate hospitalization.

In cities such as Washington D.C. where the African-American population is significantly large, HIV services for gay and bisexual men within that population are urgently needed. The HIV Prevention Community Planning Committees in Washington, D.C.,

---

[2] A cautionary note has to be made regarding the definition of the population at hand. Our discussion includes not only self-identified gay and bisexual African American men, but also other "men who have sex with men" (or MSM). Being a behavioral category, MSM are usually referred to men who engage in sexual behavior with other men, but may not self-identify as gay or bisexual. However, men who cross-dress or have undertaken gender reassignment, deserve further attention beyond our intent.

Maryland, and northern Virginia declare a shortage of community-based organization that provide HIV-related service for African American gay and bisexual men, and have called for special interventions for this population as a top priority.

Community Psychology's Response to HIV/AIDS

HIV intervention researchers and others (e.g. Hobfoll, 1998; Kelly, Murphy, Sikkema, & Kalichman, 1993) have advocated that Community Psychology can help develop more effective HIV prevention and research. As the HIV/AIDS epidemic continues to affect the African American community, however, many (e.g. Peterson, 1998) agree that, unlike in other fields such as social work (e.g. Icard, Schilling, El-Bassel, & Young, 1992) and public health, there have not been enough efforts among community psychologists to study or promote the prevention of HIV/AIDS among African American people. A special issue of the American Journal of Community Psychology (1998, Volume 26, Number 1) was dedicated to HIV/AIDS Prevention Through Community Psychology. In that issue, while two articles (St. Lawrence, Eldridge, Reitman, Little, Shelby, Brasfield, 1998; Wingood & DiClemente, 1998) reported on the HIV prevention among African American women, none addressed exclusively on African American gay and bisexual men.

Except for a few authors (e.g. Hobfoll, 1998; Kelly, Murphy, Sikkema, & Kalichman, 1993; Peterson, Folkman, & Bakeman, 1996), the efforts of Community Psychology are at their infancy stage in studying the status and prevention of HIV among African American gay and bisexual men. Hobfoll (1998) argues that Community Psychology was late in joining in the efforts of preventing HIV and AIDS, although HIV-related risk behaviors are very much related to Community Psychology's notions of empowerment, sense of community, interpersonal ties, resources, and culture. Some early prevention efforts have pioneered community based intervention research to reduce the risky sexual behaviors among African American gay and bisexual men. Tailored to facilitate healthy social and sexual contexts of African American gay and bisexual men, a number of community-based formative and intervention research (e.g. Center for Disease Control and Prevention, Behavioral Interventions and Research Branch, 1996) have used community members as agents and audience for the intervention in their naturalistic environments. Though carried out in groups, many training/intervention methods rely much on individually and behavioral interventions, and lack the intervention focused on the social and macro-systemic context. For instance, the African-American Men's Health Study (Center for AIDS Prevention Studies, 1990) modified a standard protocol derived from the San Francisco "Stop AIDS" Project to promote risk reduction behavior change among gay and bisexual African American men.

Previous work on African American women (e.g. St. Lawrence, Eldridge, Reitman, Little, Shelby, Brasfield, 1998; Wingood & DiClemente, 1998), adolescents (Bourdon, Tierney, Huba, Lothrop, Melchior, Betru, & Compoc, 1998; Rotheram-Borus, Gwadz, Fernandez, & Srinivasan, 1998; Tenner, Trevithick, Wagner, & Burch, 1998; Woods, Samples, Melchiono, Keenan, Fox, Chase, Tierney, Price, Paradise, O'Brien, Mansfield, Brooke, Allen, & Goodman, 1998; Wright, Gonzalez, Werner, Laughner, & Wallace, 1998), and gay male hustlers and their gay customers (Miller, Klotz, & Eckholdt, 1998) suggest that approaches in Community Psychology can be used to gather resources to tackle life circumstances, empower them through their social support system, teach them social skills, health HIV- related beliefs, and modify the norms of safe sex behaviors. These intervention practices are all delivered in their community settings, using concepts in community psychology. For example, St. Lawrence et al (1998) discuss the need for providing resources for African American women to respond to racism, poverty, underemployment, and unstable couples' relationships. In their study of 423 sexually active African American women, they found that condom users reported more frequent and comfortable sexual communication with partners, and that their peers also use condoms. The use of community psychology's approach to modify the peer norms of sexual behavior and communication to enhance condom use appears to be indicated for the African American population.

CURRENT MODELS OF HIV/AIDS SERVICES
FOR GAY AND BISEXUAL MEN

Like other services, agencies of HIV/AIDS prevention and intervention services tend to vary in some of these following dimensions:

- gay, lesbian, bisexual, and transgendered (GLBT) focused or generic (non-GLBT focused)
- HIV/AIDS or all public health issues, including sexually-transmitted diseases (STDs)
- Minorities targeted or mainstream
- Comprehensive services/mental health or piecemeal service/physical health
- Geography: large city or small towns
- Private funding or public clinic
- University-affiliated and research oriented or service oriented
- Conventional or alternative treatment

We will discuss two typical models of HIV/AIDS-related services exist for serving the gay and bisexual male population.

Public, General Health Clinic

The first, and more common model is the publicly funded, mainstream health clinic/service that specializes in sexually-transmitted diseases (STDs). Such STD clinics or services are often housed in or are part of a large, public general hospital. These facilities locate in almost any place, from big or suburban cities to small rural towns. The larger facility which houses these divisional STD clinics also serves the immediate geographical population for other public health issues, including infectious diseases, sexually-transmitted diseases, or other public health issues, such as violence, and public safety issues. To a great extent, they mostly provide physical health care and prevention, and do not cover other areas of health care, such as mental, emotional health, and financial health. They often provide services for the population at large because of their town, county, or state government funding. Their intervention/prevention efforts are often almost exclusively service-oriented. They tend to use standard, conventional protocols of intervention and prevention, as in any large general hospitals in big cities or smaller towns.

In theory, everyone is welcomed at these clinics, regardless of sexual orientation, race, and gender. Also, because these clinics are administered under a central executive body of city or state health departments, central mobilization of intervention and prevention efforts is possible. They, therefore, afford to have a staff with generalized skills for a broad population. This model allows easier tracking diseases and modifying risk behaviors that threat public health. Services are also less likely to be duplicated in the same geographical region, and are affordable in locales with smaller populations, such as a small town.

In reality, however, these clinics are not equipped to serve the African American MSM population. The problems associated with this model is its being part of the bigger local city/state government. In many instances, the issues of bureaucracies, red tape, and inefficiency of large organization become a hurdle for effective prevention and intervention programs. Although they are mandated to serve diverse populations, they are often over-burdened and cannot satisfy diverse needs. In other cases, they are not ready to effectively outreach or provide sensitivity to gay, bisexual, and other non-mainstream populations.

Private, Non-For-Profit Gay and Lesbian Community Health Centers

This second typical model targets the gay, lesbian, bisexual, and transgendered population. These agencies are often funded by private foundations, service grants, or community members. They provide comprehensive services in specialized community center/clinics, or wellness centers including the use of alternative and complementary treatments. They often locate geographically in the gay ghetto where the gay, lesbian, bisexual, and transgendered populations are clustered, and may have satellite sites around the main site. These health centers start in major metropolitan areas, and may branch out to surrounding towns either through its satellite sites or its magnet services that are only afforded by big cities. Because they exist around big clusters of the gay population, they almost always only exist in the center of large metropolitan centers, such as New York, Washington, Boston, Los Angeles, and San Francisco. As these centers are catered for the needs of the gay population, they are often heavily staffed or volunteered by members of the gay community. Whenever possible, they provide specialized services for different ethnic groups, such as African Americans, Latino/Latina, and Asian Americans. The intervention/prevention efforts are usually service-oriented (Misir, 1997), but may not be research-oriented and university-affiliated for some large intervention research projects. Some examples of this model are Gay Men's Health Crisis in NYC, NY; AIDS Foundation in San Francisco, CA; and the Whitman Walker Clinic in Washington, DC.

The most significant advantage of this model is its sensitivity to the special needs of the MSM population, such as those documented by authors like Garnets and Kimmel (1993). Because they are in gay ghetto of big cities, they can afford to have a gay affirmative staff, and be assisted by a large number of volunteers from the GLBT communities. The programs can expend more intervention/prevention efforts for a well-defined clientele; their array of service being in the same building, they become not only a comprehensive, one-stop service location, but also a community center like convenient service building for the gay population, which otherwise lack a publicly funded community center. In these centers, they can better provide personalized services related to HIV/AIDS, including physical, mental, emotional, financial, and legal health services, and often HIV testing, housing, drug rehabilitation, case management, advocacy, educational, library, immigration, care provider support, and other social services. Their central location in the city center often provides convenience for its clientele, and facilitates easier and more effective outreach to the targeted gay population. As a community service center, they may also serve to enhance a sense of community cohesion among the gay population.

Even with this model, except for a few very exceptional examples in the U.S., there are still a lot of unfilled gaps of needs of African American gay and bisexual male population. The African American MSM population often face very unique issues including coming out, homophobia, social isolation, rejection, depression, cultural and racial discrimination, and disadvantaged economic situations. A detailed description of those issues can be found elsewhere (e.g. Hawkeswood, 1996; Hemphill, 1991; Riggs, 1989; Roman, 1994; Simmons, 1991).

AN ALTERNATIVE, HOLISTIC MODEL

Because of the inability of either model to fulfill the specific needs of gay minorities, a holistic model is necessary for serving African American MSM. Several authors have described holistic principles involving culture-specific understanding of people of African descent. We attempt to describe below the summative characteristics of such a model.

Comprehensiveness

Safer sex and other health-related behaviors do not only require knowledge of safer sex practices and health information, but also physical and financial health, positive self-image, and social development. A comprehensive HIV service program should address multi-systemic areas of HIV-related health behaviors. Using focus groups of 17 limited-income African American MSM to discuss their needs as clients with AIDS and their expectations from the health care system, Dancy (1994) found that this population indeed expect a competent comprehensive health care system, which fulfills their financial, social, emotional, and familial needs using both traditional and complementary treatments. Such holistic model is ethnically valid for the African American population because it adopts a Black model of human being, involving the individual's intellectual, professional, spiritual and emotional components.

The model we propose should provide African American MSM a wide array of services ranging from physical health care information and services, to psychological, mental health treatment, to money management, to legal consultation clinics, and to interpersonal skills training. A comprehensive health care system allows efficient, well-coordinated services to clients deal with their complex, HIV-related risk factors and medical symptoms. For HIV-related illnesses, even the most resourceful clients may have trouble assembling all the treatment providers, social services, religious leaders, and funeral resources. An average client is therefore likely to miss some areas of necessary services. We believe that having African American MSM making their own arrangements with numerous clinics is not only inefficient, but also risky to the client's health because poorly coordinated health care may pose unnecessary requests or even contradictory and confusing opinions on African American MSM.

Afro-Centrism

A successful HIV prevention/intervention program for African-American MSM must also incorporate culture-specific beliefs and methods that the clients are familiar with. Myers (1988) calls for an optimal conceptualization of human functioning through an ancient Afro-centric psychology which encompasses a world view of a unified spiritual/material nature of reality, self-knowledge through intuition, symbolic imagery, and rhythm, high value in positive personal relationships, union of opposites, multi-dimensional, extended self, and intrinsic self-worth, and communalism. Similarly, Ntu, another Afro-centric approach which stresses mind-body-spirit harmony, balances and interconnectedness, has also been used for programs of this population (Foster, Phillips, Belgrave, Randolph, & Braithwaite, 1993).

HIV services for African American MSM should translate some of those principles into concrete programs by using a staff from or sensitive to the African American MSM community. Using an Afro-centric model for HIV prevention/intervention, Us Helping Us, a program in Washington DC, for instance, attempts to improve the well-being of the African American gay and bisexual men in a holistic manner: improving self image, social relationship, spiritual growth, safer sexual behavior, and better medical conditions. Afro-centric services for HIV MSM should therefore go beyond serving clients by merely providing with medical information, but help clients reflect deeper, personal, and interpersonal issues. The methods used can include non-conventional activities such as drama, African music, community/social events, and spiritually-oriented programs to deliver the health messages, and to help generalize the positive medical compliance and safer-sex behaviors.

Prevention

HIV services for African American MSM should use not only tertiary prevention strategies (stopping HIV-related illnesses from getting worse), but also secondary prevention (lowering the prevalence of an illness among a high risk MSM population), and primary prevention initiatives (reducing HIV infection among healthy African American men). Community psychology provides prevention approaches that are appropriate for preventing HIV/AIDS among African American gay and bisexual males. Some authors (such as, Kelly, Murphy, Sikkema, & Kalichman, 1993; Duffy & Wong, 2000) have addressed the use of community and psychological/behavioral interventions to prevent HIV/AIDS infections. For instance, community psychology stresses the social ecology of diseases and prevention, conceptualizing human behavior in its social context and environment (Kelly, 1986; Trickett, Kelly, & Vincent, 1985). Such efforts have stressed the use of key informants, such as bartenders, community leaders, and sex workers to form positive safer-sex norms. Our model, therefore, advocates the use of peers from the African American MSM to modify norms of safer sex behaviors.

In a milestone review of HIV prevention work in psychology, Kelly, et al (1993) suggested that community psychology could help develop culturally specific prevention models on a large scale to prevent HIV infection in vulnerable populations. The authors also state that evaluation approaches to encourage and motivate HIV antibody testing, and to develop community based HIV prevention campaigns are understudied but much needed. The approaches supported by community psychologists are particularly applicable for HIV prevention among the gay and bisexual African American population. Some current models of those prevention efforts indeed fit very well the community psychology prevention approaches.

Holism

The use of a holistic model for HIV prevention and intervention for African American gay and bisexual men is clearly indicated by the literature. Us Helping Us's holistic approach for the African American gay and bisexual men in DC is the closest to the ideal AIDS program that population can expect, as described by Dancy (1994). Such a holistic approach appears to be applicable to African American population on other health issues, such as cancer, and heart diseases, and for other populations and the same population in other cities and countries. A holistic model can certainly be applied to other public health concerns, such as occupational health, adolescent sexual behavioral and teen pregnancy, substance use, addictive behaviors such as gambling, and sexual addiction.

With the National Institute of Health's new initiatives of AIDS research priorities on African American population-specific interventions and prevention (NIH, 1999a, 1999b, & year unknown b) and recommendations to evaluate wellness support and alternative medicine in treating HIV/AIDS (NIH, year unknown a), community psychologists will prove to be a very promising group to provide evidence for the effectiveness of culture-specific prevention and intervention program for African American MSM.

REFERENCES

Bourdon, B., Tierney, S., Huba, G.J., Lothrop, J., Melchior, L.A., Betru, R, & Compoc, K. (1998). Health Initiatives for Youth: A model of youth/adult partnership approach to HIV/AIDS services. *Journal of Adolescent Health*, *23* (Suppl. 2), 71-82.

Center for AIDS Prevention Studies (January, 1990). *African American Men's Health Study Intervention Facilitator's Training Manual*. University of California, San Francisco, Center for AIDS Prevention Studies, Multicultural Inquiry and Research on AIDS. San Francisco: Author. Retrieved January 17, 2000 from the World Wide Web: http://HIVInSite.ucsf.edu/prevention/prevention_models/2098.297c.hmtl

Center for Disease Control and Prevention (1995). *HIV/AIDS surveillance report: U.S. HIV and AIDS cases reported through December, 1994*. Atlanta, GA: Author.

Center for Disease Control and Prevention, Behavioral Interventions and Research Branch. (1996, March 25). *What have we learned..... 1990-1995*. Atlanta, GA: Author. Retrieved January 11, 2000 from the World Wide Web: http://www.cdc.gov/nchstp/dstd/wwhl.pdf

Center for Disease Control and Prevention. (2000, January 14). HIV/AIDS among racial/ethnic minority men who have sex with men - United States, 1989-1998. *Morbidity and Mortality Weekly Report, 49* (1). Retrieved January 17, 2000 from the World Wide Web: http://www.cdc.gov/epo/mmwr/preview/mmwrhtml/mm4901a2.htm

Dancy, B.L. (1994). African American men: The ideal AIDS program. *Journal of National Black Nurses Association, 7* (1), 60-67.

Duffy, K.G. & Wong, F.Y. (2000). *Community psychology*. Needham Heights, MA: Allyn & Bacon.

Feldman, R.H., & Fulwood, R. (1999). The three leading causes of death in African Americans: barriers to reducing excess disparity and to improving health behaviors. *Journal of Health Care for the Poor and Underserved, 10* (1), 45-71.

Foster, P.M., Phillips, F., Belgrave, F.Z., Randolph, S.M., & Braithwaite, N. (1993). An Africentric model for AIDS education, prevention, and psychological services within the African American community. *Journal of Black Psychology, 19* (2), 123-141.

Hawkeswood, W.G. (1996). *One of the children: Gay Black Men in Harlem*. Berkeley, CA: University of California Press.

Hemphill, E. (ed.) (1991). *Brother to brother: New writings by black gay men*. Boston: Alyson Publication.

Hobfoll, S.E. (1998). Ecology, community, and AIDS prevention. *American Journal of Community Psychology, 26*, 133-144.

Icard, L.D., Schilling, R.F., El-Bassel, N., & Young, D. (1992). Preventing AIDS among black gay men and black gay and heterosexual male intravenous drug users. *Social Work, 37* (5), 440-445.

Kass, N., Flynn, C., Jacobson, L., Chmiel, J.S., & Bing, E.G. (1999). Effect of race on insurance coverage and health service use for HIV- infected gay men. *Journal of Acquired Immune Deficiency Syndromes and Human Retrovirology, 20* (1), 85-92.

Kelly, J.A., Murphy, D.A., Sikkema, K.J., & Kalichman, S.C. (1993). Psychological interventions to prevent HIV infection are urgently needed: New priorities for behavioral research in the second decade of AIDS. *American Psychologist, 48* (10), 1023-1034.

Miller, R..L., Klotz, D., & Eckholdt, H.M. (1998). HIV prevention with male prostitutes and patrons of hustler bars: Replication of an HIV preventive intervention. *American Journal of Community Psychology, 26*, 97-131.

Misir, P. (1997). Behavioral interventions for black and Latino men who have sex with men. *AIDS Patient Care & STDs, 11* (1), 6-8.

Myers, L.J. (1988). *Understanding an Afrocentric world view: Introduction to an optimal psychology*. Dubuque, Iowa: Kendall/Hunt Publishing.

Peterson, J.L. (1998). HIV/AIDS prevention through community psychology. *American Journal of Community Psychology, 26* (1), 1-5.

Peterson, J.L., Catania, J.A., Dolcini, M.M., & Faigeles, B. (1993). Multiple sexual partners among blacks I high-risk cities. *Family Planning Perspectives, 25*, 263-267.

Riggs, M. (Director). (1989). *Tongues Untied: Black Men Loving Black Men* [Film]. (Available from Strand Releasing Home Video, 1460 4th Street, No. 302, Santa Monica, CA 90401).

Roman, D. (1994). Fierce Love and fierce response:Intervening in the cultural politics of race, sexuality, and AIDS. *Journal of Homosexuality, 26* (2-3), 195-219.

Rosenberg, P.S., & Biggar, R.J. (1998). Trends in HIV incidence among young adults in the United States. *Journal of the American Medical Association, 17* 279 (23), 1894-1899.

Rotheram-Borus, M.J., Gwadz, M., Fernandez, M.I., & Srinivasan, S. (1998). Timing of HIV interventions on reductions in sexual risk among adolescents. *American Journal of Community Psychology, 26*, 73-96.

Simmons, R. (1991). Some thoughts on the challenges facing black gay intellectuals. In E. Hemphill (ed.), *Brother to brother: New writings by black gay men* (pp. 211-228). Boston: Alyson Publication.

St. Lawrence, J.S., Eldridge, G.D., Reitman, D., Little, C.E., Shelby, M.C., & Brasfield, T.L. (1998). Factors influencing condom use among African American women: Implications for risk reduction interventions. *American Journal of Community Psychology, 26*, 7-28.

Tenner, A.D., Trevithick, L.A., Wagner, V., & Burch, R. (1998). Seattle YouthCare's prevention, intervention, and education program. *Journal of Adolescent Health, 23* (Suppl. 2), 96-106.

Trickett, E.J., Kelly, J.G., & Vincent, T.A. (1985). The spirit of ecological inquiry in community research. In E.C. Susskind & D.C. Klein, (Eds.), *Community research: Methods, paradigms, and applications* (pp. 283-333). New York: Prager.

Wingood, G.M., & DiClemente, R.J. (1998). Relationship characteristics and gender-related factors associated with noncondom use among young adult African American women. *American Journal of Community Psychology, 26*, 29-51.

Woods, E.R., Samples, C.L., Melchiono, M.W., Keenan, P.M., Fox, D.J., Chase, L.H., Tierney, S., Price, V.A., Paradise, J.E., O'Brien, R.F., Mansfield, C.J., Brooke, R.A., Allen, D.,& Goodman, E. (1998). Boston HAPPENS Program: A model of health care for HIV-positive, homeless, and at-risk youth. Human immunodeficiency virus (HIV) Adolescent Provider and Peer Education Network for Services. *Journal of Adolescent Health, 23* (Suppl. 2), 71-82.

Wright, E.R., Gonzalez, C., Werner, J.N., Laughner, S.T., & Wallace, M. (1998). Indiana Youth Access Project: A model for responding to the HIV risk behaviors of gay, lesbian, and bisexual youth in the heartland. *Journal of Adolescent Health, 23* (Suppl. 2), 83-95.

Chapter 11

THE BLACK MALE AND RECENT
U.S. POLICY TOWARD AFRICA

Jake C. Miller[1]
Bethune-Cookman College

ABSTRACT

A major purpose of this paper is to determine the extent to which black American males have made and are continuing to make an impact on the shaping of U.S. policies in regard to Africa. It takes into consideration the obstacles that they face both in regard to being black and in promoting issues which are not usually given high priority by the general American population. The chapter also will suggest how effective black American males are likely to be in influencing U.S. policies toward Africa in the future.

Through the years African Americans have shown an interest in the United States' policies relatives to Africa, although minimal at the outset. During the decade of the 1960s their interest increased as numerous African nations entered the international arena. In years that followed, their involvement has risen and fallen depending upon the crises that arose in Africa. This chapter discusses the contributions of African Americans in the development of a more enlightened United States' approach to Africa. Consistent with the theme of this book, the chapter focuses on the role of black males, although it is not always possible to isolate their contributions from those of their female counterparts. The intent, here, is not to assess the roles of all African American males who made an impact on U.S. policies; instead, it will focus upon a few primary actors whose roles can be considered pivotal. While emphasis is

---

[1] Jake C. Miller is a professor of political science emeritus at Bethune-Cookman College with a research interest is international affairs. Among his publications are *The Black Presence in American Foreign Affairs* (1979) Washington: University Press of America, and *The Plight of Haitian Refugees* (1984), New York: Praeger. He also has written several articles for professional journals, including "African American Males in Foreign Affairs" which appeared in the *Annals of the American Academy of Political and Social Science*, 569 (May 2000), pp. 29-41.

placed upon contributions of the last two decades, con- sedition will be given to earlier contributors who helped to pave the way for more recent foreign policy actors.

HISTORIC CONTEXT

As early as 1811, black Americans had begun to reflect an interest in Africa, with Paul Cuffee founding the Society of Sierra Leone. He visited that country in 1811 and 1815 in efforts to establish channels of communication between black Americans and Sierra Leone. Reports of his African experience were made to the founders of the American Colonization Society. Among other black Americans who took an early interest in Africa, especially the colonization of Liberia, were Daniel Coker, a bishop in the African Methodist Episcopal Church, Lot Cary, a Baptist preacher and John Russwurm, a journalist. A later advocate of emigration was Henry Highland Garnett, president of the African Civilization Society.

Although the U.S. colonized Liberia in 1821, its belated diplomatic recognition did not take place until 1871. Following the establishment of this new relationship, the doors of opportunity were opened for black American males to exert their influence on policies toward Africa from inside the foreign policy arena. After selecting several whites to be minister to the country, in 1871 the United States named J. Milton Tur ner, its first African American to the post. In years that followed, appointing African Americans to head the legations in Monrovia, Liberia and Port au Prince, Haiti was considered a given. Perhaps, Turner's agenda was typical of those of the twenty-two ministers who followed him. He wrote many reports encouraging American investments in Liberia in order to lessen the European influence. After 1949, our diplomatic relations were elevated with an ambassador rather than a minister being accredited to the nation. Once again, African American males were named to that post (Miller, 1978).

Our interest in Africa was moved beyond that of Liberia by such men as Martin Delany, an abolitionist, who was best known for leading the Niger Valley Exploring Party which he undertook in 1859-1860. In his report, upon his return to the United States, he maintained that "our policy must be...Africa for the African race, and black men to rule them." By black men, he insisted, he was referring to "men of African descent who claim an identify with the race" (Uya, 1971, 82).

EARLY BLACK AMERICAN INTELLECTUALS AND AFRICA

In order to bring about desired changes in our policy toward Africa, public awareness of such a need had to first take place. To accomplish this new appraisal of Africa, such intellectuals as Carter G. Woodson, W. E. B. DuBois, and Ralph Bunche pioneered the way. They were among the few scholars, who sought to remove from Africa many of the stereotypes that the world had associated with what often was referred to as the "dark continent."

Carter G. Woodson (1875-1950) contributed greatly to the developing of a new image of Africa through the writing of such books as *The African Background Outlined*, 1936 and *African Heroes and Heroines*,1939. Equally important was his founding of the Association for the Study of Negro Life and History, which provided a mechanism by which African

Americans could be better informed on problems and potentials of Africa. *The Journal of Negro History* 1916, *Negro History Bulletin* (1937) and other publications of the Association took the message of the homeland to more than the highly intellectuals (Sulley, 1993, 99-100).

W. E. B. DuBois, (1868-1963) a graduate of Fisk University, sensing the need for a campaign to dispel ignorance in regard to Africa he launched an effort while still a student at Harvard University. His doctoral dissertation, entitled *The Suppression of the African Slave Trade in the United States of America, 1638-1870*, was published in 1896. Later as editor of the *Crisis*, the major publication of the NAACP, DuBois introduced its readers to Africa. Among his other writings on Africa were: "Inter-racial Implications of the Ethiopian Crisis," 1935; "Liberia, The League, and the United States, 1933; "The Realities in Africa: European Profit or Negro Development?", 1943; "The Africa Roots of War;" and *The World and Africa,* 1947.

DuBois also was a pioneer in the Pan African movement, serving at the 1900 conference as chairman of the committee which drafted an appeal to the world to respect the integrity and independence of Ethiopia, Liberia and Haiti. He was also a major force in later conferences. In 1963 he died in Ghana, his adopted home.

Ralph Bunche's intellectual interest in Africa also began with his doctoral dissertation, "French Educational Policy in Togo and Dahomey," 1934. Much of the research for it was undertaken in Paris and Africa. His study led him to conclude that there was a major distinction between British and French colonial policies as they related to Africa. He perceived the French policies as going "too far toward the rapid disintegration of African culture," while the British "went too far toward the preservation of native culture, to the detriment of Africa's development" (Henry, 1999, p.70).

After completing his dissertation, the Howard University professor published many African related articles and books, including: "French Educational Policy in Togoland and Dahomey (1935), "French and British Imperialism in West Africa and *A World View of Race* (1936) Likewise, he delivered many speeches and papers on Africa. Bunche also sponsored a conference on "The Crisis of Modern Imperialism in Africa and the Far East" in May 1936. Following this, he undertook a two year study on the impact of colonial rule and Western culture on Africa from their perspective. Charles Henry concluded that although Bunche's research was never published, it prepared him for his future work (Henry, p.86).

In later years, Ralph Bunche became an African specialist in the U.S. State Department, serving as associate chief of the Division of Dependent Area Affairs. With the establishment of the United Nations, he served in several roles, including that of under secretary general.

EXERTING INFLUENCE ON AFRICAN POLICIES

African Americans seeking to advance the cause of Africa faced two major obstacles. Firstly, racial attitudes and practices here in this county made it difficult for them to obtain positions of importance, and secondly, the United States gave a low priority to African affairs. The relative success of the civil rights revolution of the sixties, as well as the entry of numerous African states into the international community, however, opened the doors of opportunity, somewhat. Several African Americans were assigned to head diplomatic missions in Africa during the sixties, and this trend was followed in later years. Likewise, they also began to hold semi-important positions in the State Department. The greatest influence by African Americans, however seem to have been exerted by those who held major assignments at the U.S. Mission to the United Nations in the late seventies and by those who served in key roles in Congress. Leaders of organizations supporting African causes also began to be somewhat influential during the decade of the seventies. African Americans holding such positions will be assessed below.

ANDREW YOUNG AND DONALD MCHENRY AT THE UNITED NATIONS

During Andrew Young's tenure as U.S. representative to the United Nations, he did much to aid the African cause. What stands out most are his efforts to obtain peace in Angola and to achieve majority rule in Rhodesia (Zimbabwe) and Southwest Africa (Namibia). He waged a vigorous fight to persuade Congress to repeal the Byrd Amendment, which had made it possible for the U.S. to continue to purchase chrome from Rhodesia in violation of the UN embargo against it. After visiting Africa, Young concluded that most African leaders viewed our action in regard to the Byrd Amendment as "a test of American sincerity and commitment to majority rule in southern Africa." He appealed to legislators to strengthen his hand by repealing the Amendment prior to his assuming the presidency of the Security Council. Congress did so, therefore his "credibility with African leaders was given a significant lift at a critical early period of his service at the United Nations" (Finger, 1988, 275).

Young's struggle to change our policy toward Africa also was demonstrated through his efforts to resolve the Rhodesian crisis. He challenged the efforts of the white minority government to prevent participation of the Patriotic Front--an umbrella organization of anti-government guerrillas--in discussion of constitution revision (Jones, 1996, p. 61). Young was criticized for his friendship with Nkomo, a guerrilla leader, whom he insisted upon being involved in drafting a settlement for Rhodesia. Although many Americans favored the internal settlement, which had brought Bishop Abel Muzorewa to power as a "token president." Young succeeded in holding out for a government in which "majority rule" was the guiding principle (Jones, 69-70)

While many supporters of the African cause expressed dismay over the exit of Andy Young from the UN, they were consoled by the naming of Donald McHenry, his deputy, as his replacement. In the appointment of McHenry, President Carter indicated that he was trying to send several messages, including: "to let the world know that we staunchly are committed as a nation and as a government to ending racism and apartheid in southern Africa and we will never yield on this point." Generally, McHenry was applauded for the role that he played in laying the groundwork for a resolution of the Namibian problem.

BLACK CONGRESSMEN AND AFRICA

During the Nixon and Ford administrations when issues relative to the enhance- ment of Africa were on the back burner, the most vocal critic of our foreign policy was Congressman Charles Diggs (D) of Michigan, who headed both the House Subcommittee on Africa and the Congressional Black Caucus (CBC). Through Congressional hearings, visits to Africa and other forms of confrontations, he made his voice heard in behalf of Africa. Being a member of the majority party in the House of Representative, but not a member of the party of the president, Diggs' role in many cases was that of opposing policies of the administration. Typical of that opposition were his efforts to derail the nominations of Nathaniel Davis to be assistant secretary for African Affairs, and Kenneth Rush to be under secretary of State, considering them to be disastrous to American policies toward Africa (Miller, 144). The Congressman made history in 1971 when he resigned from the U.S. Delegation to the United Nations as a protest over our policies toward Southern Africa. During his tenure in Congress, Diggs was the most vocal spokesman for the African cause.

Congressman Mickey Leland, who represented Texas in the House of Representatives from 1979 to 1989 was an important African American voice heard in behalf of Africa After co-authoring legislation creating the House Select Committee on Hunger in 1984, he became its first chairman. According to Leland the objective of the committee is "to fashion from its assessment of hunger issues a suggested program of related legislative proposals outlining a more effective U.S. hunger policy" (Leland, 1984, p.7915).

Insisting that he recognizes no national boundaries, Leland maintained that "we all have an obligation to the 'familyhood' of the world." He decried our failure in Africa, noting that "we've raped it of its natural resources, even its humanity." Leland made six official trips to that Continent since 1982. He was a humanitarian whose concern for those in need transcended cold war politics. He did not perceive food aid as a political tool, yet he realized that by doing the right thing we would eventually win friends for the United States. In an appearance before the House Committee on Foreign Affairs, Leland warned that "A billion dollar is not too much money to spend. When we look at our military expenditures building weapons to destroy humanity..." (U.S. Cong. HR, 1985, pp. 25-26).

Committed to the cause of feeding the hungry, Leland was killed in a plane crash as he sought to help the starving of Ethiopia in 1989. In praising the efforts of Congressman Leland, Senator Edward Kennedy noted that the deceased "leaves behind his conviction that the interests of the United States in foreign affairs are best served when humanitarian responsibilities are given high priority" (U.S. Cong. HR, 32).

Congressman Charles Rangel of New York was very influential during the Clinton administration. He accompanied the President on his historical trip to Africa in March 1998, visiting Ghana, Senegal, South Africa and Botswana and on his visit to Africa in August 2000. Rangel also served Clinton in a useful role in 1997, as head of a Presidential Mission on Economic Cooperation to Ethiopia, Eritrea, Uganda, Botswana, Mauritius and Ivory Coast.

Congressman Rangel was one of the authors and a chief backer of the African Growth and Opportunity Act, which was signed by President Clinton in January 2000. Consistent with that law, "duty-free treatment" was accorded to various exports from Sub-Saharan African countries to the U.S..

Congressman Donald Payne (NJ) the ranking Democrat on the House Subcommittee on Africa, has been somewhat influential in regard to African affairs. This influence, more than likely, will increase if the Democrats regain control of the House of Represent- atives in 2002. Payne's early interest in African affairs was shown when he was arrested in a demonstration before the White House in opposition to the apartheid policies of South Africa. His interest in achieving democracy has not been limited to that country, however, he has advocated democracy throughout the world. Among resolutions sponsored by him were those condemning the practice of chattel slavery in Sudan and Mauritania, and condemning the abduction of Ugandan children and their use as soldiers. Both resolutions were introduced in 1998 (Payne, 2001).

In December 1995, Payne took a hard line against the abuses of the Nigerian government. With the encouragement of Nigerian human rights groups and governments of Africa, Payne joined with others in sponsoring a resolution calling for sanctions against Nigeria, including the prohibition of any new American investment there. In a positive light, the bill provided for an increase in assistance for "democracy building" through nongovernmental organizations in the country (U.S. Cong. 1995, pp.65-66).

Payne has made several trips to Africa, including the accompanying of President Clinton in 2000. Perhaps, his most important trips abroad, however, were his visits to Kenya and Rwanda where he performed in peacemaking roles.

If the current Bush Administration pursues a policy that ignores the African interest, then it will be the job of Congressman Payne to be the voice of Africa in the Congress.

JESSE JACKSON IN A SPECIAL ROLE

At the swearing-in ceremony for Rev. Jesse Jackson as President Clinton's special envoy to Africa on October 10,1997, Secretary of State Madeleine K. Albright perceived him as being "ideally suited" for helping this nation "to build partnerships and establish dialogues" with African nations since he is "well known to African leaders...deeply-respected by the African people..." and " has been a champion of human rights and human dignity throughout his career."In accepting the appointment, Jackson noted that "the U.S. is so blessed and so powerful, and thus has the awesome responsibility to be a force for good in the world" (Albright, 1997).

In December 1997 Jackson, as the President's and Secretary of State's Special Envoy for the Promotion of Democracy in Africa, made his first trip to Africa to visit Kenya and Zambia. His assignment there was to confer with government leaders, opposition figures, and a wide cross-section of civil society, including religious leaders (Rubin, 1997). In May 1998. Jackson visited Ethiopia, where he delivered an address "on human rights and democracy to Parliament" (Rubin, 1998). In May, 2000 Jackson visited Nigeria, Liberia, Mali, Guinea and Sierra Leone to consult with their governments concerning efforts to resolve the crisis in Sierra Leone (Boucher, 2000).

AFRICAN AMERICANS AND ECONOMIC AID FOR AFRICA

Through the years there have been numerous organizations which have focused attention on Africa. Some of these have served as means by which African Americans have been active in aiding the economic development of Africa, including Crossroads Africa, Africare. Likewise, there have been organizations that have lobbied for the African cause. Perhaps, the most familiar of recent organizations of this type are Trans-Africa and the emerging National Summit on Africa: The Africa Society. These organizations and the men who led/lead them will be discussed below.

Prior to the advent of the Peace Corps in 1960, Dr. James Robinson, a Presby- terian minister pioneered in the field of people to people programs with his Operation Crossroads

Africa. He successfully recruited young men and women for services in Africa. Speaking at a commissioning ceremony for Operation Crossroads Africa on June 21, 1961, G. Mennen Williams, Assistant Secretary for African Affairs praised the organ- ization as one "founded on the idea that a sense of community can be achieved through the active sharing of common experiences and common efforts by people of differing races, creeds, and nationalities (Dept. of State Bulletin Jul 24, 1961, pp.151-152).

While Operation Crossroads Africa, in many ways inspired the Peace Corps, Africare became a reality because of the dreams of some who served in the Corps. including, C Payne Lucas, a founder and president of Africare, who served as African Regional Director. Africare is a non-profit organization that specializes in aid programs to Africa. Currently there are 150 programs in such fields as agriculture, water, the envi- ronment, health, private sector development and emergency aid being pursued in 28 African countries. Among the contributors to Africare are corporations, foundations, U.S. Government and international organizations (africare, 2001).

For his services, Lucas has been applauded by several American presidents and more than two dozen leaders of African nations. His opinion has been sought frequently by subcommittees of both the U.S. House of Representatives and the Senate. He has been a strong supporter of the Africa Growth and Opportunity Act, perceiving it as offering new hope for the people of Africa.

Rev. Leon H. Sullivan, who as a result of his interest in improving the economic lot of African Americans founded the Opportunities Industrialization Center (OIC), reflected a similar interest in Africans. Using the model which he had employed here in the United States, he established OIC International training centers in twelve different African countries. His interest in advancing Africa also encouraged him to found the International Foundation for Education and Self-Help (IFESH) for the purpose of fighting such menaces as illiteracy, hunger and unemployment (Smith, 1998, pp.1091-1092).

In advancing the well-being of Africa, Sullivan contributed in many ways, but he is best known for his fight against apartheid in South Africa. Specifically, he is identified with the *Sullivan Principles,* which he described as "an equal rights code for corporate conduct in South Africa. According to Sullivan:

> Essentially, the principles call for an end to all discrimination against blacks in company operation equal pay for equal work; training and elevation of blacks in large numbers to supervisory and administrative jobs, including black supervision over whites, extensive aid to housing, health and other community programs; the recognition of representative, independent, free black trade unions, thereby helping empower the black workers who is the greatest hope for peaceful change in South Africa (U.S. Cong. S.,1985, p. 460).

For his developing the principles, Sullivan was praised by Senator Alan Dixon, who noted that the principles "are responsible for improving the lives of tens of thousands of blacks, Asians, and others suffering under apartheid, and provide a crucially needed impetus toward ending that abhorrent system." (U.S. Cong. S., 459)

AFRICAN AMERICANS LOBBY FOR THE AFRICAN CAUSE

According to Randall Robinson, executive director of TransAfrica, the organization "grew out of the broadly recognized need for an institutional mechanism through which African-Americans could be informed, galvanized, and moved to a focused, thoughtful participation in the formulation of U.S. foreign policy toward Africa and the Caribbean."

In his effort to influence American policies toward Africa, Randall Robinson found himself at a disadvantage--initially because members of Congressional committees did not appear to take his testimony seriously, nor most of the issues related to Africa. Realizing the obstacles he faced, he sought to bring public pressure to bear on Congress, as well as the White House and State Department. The media did not seem helpful since it was accustomed to giving the little coverage it gave to African countries with substantial white population. Typical of the inability to present the cases of smaller countries with few whites was that of the Western Sahara in which in 1980 the indigenous Polisaro Movement was engaged in a fight to claim its independence, which was resisted by Morocco. The U.S. close relations with Morocco pitted "Washington against Africa and the better part of the world (Robinson, 1998, p. 112).

In response to the Reagan's policy of *constructive engagement,* Robinson launched a more active campaign against the apartheid regime of South Africa beginning with a "sit in" on November 21, 1984 following a meeting with the South African ambassador. He and other participants presented an ultimatum which called for the immediate release of all political prisoners detained by the South African Government, including Nelson Mandela and a demand that the Government make public it s intentions to undertake "the speedy dismantlement of the apartheid system with a timetable set for the task" (Robinson, 152). The failure of Robinson and other participants to leave the embassy led to their arrest, which was followed by massive demonstrations, which inspired the organizing of the "Free South African Movement." It had as its major purpose the using of demonstrations at the Embassy as leverage in obtaining the passage of comprehensive economic sanction against South Africa (Robinson, 155).

The Movement, which was supported by a coalition of organization was able to bring effective pressure upon the Congress to adopt the Comprehensive Anti-Apartheid Act of 1986, which became a law over the veto of President Ronald Reagan. The adop- tion of this legislation and its implementation were perceived as being a decisive force in the granting of one man one vote to South Africa in 1991.

Robinson's interest in Africa was not only in achieving "one man one vote" in white minority countries, but in obtaining better treatment for Africans throughout the continent. Perhaps, chief upon the evils which he opposed was the tyrannical government of General Sani Abacha of Nigeria. As he had done in the case of South Africa, he led a protest demonstration before the Nigerian Embassy for several days, protesting his abuse of power. Earlier, Robinson had led a similar demonstration at the Ethiopian Embassy where he protested the brutality of Ethiopian dictator Mengistru Haile Mariam.

Not only did TransAfrica seek to influence policies toward Africa but to develop an awareness of critical issues related to it, as well. In order to accomplish the latter the organization published *TransAfrica*, a quarterly journal.

In 1996 there emerged a constituency-building organization called National Sum- mit on Africa, headed by Leonard Robinson, Jr., a former deputy assistant secretary of state for African Affairs. It was established with funds from the Ford and Carnegie foundations to conduct a series of forums in six cities with 15,000 participants. The purpose of these forums was to discuss U.S.- African relations. About a third of the participants were Africans living in the United States. According to Robinson, the program that was funded for three years was perceived as a campaign to promote, inform and educate Americans about Africa; to formulate a national policy plan; and to create new linkages between Americans and Africans in many sectors.

A major national summit was held February 17-20, 2000 with approximately 6,5000 delegates and observers attending. At the end of this national meeting, Robinson released its draft National Policy Plan of Action for U.S.-African Relations in the 21st Century. The summit pledge to campaign for: increasing funds to fight HIV/AIDS in Africa, banning landmines, providing greater financial aid for African refugees increasing immigration limit for refugees from Africa, increasing support for peacekeeping training and missions to Africa and passing the trade bill, the African-Growth and Opportunity Act immediately (Thompson 2001).

CONFRONTING THE SYSTEM

In efforts to exert greater influence in the making of policies toward Africa, what obstacles did African Americans face? Perhaps, the most difficult challenge was that of persuading various administrations to view Africa as an important continent in itself and not mainly as a part of a larger strategy of containing Communism. In seeking to pursue such a course, Andy Young, who was considered the leading voice of those referred to as Africanists or regionalists, was often in conflict with the globalists of which Zbigniew Brzezinski, the National Security Adviser, was the major spokesman. Among Young's goals was to convince black Africa that "the U. S. position had subordinated the East- West conflict to a concern for the welfare of Africans" and that "we would work for African solutions to African problems with a minimum of big power interference." Brzezinzki, on the other hand, viewed "Communist diplomacy and military intervention in Africa as a threat with linkage to other world trouble spots." Often in the struggle Secretary of State Cyrus Vance and his assistant secretary of state for African affairs Richard Moose sided with Young (Jones, p.67).

Leland, in his fight to provide food for the starving people of Ethiopia, also found opposition from those who expressed concern over aiding the Marxist-oriented Mengistu government. Leland responded by reminding them that "We spend much energy and moneys talking ideology when hungry people recognize no ideology." He insisted that with millions of people starving in Africa, "We don't have time to discuss whether Mr. Mengistu cares about his people, whether he is spending his government's money wisely, or whether he established a government with the right ideology" (U.S. Cong.H.,1985, p.25).

Randall Robinson of TransAfrica also viewed the Communist strategy as standing in the way of efforts to convince the government and public to pursue a more progressive policy toward Africa. He referred to the case of the West Sahara, where, in 1980 he had interest in efforts pursued by the indigenous Polisaro Movement that was engaged in a fight to claim its independence in spite of the resistance of Morocco. Although Robinson was sympathetic toward the Polisaro's claim, he found himself in a difficult fight to win American support for the cause because of its Communist strategy. The United States, which had just supplied a 235 million dollar arm package regarded Morocco as one of its most reliable friends in its efforts against Communism. The U.S. close relations with Morocco pitted "Washington against Africa and the better part of the world, while alienating war-weary desert people whose rights to independence was not morally and legally unassailable (Robinson, p.112).

Equally important as a deterrent to African American influence was/is that of legislative tradition. Leland noted that in his effort to secure support for the creation of the House Select Committee on Hunger, he faced strong opposition from those who perceived him as attempting to invade their Congressional turf. Secondly, he was not supported by those who contended that there was no need for the establishing of additional committees. Leland was victorious, however, and when the committee was created in 1984, he became its chairman.

PROJECTIONS FOR THE FUTURE

The influence of African American males in the making of future policies relative to Africa will depend on several factors, including positions which they hold within the foreign policy apparatus, and the extent to which their views are consistent with those generally held by other Americans, Historically, black Americans generally were relegated to position of little or no influence, but in recent years some have been appointed to mean- ingful foreign policy positions, including General Colin Powell, the first of his race to serve as secretary of state and Condoleezza Rice, who holds the position of national security adviser. Earlier in the Clinton administration Susan Rice held the post of assistant secretary of state for African Affairs. There appears to be a trend of naming more African Americans to positions of importance in foreign affairs. While naming more African Americans to critical foreign policy positions is a major factor in formulating a more sympathetic policy toward Africa, it is by no means the only determinant. The extent to which such a policy maker "gets the ear" of the president carries significant weight. In analyzing previous administrations, we conclude that African American males in major positions tended to exert greater influence on a positive approach to Africa during the Carter and Clinton administrations than during those of Nixon, Ford, Reagan and Bush.

Since Congress plays an important role in the making and implementation of foreign policy, the political control of the legislative body is critical to the African policy that emerges. Only if the Democrats are in control of Congress, House of Represent- atives in particular, will African Americans be in a position of power relative to foreign policy. Congressman Donald Payne can be expected to head the House Subcommittee on Africa if the Democrats come to power, and in years to come the possibility exists that he could even become head of the Foreign Relations Committee. It should be noted, that within the Republican Party, Congressman J. C. Watts, an African American, heads the House Republican Conference and, in that role, is a possible source of influence should he choose to speak out in regard to U.S. African policies.

Generally ethnic groups are expected to influence U.S. policies toward nations that they regard as their homeland. The extent to which they are successful is often dependent upon the extent of their acceptability in the overall American society. Considering that at the time of the emergence of most African nations from colonial rule African Americans were just beginning to rise from second class citizenship in the United States, it was not expected that they would be overly interested in Africa. Even today, because there are civil rights issues yet to be resolved, many African Americans insist that they cannot concentrate on problems of Africa until solutions are found to racial problems in the United States. Fortunately, however, there are those who see the two problems as interrelated and; therefore, insist that both battles be fought simultaneously.

Minorities seeking to exert influence in regard to policy-making must be able to establish coalitions in support of issue they favor while simultaneously not having to com- promise principles that they hold dearly when they reciprocate. This is not always easy to do. In earlier years we obtained Jewish support for our domestic civil rights campaign and in return we supported Jewish positions in regard to the middle East. This coalition caused us much embarrassment, however, in the Third World, especially with the Arabs. Likewise efforts to build a coalition with the Hispanic, which is now the nation's largest minority, have been complicated over issues related to African American sympathy with Castro and over the treatment of Cubans in the Miami area contrasted with the that of Haitians.

The question is often raised as to why black Americans can not exert influence on U.S. policies toward Africa as the Jewish people do in regard to Israel. Henry Jackson, in his study of African American ties with Africa responded, somewhat. He noted the influence which the Jewish population of three percent exert on policies toward Israel, contrasted with the inability of the African American population of fifteen percent to influence U.S. policies toward Africa. He attributed this failure to the lack of economic clout by blacks (Jackson, 1982, pp. 162-163).

In conclusion, the lack of knowledge concerning Africa, the inability to convince other Americans that the United States has a vested interest in Africa, the current conservative trend in the nation, the inability to form meaningful coalitions, the lack of African Americans in key foreign policy positions, the prioritizing of black interest favoring a domestic agenda over international concern, all contribute to a lack of influence by African American males in regard to current U.S. policies toward Africa.

REFERENCES

Albright, M.K. (1997, October 10). Remarks at swearing-in ceremony for Reverend Jackson as special envoy to Africa. U.S. Department of State [On-line] http://sect.state.gov.www/briefings/statements/97101.html.

Boucher, R. (2000, May 17). Presidential Envoy Jackson's trip to West Africa. U.S. Department of State Press Statement. [On-line] http://secretary.state.gov.www/briefings/statements/2000.

Finger, S. (1988). *American ambassadors at the UN*. New York: Holmes & Meier.

Henry, C. P. (1999) *Ralph Bunche: Model Negro or American other*. New York: University Press.

Jackson, H. (1982) *From the Congo to Soweto: U.S. foreign policy toward Africa since 1960*. New York: William Morrow.

Jones, B. C. (1996). *Flawed triumphs: Andy Young at the United Nations*. Lanham, MD: University Press of America.

Leland, M. (1982, April 27). A need for a select committee on hunger, House of Representatives *Congressional Record*, 97th Cong, 2nd sess., vol. 28 part 6, p. 7915.

Miller, J. C. (1978) *The black presence in American foreign affairs*. Washington, DC: University Press of America.

Payne, D. (2001) Biography of Donald M. Payne. [On-line] http://www.house.gov/payne/bio-engl.htm.

Rangel, C (2000, August 25). Cong. Rangel leads House delegation on presidential mission to Africa, News Release.

Robinson, R. (1998). Defending the Spirit: A black life in America. New York: Dutton.

Rubin, J. (1997, December.1).Reverend Jesse Jackson's trip to Africa. U.S. Department of State Press Statement.[On-line]http://secretary.state.gov.www/briefings/ statements/97.

Rubin, J. (1998, May 15).Reverend Jesse Jackson's Third Trip to Africa. U.S. Department of State Press Statement. [On-line]htt://secretary.state.gov.www/briefings/statements/ 1999.

Smith, J. C. (ed). (1998) *Notable Black American Men*. Detroit: Gale Research.

Sully. C. (1993). *The black 100*. Secaucus, NJ: Coral Publishing Group.

Thompson, J.F. (2000, March 2). National Summit action plan charts course for future Africa News Services.[On-line] http://www.africasummit.org.

U.S. Congress, House of Representatives, Committee on Foreign Affairs (1985) *African famine situation*, 99th Cong., 1st sess. Washington: U.S. Government Printing Office.

U.S. Congress, House of Representatives, Committee on International Relations, Subcommittees on Africa and International Operations and Human Rights (1995). *Recent Developments in Nigeria*. 104th Cong. 1st sess. Washington: U.S. Government Printing Office.

U.S. Congress, Senate, Committee on Banking, Housing, and Urban Affairs and Subcommittee on International Finance and Monetary Policy. (1985) *The Anti-Apartheid Act of 1985*. 99th Cong., 1st sess. Washington, DC: U.S. Government Printing Office.

Uya, O.E., (1971). *Black brotherhood*. Lexington, MA: D. C. Heath and Company.

Williams, G.M. (1961, July24). Operation Crossroads Africa. U.S. Department of State Bulletin.

Chapter 12

FOREIGN-BORN BLACK MALES: THE INVISIBLE VOICES

Festus Obiakor
Department of Exceptional Education
University of Wisconsin-Milwaukee

Black males, whether born in the United States (U.S.) or in foreign countries (e.g., Nigeria or Jamaica), confront multidimensional problems that range from misperceptions to prejudicial generalizations because of negative attributions to their race or skin color. Steele (1990), a conservative Black scholar, noted more than a decade ago that:

> The condition of being Black in America means that one will likely endure more wounds to one's self-esteem than others and that the capacity for self-doubt born of these wounds will be compounded and expanded by the Black race's reputation of inferiority.... Black skin has more dehumanizing stereotypes associated with it than any other skin color in America, if not the world. When a Black presents himself in an integrated situation, he knows that his skin alone may bring these stereotypes to life in the minds of those he meets and that he, as an individual, may be diminished by his race before he has a chance to reveal a single aspect of his personality, (p. 36)

Steele's statement has psychological, educational, socioeconomic, and political ramifications on Black males, whether they are U.S. or foreign born. In other words. Black males, unlike their White male counterparts, have the added pressure of proving themselves despite circumstances and situations.

While the above assertions are correct, it is disingenuous to downplay the energies and strengths of Black males in surviving life's complex maze. The fact remains that many Black males have been successful at different educational, socioeconomic, and political levels. For instance, for many foreign-born Blacks, misperceptions based on race and skin color have had little devastating effects on how they view and tackle successes and failures. It is logical to argue that other personality and motivational variables contribute to how they internalize or externalize misperceptions and illusory generalizations. Ogbu (1978), in his classic work, addressed this interesting phenomenon. According to him, different minority groups (i.e., voluntary, involuntary, or immigrant minorities) respond to school success and failure differently. To a large extent, this affects how these group members confront society's trials and tribulations. In this chapter, cases are used to analyze implicit and explicit motivational factors responsible for successes of foreign-born Black males in mainstream American society in spite of prejudicial expectations and gross generalizations.

ENDEMIC PROBLEMS CONFRONTING BLACK MALES

As indicated, Black males are faced with a myriad of problems. It is no surprise that many scholars (e.g., Bell, 1985, 1992; Staples, 1984) have been critical of the ideology of equal opportunity in the U.S. because of persistent racial and class stratifications. According to Staples, "the ideology of equal opportunity masks the reality of a country stratified along racial, gender, and class lines" (p. 2). He decried the complex web of informal rules and processes that impedes achievements, opportunities, and choices for Black people. He added that Blacks who attempt to take advantage of opportunities (e.g., in colleges) experience intellectual racism. He noted, for instance, that there is a pervasive perception that Black students and faculty are unqualified and intellectually inferior to their peers and colleagues. As a consequence, affirmative action regulations designed to facilitate the recruitment and retention of black students, staff, and faculty are now abused, counterproductive, and even unworkable (Staples, 1984, 1986). As Staples (1984) pointed out, "no college has lost a contract because of failure to comply with affirmative action regulations nor does the government follow-up on how well schools implement their promises to remedy racial and gender imbalances in their work force" (p. 8). Staples (1986) acknowledged the huge presence of the "old boy" network and of what he calls the "new racism" which (a) tends to deny the existence of racism or the responsibility for it; (b) opposes quotas and affirmative action regulations; (c) calls for reduction in welfare, food stamps, and public housing; (d) defends phony meritocracy; and (e) relies heavily on standardized tests that are not valid predictors of quality performance. Banks (1999), Grossman (1998), Obiakor (1994, 1999), and West (1993) confirmed that race still matters in American society, and because it matters, pro-active efforts must be made to alleviate its devastating effects.

Many of the aforementioned problems have been acknowledged, in some measure, by many conservative Black scholars (e.g., Loury, 1985, 1992; Sowell, 1993; Steele, 1991); however, how these problems can be resolved is usually the bone of contention. Loury decried the long-held belief that racism is the only impediment to opportunities and choices in all facets of American life. According to him, "the price and self-respect valued by aspiring peoples throughout the world cannot be the gift of outsiders—they must derive from the thoughts and deeds of the peoples themselves. Neither the guilt nor the pity of one's oppressor is a sufficient basis upon which to construct self-worth" (p. 11). While Loury does not condone racism and discrimination in the provision of opportunities and choices, he castigates the Black community for what he calls the "enemy-without" and the "enemy-within." The enemy-without includes implicit and explicit racism at all levels; and the enemy-within includes Black-on-Black crime, self-destructive tendencies, drug abuse, teenage pregnancy, and excessive reliance on government support. Like many Blacks, Loury recognizes the role of the government in resolving the critical problem of the "underclass" in society; he nevertheless advocates the building of constructive, internal institutions that could integrate efforts of Black business, academic, and political elites. As he succinctly put it, "no people can be genuinely free so long as they look to others for their deliverance" (p. 1). There is enough data to suggest that foreign- born Blacks try to look within themselves for deliverance (Obiakor, Obi, & Grant, 2000).

Many foreign-born Black males find themselves entangled in the web of racism, prejudicial perceptions, xenophobia, discriminatory generalizations, and problems of adjustment to their new environment. For instance, my personal experiences and interactions with people have exposed me to negative assumptions about Africa, its diaspora, and its descendants, most of whom are Black. These assumptions include (a) Africa is a "dark" continent; (b) Africans are dark-skinned; (c) Africans are cannibals who live in jungles and in huts; (d) Africans do not have roads, streets, and lights; (e) Africans are short; (f) African men are chauvinists; (g) African men have two or more wives; and (h) African women are not free (Obiakor, 1990-91). There are other sad examples. A few years ago, efforts were made by some scientists in the medical field to attribute the origin of the Acquired Immune Deficiency Syndrome (AIDS) virus to Haiti, West Indies. Today, in the news and on television, high-powered efforts are also made to attribute the origin of AIDS to African monkeys. These sad notations have far-reaching implications on how men from these places are viewed as they socially interact in mainstream American society. More than two decades ago, Mojekwu, Uchendu, and Hoey (1978) remarked that the leading misconception is that "if you have seen one African, you have seen them all" (p. 11). Similarly, there exists a dangerous supposition that all Black people respond monolithically to societal and racial problems in the same fashion—this supposition looks at and treats all Blacks as one. In reality, the histories and experiences of Blacks (as framed by slavery and colonization) preimposes how they respond to issues of opportunities and choices (Arthur, 2000; Ogbu, 1978).

PERTINENT CASES AND IMPORTANT REVELATIONS

Foreign-born Blacks like other minorities in America appear to confront a myriad of problems that range from implicit misconceptions to explicit xenophobia. Consider the following examples. Rodney King was brutally beaten by some members of the Los Angeles Police Department (LAPD) who were initially exonerated until they were finally found to violate his civil rights. Abner Louima was also brutally beaten and dehumanized by some members of the New York Police Department (NYPD). In addition. Amadou Diallo was shot and killed by some NYPD members who were exonerated from the crime. These cases reveal similar trends of racial abuse, police brutality, and domination of these Black men by overzealous White police officers. Although these problems are similar, all Blacks do not respond to issues of race and discrimination in a monolithic fashion. Just like other immigrant minorities, foreign-born Blacks respond to societal imperatives differently (see Arthur, 2000; Obiakor et al., 2000; Ogbu, 1978).

To properly explore multidimensional problems that confront foreign-born Black males and their techniques for dealing with them, I have used *cases*. My effort is to "create experiences that embody cultural meanings, and cultural understandings that operate in the 'real' world" (Denzin, 1995, p. 8). These cases reveal experiences and self-stories that make up important events in people's lives. Denzin explained that they open "a parallax of discordant voices, visions, and feelings"—and "yield to a cacophony of voices demanding to be heard (and seen)" (p. 18). Colbert, Desberg, and Trimble (1996) explained that cases provide powerful means of learning through experiences and concluded that "cases represent an interesting paradox in that they are deeply personal evolving out of an individual's experiences" (p. xiii).

Based on the 10 cases presented below, I have illuminated data points necessary for furthering research and policy on Black men from African and Caribbean nations. These cases have resulted from personal interactions and telephone interviews with people who immigrated to the U.S. from different predominantly Black nations. These individuals live in different locations of the U.S. and are engaged in different professional careers. They were asked 6 open- ended questions, namely: (1) What is your name? (2) Where are you originally from? (3) When did you come to the U.S.? (4) What problems did you encounter? (5) How did you tackle your problems? (6) What do you do right now? To get detailed information, each interview session lasted from 45 to 60 minutes. Participants were given leeways to share their views. For confidentiality purposes, I did not use real names of those interviewed. I also felt that it was unnecessary to give exact work locations of those interviewed to avoid unnecessary fears that could prejudice subject responses.

Case #1

Eze came originally from Nigeria to the U.S. in 1979, more than 22 years ago. He indicated that he has consistently endured discrimination since coming to the U.S. According to him, "I faced xenophobia and racism when I was working on my Master's and Doctoral degrees." He noted that his professors looked down on him and refused to provide him with opportunities to grow. This lack of support continued when he graduated. He was unable to get jobs in his area of expertise (i.e., geological sciences). Eze did not give up in spite of his predicament. He noted that perseverance, persistence, hard work, and his family values have been instrumental to his survival. At present, he is an Associate Professor at a university in the state of Texas.

Case #2

Usman came originally from Mali to the U.S. in 1978, more than 23 years ago. He indicated that he lacks networks and opportunities. He also noted that he has experienced implicit and explicit racism, and tremendous job discrimination and xenophobia. He has been surprised by the fact that all his peers who earned engineering degrees at the same time as he did got steady, better-paying jobs than him. Although Usman's problems seem to be multidimensional, he explained that his assertiveness, perseverance, self-assuring behavior, and hard work have been beneficial to him. He added that his family values have also been very helpful. At present, he is an Engineer working for a private company in the District of Columbia.

Case #3

Abebe came originally from Ethiopia to the U.S. in 1975, more than 26 years ago. He explained that he has experienced racism, job discrimination, lack of support, and what he calls "White superiority complex." He added that people seem to be indifferent in the U.S. For instance, he complained that many people never take him seriously, and to a large extent, this has been responsible for his inability to land employment in his field of study. Abebe has been able to earn his doctorate degree and establish his own business. He credits his success to his belief in himself and God, individual initiative, persistence, and hard work. As he pointed out, 'I return favors and love people regardless of race, religion, political affiliation, or place of origin." Presently, he is a Private Entrepreneur who operates his business in the state of Kansas.

Case #4

Ndungu came originally from South Africa to the U.S. in 1993, more than 8 years ago. In his few years in this country, he has experienced racism, job discrimination, and xenophobia. He indicated that he went through several job fairs that were fruitless. At first, he felt like giving up in the face of adversities. Although Ndungu encountered multidimensional problems, he has been able to survive. He credits his success to perseverance, dedication, determination, and his ability to relate cross-culturally to others. At present, he is a Financial Analysis for an international engineering company that is located in the state of Kansas.

Case #5

Awe came originally from Zimbabwe to the U.S. in 1965, more than 36 years ago. He indicated that he has experienced ethnocentrism and chauvinism in scholarships, and closed mindedness while in school. At work, his problems included lack of professional respect and recognition, and racism in faculty promotion. Sometimes, he felt unwanted and resented by his peers and colleagues. Awe has been able to tackle his myriad problems through perseverance, hard work, dedication, and family values. He has never believed in giving up. Right now, he is an Associate Professor of a university in the state of Pennsylvania.

Case #6

Jack came originally from Jamaica to the U.S. in 1969, more than 32 years ago. As he indicated, "I have been through so many trials and tribulations." He acknowledged that great opportunities have come his way since coming to the U.S., but added, "I will never forget my negative experiences in my job at a vacuum cleaning company in Illinois when a colleague referred to me as a second class citizen or when my wife and I experienced a housing discrimination." He also recounted not being allowed to swim in the swimming pool of his apartment complex. In spite of his problems. Jack believes the U.S. is a great country that has given him and his family the opportunity to maximize their fullest potential. In his words, "my secrets to survival include personal confrontation, assertiveness, perseverance, and educational training." Right now, he is a successful Sub-contractor in the state of Florida.

Case #7

Mohammed came originally from Trinidad to the U.S. in 1976, more than 25 years ago. He noted that he has experienced overt racism and discrimination. According to him, "it is difficult to solidify friendships in the U.S. It's like no one gives a damn." He has, however, managed to survive in spite of all odds. Mohammed noted that he has succeeded because of individual initiative, persistence, family values, and what he calls "inner perseverance." At present, he is an Accountant for a Fortune 100 company in the state of New Jersey.

Case #8

Jean came originally from Haiti to the U.S. in 1991, more than 10 years ago. In his opinion, he has never experienced racism. In his words, "people comment on my accent. I do not go looking for racism, but I know I have experienced mild discrimination, and Black skin carries with it some form of prejudice." Jean noted that he increased his success potential in the U.S. through hard work, good education, perseverance, and determination. According to him, "I set high goals for myself." At present, he is a Software Engineer of a Fortune 500 company in the state of Illinois.

Case #9

Victor came originally from Guyana to the U.S. in 1964, more than 37 years ago. While in school, he encountered professors who doubted his intelligence and ignored whatever he said. He had problems adjusting to the educational system (e.g., the great emphasis on multiple-choice tests). At work, he had employers who did not expect him to be as smart as they were and those who talked down to him. Those individuals apologized after the fact and made statements such as, "you are different from other Blacks in America." Victor has encountered people who smiled at him but meant no good. On one occasion, he was promised an apartment over the phone only to be denied when it was found he was Black. He was also shocked to learn, on several occasions, that some of those who he called friends talked negatively about him in his absence. In his words, "Whites think you should be subservient to them even when you are more qualified than they will ever be." At present, Victor is a Teacher in a junior high school in the state of Florida. In addition, he is an Adjunct Professor of a junior college in the same state. He credits his success to working twice as hard, learning to adjust to the system, support from friends and family members from his home country, strength of character, refusing to give up or be subordinate, refusing to allow people to let him feel less than he is, and never allowing people to make him think they are better than him.

Case #10

Steve came originally from Barbados to the U.S. in 1969, more than 32 years ago. He indicated that his first experience with education in the U.S. was positive because he was recruited for his doctoral degree by the chairperson of the department. In his words, "my first negative experience was with African Americans. Now, I can understand their frustration. I never experienced a housing discrimination. However, my children, while playing n the streets, were called 'niggers' a time or two. I also found feces on my doorsteps." Steve has been able to survive and succeed. At present, he is a Full Professor of a university in the state of Virginia. He credits his success to working twice as hard, learning to adjust to the system, support from family in his home country, strength of character, refusing to give up in the face of adversity, and developing relationships with core people.

FROM INVISIBLE VOICES TO VISIBLE ACTIONS

From subject responses, foreign-born Black males experience similar racist and prejudicial patterns of behavior as other minorities in the American society. Ironically, their voices are invisible in the discourse on race since they do what they must do to survive. They frequently have the added burden of proving themselves not just to the dominant Whites, but also to their Black brothers and sisters born in the U.S. Their willingness to endure racism because of their immigrant status does not in any way downplay the fact that they experience racism or other forms of dehumanizing experiences. Subject responses reveal that all foreign-born Black males (i.e., 100 of the subjects) have endured implicit and explicit racism, prejudicial expectations, and illusory generalizations. Some of them recalled specific traumatic experiences, adjustment problems, and identity crises that they have endured. In spite of their respective problems, subject responses reveal high motivational levels and visible actions for all foreign-born Black males. Many had credited their survival to hard work, perseverance, self-assurance, and family values. And, many had developed intrinsic and extrinsic motivational techniques (e.g., hard work and belief in God) to tackle their predicaments. Based on subject responses, they all seem to be self-aware, self-responsible, and self-empowered as they endeavor to create opportunities and choices for themselves (see Obiakor, 1993).

As immigrant minorities, foreign-born Black males appear to reject offensive definitions of their status, which they sometimes consider better than it was in their countries of origin. In addition, they appear to devote less time to internalizing the effects of discrimination (see Ogbu, 1978, 1990). As a consequence, the promises of wealth, opportunity, and freedom are motivational forces that sometimes inflaence their survival strategies. It is logical to assume that foreign-born Black males overcome socioeconomic, cultural, and linguistic problems that they face by quickly adapting to new cultural challenges in their host society. As Ogbu (1978, 1990) concluded in his works, to a large degree, they begin to define "quality" from the perspective of the dominant White society.

Foreign-born Black males seem to put lots of credence on their family values. For these men, "the family is a cultural entity that will be difficult to drastically change because of its role as the cornerstone of the African culture. It is the dominant connecting force that provides a source of socio-cultural continuity. The African family unifies the delicate rough edges of the community" (Obiakor, 1990-91, p. 3). Earlier, Fafunwa (1975) and Madu (1978) acknowledged the roles of the Black family before the slavery and colonization of the White powers. For instance, Fafunwa noted that traditional African education prepares individuals to "develop latent physical skills, inculcate respect for elders and those in position of authority, develop character, acquire specific vocational training and develop a healthy attitude toward honest labor, develop a sense of belonging and to participate actively in family and community affairs, and to understand, appreciate and promote the cultural heritage of the community at large" (p. 20). These principles of traditional Black family life in Africa and the Caribbean seem to be comparable with dominant traditional principles of survival and uplift of White America. Obviously, foreign-born Black males appear to succeed in mainstream American society because of the strong sense of character impacted upon them by their respective families (Obiakor, 1992b). Their rough edges are usually smoothed before they come to the U.S. By so doing, they are prepared to tackle all kinds of problems to make themselves and their families proud (Arthur, 2000).

Although there are some foreign-born Black males who abuse drugs and commit crimes, many of them are dedicated and committed to tasks. In fact, many rely on their personal values to succeed in their education, job, and advancement despite endemic problems associated with immigrating to a society where race continues to matter. Based on these values, one can correctly argue that they are motivated to succeed because of their self-knowledge of who they are. They do not view themselves as "victims"—they tend to have accurate self-understanding of their personal characteristics. They also tend to have accurate self-esteem (i.e., a self-descriptive behavior that reflects self-love or self-evaluation). Finally, because of the traditional respect of honest labor in their cultural upbringing, they develop accurate self-ideals (i.e., self- empowerment or an ability to expend efforts to achieve goals). Since foreign-born Black males are able to self-analyze, they make functional goal-directed decisions (Obiakor, 1992a, 1995, 1996). Their personal survival is remarkable because they do not feel hopeless, have high expectations, and understand the importance of effort or the importance of succeeding in the face of failure (Graham, 1997; Obiakor et al., 2000).

Foreign-born Black males do not internalize prejudicial judgments with as great intensity as their U.S.-born counterparts. Their immigrant status creates different contexts and circumstances. They try to have realistic expectations, avoid unnecessary assumptions, and create rewarding environments. They do not wait for ready-made governmental answers—they sometimes create answers to their fundamental problems. They are usually information seekers who see no boundaries. It is no surprise that they live in areas where U.S.-born Blacks might find uncomfortable. It does not necessarily mean that they condone retrogressive racist behaviors, it only means that they are willing to collaborate, consult, and cooperate with individuals whose behaviors they even find repulsive. In general, foreign-born Black males tend to be success oriented. They also tend to know who they are, learn the facts when they are in doubt, change their thinking, use resource persons, build self-concepts, learn and teach with divergent techniques, make the right choices, and continue to learn (Obiakor, 1994, 1998, 1999; Obiakor et al., 2000).

CONCLUSION

In this chapter, 10 *cases* have been used to expose how foreign-born Black males turn their invisible voices into visible actions. Although these cases might have generalizability problems across subjects or even settings, they unveil real persons, problems, situations, and solutions. As other African Americans, foreign-born Black males encounter multidimensional problems that range from misperceptions to prejudicial generalizations due to negative attributions to their race or skin color. But, as immigrant minorities, they solve their myriad problems proactively and consistently. Their goals usually are to better themselves and free themselves from socioeconomic and political shackles sometimes imposed on them by their home countries. As it appears, foreign-born Black males view education not as "White" people's prerogative but as an instrument for societal survival and advancement. They do not belabor the issue of racism—even when they find it repugnant—they find innovative ways to deal with it. The hub of their strength is family values—they do not want to disappoint their families. For most of them, their families have invested so much in their education—as a result, it behooves them to educate themselves to increase cultural and socioeconomic continuities (Arthur, 2000; Obiakor et al., 2000).

Based on the analyses of the cases, it is reasonable to conclude that foreign-born Black males develop accurate self-knowledge, self-love, and self-empowerment that assist them in making functional, goal-directed decisions. In an era when many Black males are in jail or in trouble with the justice system, policy makers and community leaders must make efforts to tap on the talents and energies that foreign-born Black males bring into mainstream America. The Black community must also incorporate their talents in their struggles for equal opportunity and racial justice. Collaboration, consultation, cooperation, discourse, and dialogue must be fostered at all levels to include foreign-born Black males' multiple voices— they are forces of a developing social struggle. When they are buried beneath the visible surface, they tend to explode like time bombs in unexpected fashions.

REFERENCES

Arthur, J. A. (2000). *Invisible soioumers: African immigrant diaspora in the United States.* Westport, CT: Praeger.

Banks, J. (1999). *An introduction to multicultural education* (2nd ed.). Boston: Allyn and Bacon.

Bell, D. (1985). *And we are not saved: The elusive quest for racial justice.* New York: Basic Books.

Bell, D. (1992). *Faces at the bottom of the well: The permanence of racism.* New York: Basic Books.

Colbert, J. A., Desberg, P., & Trimble, K. (1996). *The case for education: Contemporary approaches for using case methods.* Boston: Allyn and Bacon.

Denzin, N. K. (1995). The experiential text and the limits of visual understanding. *Education Theory, 45,* 7-18.

Fafunwa, A. B. (1975). *History of education in Nigeria.* London: McMillan.

Graham, S. (1997). Using attribution theory to understand social and academic motivation in African American youth. *Educational Psychologist, 32,* 21-34.

Grossman. H. (1998). *Ending discrimination in special education.* Springfield, IL: Charles C. Thomas.

Loury, G. C. (1985). The moral quandary of the Black community. *The Public Interest. 79,* 9-22.

Loury, G. C. (1992). Why Steele demands more of Blacks than of Whites. *Academic questions: A publication of the National Association of Scholars, 5,* 19-23.

Madu. O.V. (1978). Kinship and social organization. In C. C. Mojekwu, V. C. Uchendu, & L. F. V. Hoey (Eds.), *African society, culture and politics: An introduction to African Studies* (pp. 76-90). Washington, DC: University Press of America.

Mojekwu, C. C., Uchendu, V. C., & Hoey, L. F. V. (1998). *African society, culture and politics: An introduction to African studies.* Washington, DC: University Press of America.

Obiakor, F. E. (1990-91). Family life in Africa: Revisiting the mismeasured custom. *Minority Voices. 13-14,* 3-5.

Obiakor, F. E. (1992a). Self-concept of African American students: An operational model for special education. *Exceptional Children. 59.* 160-167.

Obiakor, F. E. (1992b). Self image and fatherhood. *Vision Chattanooga: A publication of the Chattanooga Resource Foundation. 2,* 7.

Obiakor, F. E. (1994). *The eight-step multicultural approach: Learning and teaching with a smile.* Dubuque, IA: Kendall/Hunt.

Obiakor, F. E. (1995). Self-concept model for African American students in special education settings. In B. A. Ford, F. E. Obiakor, & J. M. Patton (Eds.), *Effective education of African American exceptional learners: New perspectives* (pp. 71-88). Austin, TX: Pro-Ed.

Obiakor, F. E. (1996). Self-concept: Assessment and intervention for African American learners with problems. In N. Gregg, R. S. Curtis, & S. F. Schmidt (Eds.), *African American adolescents and adults with learning disabilities: An overview of assessment issues* (pp. 15-28). Athens, GA: The University of Georgia/Roosevelt Warm Springs Institute for Rehabilitation, Learning Disabilities Research and Training Center.

Obiakor, F. E. (1998, August 24). Make your own destiny. *Emporia State University Bulletin. 8,* p. 17.

Obiakor, F. E. (1999). *Beyond the steps: Multicultural study guide.* Dubuque, IA: Kendall/Hunt.

Obiakor, F. E., Obi, S. 0., & Grant, P. (2000). Foreign-born African American males: turning barriers into opportunities. *The Annals of the American Academy. 569,* 135-148.

Ogbu, J.U. (1978). *Minority education and caste.* San Francisco: Academic Press.

Ogbu, J. U. (1988). Human intelligence testing: A cultural ecological perspective. *National Forum: The Phi Kappa Phi Journal, 68,* 23-29.

Ogbu, J.U. (1990). Understanding diversity: Summary statements. *Education and Urban society. 22,* 425-429.

Sowell, T. (1993). *Inside American education: The decline, the deception, the dogmas.* New York: The Free Press.

Staples, R. (1984, March/April). Racial ideology and intellectual racism—Blacks in academia. *The Black Scholar,* pp. 2-17.

Staples, R. (1986, April 27). The dwindling Black presence on campus. *New York Times Magazine,* pp. 46-62.

Steele, S. (1990, October 3). The "unseen agent" of low self-esteem. *Education Week,* p. 36.

Steele, S. (1991). *The content of our character: A new vision of race in America.* New York: Harper Perennial.

West, C. (1993). *Race matters.* New York: Vintage Books.

Chapter 13

TOWARD REPAIRING THE BREACH: THE FUTURE OF THE BLACK MALE IN WHITE AMERICA

Jacob U. Gordon
The University of Kansas

In the preceding chapters, attempts were made to examine the condition and circumstances of the more than 14 million African-American males in white America. In doing so, the aspirations, achievements, challenges and failures of the African-American male have been documented. We must now examine the prospects for the African-American male in the future. What exactly are the prospects? What is the vision of Black American leadership for African-American men and boys in the 21st century and beyond? Will the young, black, and male in America become an endangered species? And how will America respond?

The publication, "Repairing the Breach" in 1996 was a report of the National Task Force on African-American Men and Boys. In 1992, the W.K. Kellogg Foundation assembled a distinguished group of forty-seven individuals that formed the National Task Force on African-American Men and Boys (See appendix for a complete list). The group considered, among other things, the symptoms and the underlying problems of illiteracy, unemployment, poverty, drugs, crimes and violence, incarceration, and homicide among African-American men and boys. It highlighted key ways to support family life, reclaim the streets and rebuild civil society in America's communities. The Task Force Director and Editor of the volume was Dr. Bobby William Austin. The group was chaired by Andrew J. Young, former U.S. Ambassador to the United Nations. The publication highlighted a variety of critical issues, including the following: a profile of African-American males, civic story telling and public kinship, grassroots civic leadership, civic dialogue, youth, violence, and the global context.

The report explored three concepts: (1) the concept of the Human Condition and Human Development. This idea focused on the common good and connects human to human. (2) the concept of polis, signifying that members of a society have both rights and duties, and (3) the concept of public work, based on the following seven principles (Boyte, 1995):

1. Public work involves the contributions everyday people make to the common wealth. It involves non-violence, and human dignity and individual accountability.
2. Public work means learning to work effectively with people with whom you do not agree or may not even like.
3. Public work involves craft and skills, as well as pride in work. Citizenship is public work that must be developed.
4. Public work is visible and involves civic storytelling about ordinary people doing extra-ordinary things for each other and the community.
5. Public work puts experts on tap, not on top. Government officials must see themselves as citizens, working with people, not doing things to or for them. Our institutions must become civic public spaces.
6. Public work means that different groups work together, with focus and seriousness, so that people can hear one another and understand each other's stories of injustice, deprivation, suffering, and oppression.
7. Public work develops, in those people who do it, a sense of self, as well as skills and accountability.

Among other things, the Task Force report provided information and ideas which organizations and individuals can use to begin the process of transforming communities. The intent was to create long term structures for sustained intervention for African-American males in trouble. In this connection the document viewed systems change as an imperative in which many ideas can be brought together, so that crime and violence are reduced, thus improving quality of life for all Americans, especially the most vulnerable. Finally, the publication provided some far-reaching recommendations that created the Village Foundation, and the anvil on which the Foundation was to build its plans of action

About 65 recommendations were made by the Task Force in the publication. The following is a summary of the key recommendations:

1. A philanthropic organization be created that will address the plight of black males and proclaim the contributions that they have made to American society. This proposed organization would orchestrate a crusade for building a new consensus among African-Americans and attempt to successfully deal with government to stimulate systemic change relative to African-American men and boys. The organization would continue the dialogue initiated by the National Task Force on African-American Men and Boys aimed at creating a new community democracy, one that will authentically empower the black community, foster a new consensus, and empower individuals to become leaders. The proposed philanthropic organization or National Foundation be charged with creating a National Task Force on the "Education and Economic Empowerment of the African-American Community." This task force would identify successful education and economic empowerment programs, organize community dialogues using the focus group concept and latest technological tools, devise new strategies that would be effective in restructuring the American education system for improved educational outcomes, and reengineering the workplace for increasing employment and greater participation of African-Americans in the economy. The task force would also sponsor a summit

meeting designed to develop strategies for confronting the issues negating the education and economic empowerment of the African-American community.

2. The proposed task force should be charged with the creation of five centers of excellence strategically located in different areas of the country to serve as catalysts for stimulating change in the education and employment systems.

3. A new organization, possibly called the National Foundation for African-Americans, be created to address the plight of black males and proclaim the contributions they have made to our society. Such an organization would challenge federal and state governments to foster change relative to African-American men.

4. The Study Circles Resource Center, the national Dialogues on Race, and other efforts should be supported; they and other "structures for dialogue" that directly organize dialogues concerning race and thereby challenge widespread misperceptions as they foster new understanding.

5. A Technology Center Study Group should be established. This study group would be charged with developing the prototype for an extended school day after-school program, focusing on science, math, computer science, and entrepreneurship; and would be a joint venture between private industry, the community, and possibly the educational system. This program would work year-round, and it would bring to bear upon boys throughout these communities the very best in computer services so that they can become proficient in the creation of new knowledge.

6. A center be established for the development of media production, which would include film, recordings, and drama. This center would develop those civic stories that could be placed in the canon of stories that are told to young boys within our society. This media center would create original movies, dramas for film, and recordings that could be used in households, as well as for general marketing purposes. Further, this center would have some relationship with the nation's historically black colleges and universities.

7. A national historic areas project be established that would encourage communities and families to plan visits for these boys to national historic monuments, parks, houses, and museums within the United States which specifically reference African-Americans.

8. A nationwide library program for boys be developed. The strategy would be to increase the use of public libraries by African-American males, which would in turn open the door of knowledge about themselves and their culture to the rest of the world.

9. An international summit on African-American men be convened which would look at their image worldwide and how that image is distributed, studied, and discussed. The Task Force recommends that programs be developed which would provide opportunities for black males to interact with positive role models and to actively participate in activities that would enhance their ability to think positively of themselves and others.

10. Community centers be created with linkages to existing parts of the community that give boys opportunities to: (1) participate and to succeed; (2) get early and frequent messages about what is important and the responsible role of fathers in families; (3) participate in work programs with African-American men to develop positive work skills; and (4) develop a sense of caring for themselves and, in turn, caring for others.

Each community would, where necessary, establish parenting programs for teen mothers and fathers.

11. The establishment of a National Foundation for Teaching and Entrepreneurship.
12. A recommendation to establish George Washington Carver Clubs throughout the United States for young African-Americans was also made.

As one reviewer puts it, "Repairing the Breach raises issues critical to the American social fabric, elevating them from dialog to a credible plan of action." (Rodriguez, 1996)

If these recommendations are to become a reality, effective leadership is an imperative. The person behind the success of the National Task Force and the implementation of the recommendations of the Task Force was Dr. Bobby William Austin. He now serves as the President and Chief Executive Officer of the Village Foundation.

Bobby William Austin, husband, father, philanthropist, scholar and activist, is President and CEO of the Village Foundation. His breadth of vision and depth of knowledge uniquely qualified Dr. Austin to guide all aspects of this vitally important organization. He earned a B.A. in economics and sociology from Western Kentucky University; and M.A. in sociology from Fisk University; a doctorate in sociology from McMaster University in Canada; a diploma from the graduate School of Education at Harvard University and an Honorary Doctorate from Central Michigan University.

From 1989 to 1997, Dr. Austin held various executive positions at the W.K. Kellogg Foundation, including Director of the African-American Men and Boys Initiative and assistant director of the Kellogg National Fellowship Program. As the Executive Director of the National Task Force on African-American Men and Boys, he wrote, with the assistance of a writing committee, and edited its seminal report, *Repairing the Breach: Key Ways to Support Family Life, Reclaim Our Streets and Rebuild a Civil Society in America's Communities*, a work that has garnered national attention as visionary. It is described as "the movement to save America," by Washington Post syndicated columnist William Raspberry.

As Special consultant in American Culture to the Honorable Joseph Duffey, Former Chair, National Endowment for the Humanities, he has written extensively on our American common culture. Dr. Austin founded and was editor of the *Urban League Review*, a national research and policy journal of the National Urban League, and has a number of monographs, articles and artistic works to his credit. He edited *What a Piece of Work is Man* while at Kellogg, and is a Senior Fellow at the James MaGregor Burns Leadership Academy.

He taught at Georgetown University and lectured at other universities and colleges as well as served as executive assistant to the President of the University of the District of Columbia (UDC) and as an assistant to the UDC Board of Trustees and the late Honorable Ronald H. Brown. Dr. Austin was staff director of the D.C. Statehood Constitutional Convention responsible for maintaining D.C. Statehood historical papers and editing its legislative history. In addition, he served as campaign speech writer and issue director for former Housing and Urban Development Secretary the Honorable Patricia Roberts Harris and former Washington D.C. Mayor the Honorable Sharon Pratt Kelly. Because of his unique blending of philanthropy, politics, scholarship and application of leadership knowledge to solving problems, he was made a Fellow of the American Academy of Political and Social Science in 1999.

He is a recipient of the Kellogg National Fellowship award and is listed in *Who's Who in Black America, Outstanding Young Men of America*, and the International Dictionary of Biographies and the international edition of *Men of Achievement*.

Dr. Austin serves as a board member for The National Housing Trust. He has served on the boards of the National Institute for Urban Wildlife, the D.C. Repertory Theater and the Capitol Ballet Guild of Washington D.C. and as a member of the Atlantic Council of the United States, the Academic Council on the United Nations System, the Global Education Association, the American Culture Association and American Sociological Association. He is publisher of *Sirius B*, the online magazine of the Village Foundation; and a member of the Board of Advisors of the United Nations Development Program, NetAid. He is also a Deacon at the People's Congregational Church, Washington, D.C.

Dr. Austin is a native of Bowling Green, Kentucky. While pursuing his doctorate at McMasters University, he met Ms. Joy Ford Georgetown Guyana and they married two years later. Joy Ford Austin is now the Executive Director of the District of Columbia Humanities Council. From their union of 28 years they have four children: Sushama, a documentary film student at Harvard University; Julian, a dental student at MeHarry Medical School, Nashville, Tennessee; Leah, a fashion design student at Instituto Magliano in Milan, Italy, and Ariana, a senior at St. John's Catholic High School, Washington, D.C.

In anticipation of the creation of the Village Foundation in 1997, by The W.K. Kellogg Foundation, Dr. Austin organized 32 national demonstration programs that focused on African-American men and boys. These programs were first funded by the W.K. Kellogg Foundation.

According to its 1997-1999 Annual Report, the Village foundation is a national community-based 501 (c) 3 organization, incorporated in Alexandria, Virginia, in 1997. The mission of the Village Foundation is "to repair the breach between African-American men and boys and the rest of U.S. Society. (Annual Report, 1999). Its long-term (25-year) mission is to concentrate on comprehensive programs which focus on early intervention, mentorship, and skill-building of African-American men and boys through philanthropy. Fulfilling the long-term goal of the Village Foundation was based on accomplishing the following:

- creating, and supporting long-term, sustained intervention system
- creating mechanisms that allow African-American males to understand and involve themselves with the social contract by reconnecting them first to their ethnic community and then to the larger civic society
- bridging the gap that exists between the nation and a marginalized segment of African-American males

To fulfill its long-term and short-term mission and goals, the Village Foundation developed a mobilization strategy. The Foundation's strategy consisted of six interconnected programs - - The Pathways Network:

1. National African-American male Collaboration (NAAMC)
2. The Andrew Jackson Young American Futures Institute and Think Tank
3. Institute for Economic Education and Empowerment
4. Institute for Community and Race Relations

5. The Media Center
6. The Technology Project

From time to time the Foundation initiated special activities. One such activity was the Foundation's opinion survey conducted by the Gallup Organization to gauge the perceptions of Black and White with regard to African-American men and boys in American society. Similar surveys will be repeated every five years. A brief review of the Foundation's mobilization strategy is necessary for a better understanding of the foundation's programmatic development and implementation. First we begin with the

(1) National African-American Male Collaboration (NAAMC).

In 1998 the Village Foundation formally adopted (from the W.K. Kellogg Foundation) and began funding its first Pathway in the Network, the NAAMC, Inc. Formally the Kellogg Foundation African-American Men and Boys Initiative, NAAMC was a network of 32 grassroots, direct service providers that offered services to African-American men and boys. Their programs included a wide array of programs. The group aims to help grantees deliver multifaceted comprehensive interventions in the form of well-conceived projects. NAAMC became a national non-profit, tax exempt 501 (c)3 organization incorporated in Chicago, Illinois in 1998. At the time of writing, its officers were listed as follows: Horace Turnbull, President; Paul Hill, First Vice President; Charles Beady, Jr., Second Vice President; Pat Bell-Hilliard, Secretary; Eddie Staton, Treasurer; Charles Ballard, Parliamentarian; Jacob U. Gordon, Research & Public Policy Chair; John Wilson, Development Chair; Joseph Marshall, Programs Chair; E. Ajamu Babalola, Membership Chair; Linda Broadous Miles, Public Relations Chair; and Hurley Jones, Special Projects Chair. Its national Secretariat was housed at the Jane Addams Hull House Association in Chicago under the leadership of Gordon Johnson who also served as the President and CEO of the Hull House Association. The following are the 32 organizations: African-American Male Leadership Academy at the University of Kansas, Alpha Phi Alpha Fraternity, Inc., Al Wooten Jr. Heritage Center's Boys too Men Project, Athletes Against Drugs, The Boston Health CREW Project, The Boys Choir of Harlem Program, The Boys to Men, Careers and Life United in Boseon, The Duke Ellington School of the Arts, East End Neighborhood House Rites of Passage Institute, Ervin's All American Youth Club, Inc., Federation of Southern Cooperatives/ Land Assistance Fund African-American Mena nd Boys Program, The Greater Boston Morehouse College Alumni Association Building Bridges Program, Men Against Destruction - Defending Against Drugs and Social Disorder (MAD DADs Inc.), National Center for Youth Entrepreneurship Champs Cookies Y.E.S. (Youth Entrepreneurship Society), The National Foundation for Teaching Entrepreneurship, National Institute for Responsible Fatherhood and Family Revitalization, The National Trust for the Development of African-American Men, National Urban Coalition M. Carl Holman Leadership Development Institute, The No Dope Express Foundation, The Omega Boys Club, The Omega Little Brothers Program, 100 Black Men of America, Inc., Opportunities Industrialization Centers of America, Inc., Our Family Table foundation Youth Internship and Hob Training Program, The Pathways Community Development Corporation, the Peoples Cultural Arts Project of the Peoples Congregational United Church of Christ, Piney Woods Country Life School, Project 2000, Project Keep Hop Alive, and The Youth Leadership Academy.

(2) The Andrew Jackson Young American Futures Institute and Think Tank (AFI) named in honor of Ambassador Andrew Young, Chairman of the National Task Force and the Village Foundation Board of Directors, the Futures Institute and Think Tank was designed to address the specific needs of African-American men and boys by concentrating on career development, vocational and educational counseling, referral services and public policy. A clearinghouse on African-American males opened in May, 1999 with the 1-877-THE-MALE hotline that offers boys and their families information about the growing inventory of national, regional and local African-American youth service programs.

(3) Institute for Economic Education and Empowerment (IEEE). The mission of IEEE is to help impoverished communities - primarily inner-city neighborhoods in major metropolitan areas where the majority of African-American men and boys live - achieve new prosperity. Its objective was to make economics, business and entrepreneurship the foundation and focal point from which social, educational and other types of benefits were derived. It would develop, promote and facilitate programs to empower African-American men and boys to take advantage of their own capabilities and establish self-sufficiency.

(4) The Institute For Community and Race Relations. This pathway has as its goal to build a more integrated society by creating a national dialogue among the races. A major objective of this effort is the achievement of greater tolerance and understanding of the issues facing African-American men and boys in today's society by providing support to new and existing dialogues between cultures and ethnic groups. The strategies for the dialogues included conferences, workshops, websites, and the use of the media. The first conference was held at the Race Relation's Institute of Fisk University, Nashville, Tennessee, in 1997.

(5) The Media Center. The Center was designed to train African-American adolescents and men in film and video production, animation, sound recording and other media. The Center's mission is the accurate portrayal of African-American men and boys in the media without distortions based on stereotypes, misconceptions and myths about African-Americans. Thus the Center was to use the media arts as an empowerment strategy for African-American men and boys. Its specific objectives include the development of African-American male media skills, positive values, self-sufficiency, enlightened and strengthened overall sense of self-determination effective and responsible parenting, reduction of delinquency or criminal behavior, creative leadership and self-esteem etc..

(6) The Technology Project. The Project was designed to help "information poor" African-American boys learn about, gain access to and use current technology at sites, such as churches, public housing, libraries and after-school programs. The first of its activity was the Virtual Academy, a networked high-tech learning center that was helping to bridge the digital divide by simplifying the latest education technologies so that even beginning learners can benefit from its state-of-the-art- e-learning. A lone-term goal of the Technology Project was to sponsor a multi-media laboratory for the demonstration, production, and distribution of original software, courseware and art on both video and CD-ROM formats.

Other special projects of the Village Foundation included a National Literacy Campaign, the Village Success Club, and the Global Outreach. The National Literacy Campaign was designed to address the problem of illiteracy in America, especially among African-Americans. According to a press release by the Village Foundation on October 17, 2000, African-American Males were at highest risk for illiteracy (Village Foundation, 2000). Nearly 40% of African-American adults fall in the lowest "prose" literacy level, which measures a person's ability to comprehend printed information written in sentence form, while only 21% of the entire adult population falls within this category, according to the National Center for Education Statistics. The report pointed out that the gap was worse for "quantitative" literacy, which took into account a person's ability to process numeric information. Forty-six percent of African-American adults scored in the lowest level in this category, while the nation wide average was only 22%. In the category of "document" literacy, 43% of African-American adults scored in the lowest level, while the nation wide average in the lowest level was only 23%. The situation was found to be far worse for young African-American males, who routinely scored 12 to 17 points lower than young African-American females on all literacy inventories, leaving African-American males with the lowest scores among the native English-speaking population. Thus the National Campaign was to close the literacy gap among African-American males by sponsoring community-level literacy programs, in cooperation with their local-area "partners," for young Black men nationwide. The Campaign Kick-Off Summit took place October 11, 2000 at the St Regis Hotel in Washington D.C. Participants represented many states and organizations, including the Leadership Institute of Chicago, B & C Associates of High Point, North Carolina, the U.S. Department of Labor, reporters, as well as about 100 community-based partner groups from around the country.

Another important recent initiative was the U.S. Department of Agriculture and Village Foundation joint venture to save African-American family farms. In a bold and unprecedented step to rescue African-American family farms from threatened dissolution, the U.S. Department of Agriculture and a privately endowed charitable foundation have agreed to create a joint Board to address several immediate problems that require funding and technical assistance. According to a press release on December 11, 2000, the alliance will allow the Village Foundation to begin petitioning private and public entities to create a 250-million dollar fund to do the following.

- Provide technical assistance for individual farm owners.
- Provide grants to aid farm families.
- Provide revolving farm, equipment and land purchasing loans
- Provide families with training on how to obtain loans and credit
- Establish a financial co-op to help create new market systems.
- Establish worldwide networks and contacts for new marketing venues
- Create seminars, work groups and travel experiences to introduce African-American farmers to new farming techniques
- Organize and coordinate a bi-annual farm forum, that would help keep Congress, the American Public and the press informed on important African-American family farm issues

Department of Agriculture figures, and other unofficial research show the number of African-American farm families dropped from 160,000 in 1930, to just 18,000 in 1997. In comparison, white farm family numbers dwindled down only from 2.7 million to 1.8 million (Jarrett, 2000).

Dr. Bobby William Austin, President and CEO of the Village Foundation, commenting on the figures said, "Although both group's numbers dropped, black farmers and their families are in a free fall with no end in sight. This is the primary reason why we are entertaining this important agreement with Secretary Dan Glickman and the Department of Agriculture. We are, and will continue to be, committed to creating communities grounded in cooperation, industry, self-reliance and prosperity." (Press Release, 2000).

The Village Success Club (VSC) was organized in 1999 as a two-phased literacy model, (Reading Gets You There project and the media literacy), that was made available to all African-American boys in the nation. At the core of VSC was the guarantee that African-American young men and boys were imbued with an all inclusive set of values, skill sets, ethics and morals – that will undergird the potential for African-American young men to become broadened and innovative members of the body politic. In order to be contributing citizens in a civil society, participants in VSC and the Pathways, the Foundation has adopted Seven Competencies: Literacy, Education, Citizenship, World View, Service to Humanity, Entrepreneurship, American Cultural History and Compassion.

The Global Outreach. As a matter of policy the Village Foundation is represented on the advisory board of the Poverty Eradication Committee of the United Nations Development Program (UNDP, 1995). The Foundation also partnered with UNDP on NetAid, a worldwide broadcast and cybercast of a "global music extravaganza". Other global outreach activities were developed in France, Germany, England, South Africa, Botswana, and many Francophone nations. The Foundation sponsored a Francophone Male Conference in Washington, D.C. in October, 2000.

The future of African-American men and boys in America is dependent on several factors: leading social indicators, demographic trends, the color line, public policies (including profiling, affirmative action), and globalization.

By virtually every official index - - mortality, crime, incarceration, health, homicide, life expectancy, education, income, death penalty, unemployment, marital status - - African-American men and boys have emerges as one of the nation's most troubled racial groups in American Society (Gordon, 1994). In another study, Jewelle Taylor Gibbs described the status of black males in contemporary American society. "They have been miseducated by the educational system, mishandled by the criminal justice system, mislabeled by the mental health system, and mistreated by the social welfare system (Gibbs, 1998). A recent analysis of demographic changes in America supports the view that by 2010, children of color will represent the majority of young people in California, Florida, New York, and Texas - - the states that will account for a third of the nation's youth (Washington and Andrews, 1998). By the middle of the 21st century, demographers forecast that Americans of color will represent a majority of the overall U.S. population (Hodgkinson, 1992). People of color is a broad term applied to a diversity of racial and ethnic groups who are not non-Hispanic European Whites (African, Latino/Hispanic, Asian-Pacific Islander, and Native American descent).

There is abundant evidence that black males are portrayed by the mass media in a limited number of roles, most of them deviant, dangerous, and dysfunctional. This constant barrage of predominantly disturbing images have inevitably contributed to the public's negative stereotypes of black men, particularly of those who are perceived as young, hostile, and impulsive. This public image of the black male has exacerbated the racial hatred between black and white America. In spite of several civil rights bills designed to eliminate racial discrimination, racial harmony in America remains a noble dream. The removal of social and institutional barriers that society has created for African-American men and boys continue to be a major challenge to American democracy. Another major challenge is the concept of individual rights and responsibilities in our democracy. African-American men and boys must therefore be held accountable for their behaviors.

As the American society continues to experience demographic changes, so is the rest of the world. A global perspective and the national trend should shed light on the impact of globalization in American life. The Director of the Center for Demographic Policy, Dr. Harold Hodgkinson, challenged us all to take a clearer look at population characteristics – both for today and for the future. The following are statistics gathered by Hodgkinson to highlight trends:

Worldwide
- Of the 5.7 billion people on the planet, only 17 percent are White, dropping to 9 percent by 2010.
- Most young girls in the *world* will have to combine making a living with raising children.
- Many other nations have higher rates of unmarried births than the United States – 50 percent in Sweden and 33 percent in France, compared to 30 percent in the United States.

United States
- Half of all people in the United States live in suburbs, a quarter in core cities, and a quarter in small towns/rural areas.
- Only a quarter of U.S. households consist of a married couple with one or more children at home.
- A quarter of households consist of people living alone.
- An eighth of households are single mothers with children.
- There are now over 56, 000 people in the United States who are over 100 years of age, and the *third* quarter of human life is now age 50 to 75.
- The greatest increase in poor families since 1990 has occurred in close-in suburbs, not in core cities.
- Between 1970 and the early 1990's, the poverty rate increases were greater for Whites (38%) than for African Americans (19%).

Mothers (U.S.)
- Over 70 percent of school-age children have working mothers.
- *Most* unmarried and teen mothers are White; neither *percentages* are African American and Hispanic.

Children
- Children under 6 are more likely to be poor than any other age group of Americans.

- In 1950, 40 percent of the poor were elderly and 10 percent were children; but in 1990, 40 percent of the poor were children and 10 percent were elderly.
- Over 20 percent of U.S. children are being raised below the poverty line, the highest percentage of all NATO nations.
- Sixty-two percent of poor young children live with at least one parent/relative who works (1994). Only 28 percent of poor young children lived with parents on welfare.
- Between 1970 and the early 1990's, young-child poverty increased faster in the suburbs (59%) than cities (34%).
- In the year 2010, the number of children of immigrants will rise to 9 million, representing over one-fifth of the school-age population.

Transiency
- 43 million Americans move every year, more than any other nation.
- Transiency is the greatest enemy of family stability, school dropouts, and a major predictor of high crime rates.

The process of globalization makes it imperative for the United States to take a proactive stance toward repairing the breach. The problems discussed in this volume will not go away by simply ignoring them. Because the future of America is inextricably tied with the future of its citizens, including African-American men and boys, there should be a national policy to invest in its most vulnerable population like the African-American male. The failure to find immediate solutions to this most troubled segment of the American population will be very costly in material and human terms to society overall. The Village Foundation, viewed as a catalyst for change, appears to be a national model that promises to be exemplary.

Although the future of African-American men and boys may appear to be bleak now, there are reasons to believe that the "endangered species" thesis may be ill-informed. Throughout American history African-Americans 'strove with much dignity and discernible effect to be true to themselves and their ideals of freedom against overwhelming odds and adverse circumstances" (Gates and West, 2000). And as Black Americans have always shaped America, the 21st century may very well be another African-American century. African-American men and boys understand, as Gates and West put it, "that more democracy is always a possibility if they are willing to carry on the precious heritage with vision, courage, and compassion."

REFERENCES

Anderson, Alan B. (1986). *Confronting the Color Line: The Broken Promise of the Civil Rights Movement in Chicago.* Athens: University of Georgia.

Austin, Bobby William (1992). *What a Piece of Work is Man.* Battle Creek, Michigan: W.K. Kellogg Foundation.

Austin, Bobby William (1996). *Repairing the Breach.* Chicago: Noble Press, Inc.

Boyte, Harry (1995). "Citizenship and Young African-Americans" (Speech delivered to the National Task Force on African-American Men and Boys, the Martin Luther King, Jr., Center for Non-Violent Social Change, Atlanta, Georgia).

Gates, Jr. Henry Louis and West, Cornel (2000). *The African American Century*. New York: The Free Press.

Gibbs, Jewelle Taylor (1998). *Young. Black, and Male in America. An Endangered Species*. New York: Auburn House.

Gordon, Jacob U. and Majors, Richard (1994). *The American Black Male. His Present Status and His Future*. Chicago: Nelson Hall.

Hodgkinson, Harold (1992). *A Demographic Look at Tomorrow*. Washington, D.C.: The Institute for Educational Leadership.

Jarrett, Vemon (2000). "Black Illiteracy Embarrassing But No One-Way Street" in *Chicago Defender*, October 11 issue.

The Kerner Commission Report (1968). *Report of the National Advisory Commission on Civil Disorders*. New York: Bantam Books.

National Center for Education Statistics.

Rodriguez, Max (1996). *OBR The Black Book Review*.

United Nations Human Development Program (1995). *Human Development Report*. New York: Oxford University Press.

U.S. Dept. of Justice (1998). *One America in the 21st Century: The President's Initiative on Race*. Washington, D.C.: The White House.

Village Foundation (2000). *The Village Foundation Annual Report 1997-1999*. Alexandria, Virginia: Village Foundation Press Release, October 17, 2000.

Village Foundation and the U.S. Department of Labor (2000). The Village Foundation's National Literacy Campaign Kick-Off Summit, Washington, D.C.: October 11, 2000.

Washington, Valora and Andrews, J.D. (1998). *Children of 2010*. Washington, D.C.: National Association for the Education of Young Children.

APPENDIX 1

NATIONAL TASK FORCE ON AFRICAN-AMERICAN MEN AND BOYS

The Task force consists of forty-seven individuals. The Chairman was the former Ambassador to the United Nations and former Mayor of the City of Atlanta, Andrew J. Young, who served as co-chair of the Atlanta Olympic committee. The Task Force Co-Chairs were the Reverend Calvin Butts of the Abyssinian Baptist Church in New York City, and Mr. Bertram Lee, the President/Director of Albimar Communications, Inc., in Washington, D.C. The Task Force Executive Director was Bobby Austin of the W.K. Kellogg Foundation in Battle Creek, MI.

The other members of the Task Force were:

- Ewart G. Abner, Executive Assistant to the chairman, Gordy Company, Los Angeles, CA
- Dennis Archer, Mayor, Detroit, MI
- George Ayers, President, Ayers and Associates, Reston, VA
- Lerone Bennett, Johnson Publishing company, Chicago, IL
- Chuck Blitz, Executive Director, Social Ventures Network, Santa Barbara, CA
- Senator William Bowen, Grandin House, Cincinnati, OH
- Peggy Cooper Cafritz, Founder/Vice President for Development, Duke Ellington School of the Arts, Washington, D.C.
- Milton Davis, National President, Alpha Phi Alpha Fraternity, Tuskegee, AL
- Tommy Dortch, ACMC-Atlanta, Inc., National 100 Black Men, Atlanta, GA
- David Driskell, Professor of Art, University of Maryland, College Park, MD
- Gerald Freund, President, Private Funding Associates, New York, NY
- Anthony Fugett, Director, TLC Beatrice International Holdings, Inc., New York, NY
- Jeffrey Furman, Board of Directors, Ben and Jerry's Ice Cream, Ithaca, NY
- C.E. Gibson, President, Federation of Masons of the World and Eastern Stars, Detroit, MI
- Tyrone Gilmore, Sr., Grand Basileus, Omega Psi Phi Fraternity, Inc., Spartanbury, SC

- Joseph J. Givens, All Congregations Together, New Orleans, LA
- John Goss, IBPO-Elks of the World, Knoxville, TN
- Robert L. Harris, Grand Polemarch, Kappa Alpha Psi Fraternity, Inc., San Francisco, CA
- Frances Hesselbein, President/CEO, Peter F. Drucker Foundation, New York, NY
- Vemon Jarrett, columnist, Chicago Sun Times, Chicago, IL
- Timothy Jenkins, Publisher/CEO, Unlimited Visions, Inc., Washington, D.C.
- Sharon Pratt Kelly, Mayor, Washington, D.C.
- Debra Lee, President/CEO, Black Entertainment Television, Washington, D.C.
- Reverend Michael Lemmons, Executive Director, Congress of National Black Churches,
- Washington, D.C.
- Rick Little, President, International Youth Foundation, Battle Creek, MI
- O.C. Lockett, President General, Grand Masonic Congress, USA, Detroit, MI
- Haki Madhubuti, Founder/Publisher. Third World Press, Chicago, IL
- Marilyn Melkonian, President, Telesis corporation, Washington, D.C.
- E.L Palmer, Executive Director, Comprand, Inc., Chicago, IL
- N. Joyce Payne, Director, Office for the Advancement of Public Black Colleges, Washington, D.C.
- Wilbur Peer, Administrator, Rural Development Administration, Department of Agriculture, Washington, D.C.
- Huel Perkins, President, Sigma Pi Phi Fraternity, Louisiana State University, Baton Rouge, LA
- John Perking, President, John Perkins Foundation, Pasadena, CA
- Henry Ponder, President, Fisk University, Nashville, TN
- Reverend Samuel D. Proctor, Rutgers University, New Brunswick, NJ
- Kay George Roberts, Professor of Music, University of Massachusetts, Cambridge, MA
- Michael Schultz, Producer/Director, Four Winds Film Corporation, Santa Monica, CA
- Georgia Sorenson, Director, Center of Political Leadership, and Participation, University of Maryland, College Park, MD
- Nelson Standifer, Director. Midnight Basketball Leagues, Inc., Hyattsville, MD
- William Stanley, National President, Phi Beta Sigma, Atlanta, GA
- Joe Stewart, Senior Corporate Vice President, Kellogg Company, Battle Creek, MI
- Bernard Watson, Chairman, HMA Foundation, Inc., Philadelphia, PA
- Robert L. Watson, President/CEO, Lauren, Watson and Co., Phoenix, AZ
- Cordell Wynn, President, Stillman College, Tuscaloosa, AL

APPENDIX 2

Table A1. Poverty Thresholds in 2000, by Size of Family and Number of Related Children Under 18 Years (Dollars)

Size of family unit	Weighted average thresholds	Related children under 18 years								
		None	One	Two	Three	Four	Five	Six	Seven	Eight or more
One person (unrelated individual)	8,794									
Under 65 years	8,959	8,959								
65 years and over	8,259	8,259								
Two persons	11,239									
Householder under 65 years	11,590	11,531	11,869							
Householder 65 years and over	10,419	10,409	11,824							
Three persons	13,738	13,470	13,861	13,874						
Four persons	17,603	17,761	18,052	17,463	17,524					
Five persons	20,819	21,419	21,731	21,065	20,550	20,236				
Six persons	23,528	24,636	24,734	24,224	23,736	23,009	22,579			
Seven persons	26,754	28,347	28,524	27,914	27,489	26,696	25,772	24,758		
Eight persons	29,701	31,704	31,984	31,408	30,904	30,188	29,279	28,334	28,093	
Nine persons or more	35,060	38,138	38,322	37,813	37,385	36,682	35,716	34,841	34,625	33,291

Source: U. S. Bureau of the Census, Current Population Survey.

Available at http://www.census.gov/hhes/poverty/threshld/thresh00.html, Accessed 30 January 2002.

Table A2. Years of School Completed by People 25 Years and Over, by Age, Race, Household Relationship, and Poverty Status: 2000 (Numbers in thousands)

	All Races			White			Black		
		Below poverty level			Below poverty level			Below poverty level	
	Total	Number	Percent of total	Total	Number	Percent of total	Total	Number	Percent of total
All Education Levels									
Male									
Total	84,637	6,014	7.1	71,441	4,456	6.2	9,043	1,162	12.9
25 to 34 years	18,451	1,421	7.7	14,937	1,032	6.9	2,317	273	11.8
35 to 54 years	40,755	2,642	6.5	34,187	1,903	5.6	4,584	565	12.3
55 to 64 years	11,253	888	7.9	9,755	705	7.2	1,032	135	13.0
65 years and over	14,179	1,063	7.5	12,562	816	6.5	1,110	190	17.1
65 to 74 years	8,187	575	7.0	7,235	459	6.3	652	87	13.3
75 years and over	5,992	488	8.2	5,326	357	6.7	458	103	22.4
Female									
Total	92,385	9,597	10.4	76,612	6,795	8.9	11,307	2,272	20.1
25 to 34 years	18,989	2,472	13.0	14,930	1,706	11.4	2,829	609	21.5
35 to 54 years	42,065	3,477	8.3	34,468	2,328	6.8	5,432	914	16.8
55 to 64 years	12,532	1,353	10.8	10,654	976	9.2	1,367	315	23.1
65 years and over	18,799	2,296	12.2	16,560	1,785	10.8	1,680	434	25.8
65 to 74 years	9,691	1,017	10.5	8,369	731	8.7	978	230	23.5
75 years and over	9,108	1,279	14.0	8,191	1,055	12.9	701	204	29.1

Household Relationship								
In families	137,642	8,810	6.4	115,617	6,221	5.4	14,927	1,974	13.2
In married-couple families	114,141	5,167	4.5	99,231	4,214	4.2	8,943	527	5.9
In married-couple families - husband	54,534	2,515	4.6	47,731	2,050	4.3	4,233	260	6.1
In married-couple families - wife	53,430	2,434	4.6	46,744	1,991	4.3	3,962	233	5.9
In families with female householder, no spouse present	17,050	3,069	18.0	11,500	1,620	14.1	4,828	1,303	27.0
Unrelated individuals - Male	18,444	2,573	14.0	14,930	1,826	12.2	2,678	611	22.8
Unrelated individuals - Female	20,478	4,077	19.9	17,122	3,074	18.0	2,695	837	31.1
No High School Diploma								
Male								
Total	13,213	2,373	18.0	10,891	1,840	16.9	1,785	448	25.1
25 to 34 years	2,318	534	23.1	1,967	434	22.1	247	85	34.4
35 to 54 years	4,640	849	18.3	3,829	646	16.9	624	164	26.3
55 to 64 years	1,925	323	16.8	1,508	262	17.4	325	53	16.3
65 years and over	4,330	667	15.4	3,587	498	13.9	590	146	24.8
65 to 74 years	2,247	360	16.0	1,876	279	14.9	304	72	23.7
75 years and over	2,083	307	14.7	1,711	219	12.8	286	74	25.9
Female								
Total	14,555	3,778	26.0	11,346	2,636	23.2	2,445	951	38.9
25 to 34 years	2,133	829	38.9	1,681	591	35.2	355	190	53.5
35 to 54 years	4,550	1,209	26.6	3,445	809	23.5	821	316	38.4
55 to 64 years	2,207	538	24.4	1,662	368	22.1	408	148	36.3
65 years and over	5,664	1,202	21.2	4,558	867	19.0	861	298	34.6
65 to 74 years	2,546	498	19.6	1,980	324	16.3	424	150	35.5
75 years and over	3,118	704	22.6	2,578	543	21.1	437	148	33.8

Household Relationship								
In families	20,651	3,448	16.7	16,706	2,540	15.2	2,849	715	25.1
In married-couple families	15,392	2,082	13.5	13,125	1,765	13.4	1,451	215	14.8
In married-couple families - husband	7,593	1,058	13.9	6,519	914	14.0	779	102	13.1
In married-couple families - wife	6,339	916	14.4	5,422	763	14.1	585	97	16.6
Unrelated individuals	3,733	1,157	31.0	2,444	629	25.7	1,112	463	41.6
Unrelated individuals – Male	3,092	959	31.0	2,417	691	28.6	585	250	42.9
Unrelated individuals – Female	3,938	1,690	42.9	3,027	1,191	39.4	796	433	54.5

High School Diploma, No College

Male

Total	26,856	1,949	7.3	22,389	1,335	6.0	3,577	491	13.7
25 to 34 years	5,953	419	7.0	4,691	279	6.0	1,023	114	11.1
35 to 54 years	13,050	987	7.6	10,661	631	5.9	1,936	290	15.0
55 to 64 years	3,597	308	8.6	3,142	229	7.3	345	60	17.5
65 years and over	4,256	235	5.5	3,894	195	5.0	272	27	9.9
65 to 74 years	2,451	123	5.0	2,211	103	4.7	178	13	7.2
75 years and over	1,805	111	6.2	1,683	92	5.5	94	14	15.1

Female

Total	30,893	3,361	10.9	25,953	2,401	9.3	3,784	831	22.0
25 to 34 years	5,069	891	17.6	3,906	577	14.8	935	278	29.7
35 to 54 years	13,645	1,298	9.5	11,120	871	7.8	1,920	371	19.3
55 to 64 years	4,860	465	9.6	4,258	354	8.3	454	93	20.4
65 years and over	7,319	707	9.7	6,668	599	9.0	475	90	18.9
65 to 74 years	3,824	329	8.6	3,429	275	8.0	294	39	13.1
75 years and over	3,495	377	10.8	3,239	324	10.0	181	51	28.3

Household Relationship								
In families	36,912	1,743	4.7	32,379	1,427	4.4	3,152	187	5.9
In families	16,510	775	4.7	14,492	620	4.3	1,503	96	6.4
In married-couple families - husband	18,216	900	4.9	16,198	757	4.7	1,301	73	5.6
In married-couple families - wife	6,214	1,174	18.9	4,165	591	14.2	1,816	547	30.1
Unrelated individuals - Male	5,768	837	14.5	4,478	554	12.4	1,115	232	20.8
Unrelated individuals - Female	6,259	1,296	20.7	5,365	1,006	18.7	750	266	35.4

Some College, No Bachelor's Degree

Male

Total	20,877	1,032	4.9	17,754	776	4.4	2,247	165	7.3
25 to 34 years	4,960	266	5.4	4,050	178	4.4	636	56	8.7
35 to 54 years	10,878	529	4.9	9,152	405	4.4	1,286	84	6.5
55 to 64 years	2,485	157	6.3	2,214	131	5.9	199	17	8.4
65 years and over	2,555	81	3.2	2,338	61	2.6	126	9	7.1
65 to 74 years	1,599	48	3.0	1,440	43	3.0	92	2	1.9
75 years and over	956	33	3.4	898	18	2.0	34	7	(B)

Female

Total	24,502	1,665	6.8	20,364	1,173	5.8	3,229	383	11.9
25 to 34 years	5,827	498	8.5	4,529	350	7.7	982	102	10.4
35 to 54 years	12,155	682	5.6	9,941	445	4.5	1,737	190	10.9
55 to 64 years	2,978	221	7.4	2,580	148	5.7	332	62	18.7
65 years and over	3,543	264	7.4	3,314	229	6.9	179	30	16.5
65 to 74 years	1,920	124	6.4	1,765	96	5.4	128	25	19.2
75 years and over	1,622	140	8.6	1,550	133	8.6	51	5	(B)

Household Relationship								
In families	35,581	1,522	4.3	29,888	1,023	3.4	4,232	361	8.5

Household Relationship									
Household Relationship	35,581	1,522	4.3	29,888	1,023	3.4	4,232	361	8.5
In families	29,493	813	2.8	25,605	633	2.5	2,646	84	3.2
In married-couple families	13,600	383	2.8	11,922	287	2.4	1,160	46	4.0
In married-couple families - husband	14,486	402	2.8	12,642	326	2.6	1,258	36	2.9
In married-couple families - wife	4,618	605	13.1	3,130	308	9.8	1,343	261	19.4
Unrelated individuals - Male	4,575	499	10.9	3,822	377	9.9	576	93	16.1
Unrelated individuals - Female	5,057	631	12.5	4,273	510	11.9	643	90	13.9
Bachelor's Degree or More									
Male									
Total	23,691	659	2.8	20,407	505	2.5	1,435	59	4.1
25 to 34 years	5,220	202	3.9	4,229	140	3.3	411	19	4.6
35 to 54 years	12,187	278	2.3	10,544	221	2.1	737	27	3.7
55 to 64 years	3,246	99	3.0	2,891	83	2.9	164	5	3.1
65 years and over	3,037	81	2.7	2,743	61	2.2	123	8	6.3
65 to 74 years	1,890	44	2.3	1,709	34	2.0	78	0	0.5
75 years and over	1,147	37	3.2	1,034	27	2.6	44	7	(B)
Female									
Total	22,436	794	3.5	18,950	587	3.1	1,849	17	5.8
25 to 34 years	5,961	254	4.3	4,815	187	3.9	557	40	7.1
35 to 54 years	11,715	288	2.5	9,962	203	2.0	953	38	4.0
55 to 64 years	2,486	129	5.2	2,154	106	4.9	173	13	7.3
65 years and over	2,274	123	5.4	2,019	91	4.5	166	16	9.9
65 to 74 years	1,401	66	4.7	1,195	37	3.1	133	16	12.3
75 years and over	873	57	6.5	824	54	6.5	32	0	(B)

Household Relationship

In families	35,856	713	2.0	30,655	520	1.7	2,376	82	3.4
In married-couple families	32,344	529	1.6	28,121	388	1.4	1,694	42	2.5
In married-couple families - husband	16,831	300	1.8	14,798	229	1.6	792	15	2.0
In married-couple families - wife	14,389	217	1.5	12,482	146	1.2	819	26	3.2
Unrelated individuals - Male	5,009	278	5.5	4,213	204	4.8	402	36	8.9
Unrelated individuals - Female	5,224	460	8.8	4,456	367	8.2	506	48	9.5

ABOUT THE CONTRIBUTORS

Leon T. Andrews, Jr. MA. is currently a Ph.D. candidate at the University of Michigan. He co-authored *The Black Male and the U.S. Economy* (2000).

Oscar A. Barbarin, Ph.D. is the L. Richardson and Emily Preyer Bicentennial Distinguished Professor for Strengthening Families in the School of Social Work, and Senior Investigator at the Frank Porter Graham Child Development Center at the University of North Carolina, Chapel Hill. He earned a Ph.D. in clinical psychology at Rutgers University in 1975 and completed a post-doctoral fellowship in social psychology at Stanford University in 1983. He is President-Elect of the American Orthopsychiatric Association, Chair of the Black Caucus of the Society for Research in Child Development and a Fellow in APA's Division 27 Society for Community Research and Action. His research on African American children and families has explored the effects of social risks on mental health. One aspect of his work is the development of screening tools for the early detection of factors that interfere with the academic and psychological adjustment of children. Professor Barbarin has served as a consulting editor for several research journals including Psychological Assessment, a Journal of Consulting and Clinical Psychology and Journal of Black Psychology and the American Journal of Orthopsychiatry. In addition, he has served as a program and research consultant with Head Start programs and the State of Michigan Sickle Cell Program.

Jacob U. Gordon, Ph.D., LL.D., is Professor of African and African-American Studies and Research Fellow in the Institute for Life Span Studies at the University of Kansas. He is also the Executive Director of the Center for Multicultural Leadership Studies. Dr. Gordon is the author of 16 books, including this volume, *The African-American Male: An Annotated Bibliography* (1999), *The African-American Male: His Present Statues and Future* (1994); *The African Presence in Black America* (In-Press); numerous articles in academic journals, chapters monographs and research reports. He is a member of several professional organizations including life membership in the Association for the Study of African-American Life and History: African Studies Association, the American Historical Society and the Phi Beta Delta. Dr. Gordon is a recipient of many honors and awards for research, teaching, and public service.

William B. Harvey, Ph.D. is Vice President for Minority Affairs at the American Council on Education in Washington, D.C. Prior to his present position. Dr. Harvey was Dean of the School of Education at the University of Wisconsin, Milwaukee. He is co-editor, with James R. Valadez, of *Creating and Maintaining a Diverse Faculty*, a volume in the series *New Directions for Community Colleges*, co-author of *Affirmative Rhetoric, Negative Action: African-American and Hispanic Faculty at Predominantly White Institutions*, and editor of *Grass Roots and Glass Ceiling: African-American Administrators in Predominantly White Colleges and Universities*.

Susan Williams McElroy, Ph.D. is assistant professor of economics and education policy at the H. John Heinz III School of Public Policy and Management at Carnegie Mellon University. Her research interests include racial and gender inequality in the U.S. labor market and the role of education in economic status.

Garry A. Mendez, Jr., is currently the founding president of the National Trust for the Development of African-American Men. The organization concentrates on solving problems through the use of African and African American values. Prior to founding the Trust, Mendez was a visiting fellow at the U.S. Department of Justice, National Institute of Justice, where he worked on developing and evaluating a program that he designed, Crime Is Not a Part of Our Black Heritage. He earned his doctorate at the University of Michigan.

Jake C. Miller is a professor of political science emeritus at Bethune-Cookman College, where he taught for 22 years. Prior to that he taught at Fisk University. Among his publications are *The Black Presence in American Foreign Affairs* (1979) and *The Plight of Haitian Refugees* (1984). He also has written several articles for professional journals. He is a recipient of many awards and honors, including the Mary McLeod Bethune Legacy Award (1996); Distinguished Alumni Citation by the National Association for Equal Opportunity in Higher Education (1988); and the United Negro College Fund Distinguished Scholar (1986-1987).

Bridgitt Mitchell, M.A. (ABD) is Assistant Professor of Early Childhood Education at Johnson County Community College in Overland Park, Kansas. Her doctoral work at the University of Kansas was in Human Development. Prior to joining the faculty at the Johnson County Community College, Bridgitt had several years of experience in teaching pre-school and kindergarten children. To her credit are numerous research reports and papers presented at professional conferences.

Festus E. Obiakor is a professor in the Department of Exceptional Education, University of Wisconsin-Milwaukee. A teacher, scholar, and consultant in the field of special education, he is the author or coauthor of more than 100 publications, including books and articles.

Robert B. Sanders, Ph.D., is a biochemist, educator, administrator, and consultant. Dr. Sanders was the author or co-author of more than 57 articles and publications on topics in biochemistry, endocrinology, biology of reproduction, and pharmacology. He was a professor, an associate dean of the Graduate School, and an associate vice chancellor at the

University of Kansas. He was a visiting scientist at the Battelle Memorial Institute Pacific Northwest Laboratories, a visiting professor at the University of Texas Medical School Houston, and a program director at the National Science Foundation. He was a consultant for the National Science Foundation, the National Institutes of Health, the Department of Education, ALZA Corporation, and Interx Research Corporation. He was the Director of the Kansas-Nebraska-Oklahoma Regional Junior Science and Humanities Symposium for more than 20 years. He received awards and research grants from the American Cancer Society, the Battelle Memorial Institute, the National Institutes of Health, the National Science Foundation, and the U.S. Department of Education.

Dominicus W. So received his Ph.D. in Clinical/Community Psychology in 1997 from the University of Maryland, College Park. He is Assistant Professor of Psychology at Howard University in Washington, D.C., is a historically black university, where he trains graduate students to be doctoral level psychologists, and teaches psychopathology and psychotherapy. He commits to the understanding of physical health, mental health, and HIV issues of ethnic and sexual minorities. He has researched and presented papers on HIV prevention among ethnic minorities. He has previously served as a consultant for a HIV prevention program in Washington, D.C. As a consultant, he has directly experienced the local community issues of Washington and physchosocial issues related to the behavioral aspects of HIV prevention of ethnic minorities. He has often been active in the clinical work and HIV prevention work with minorities. He has also developed an interest and expertise in the area of holistic health, integrating clinical/community psychology, minority help seeking behavior, complementary/alternative medicine, spirituality, culture, and Internet usage for research and teaching.

Peter Ukpokodu, Ph.D. is Chair of the Department of African and African-American Studies at the University of Kansas where he teaches courses on African and African-American Theatre and African Culture. He is the author of Sociopolitical Theatre in Nigeria and African Political Plays. His articles and essays have been published in *The Drama Review, The Harvard Journal of African-American Public Policy, The African American Encyclopedia, Theatre Research International, Theatre Annual,* and *The Literary Griot,* among others. He is a Phi Beta Delta Scholar, an Award-winning published poet, and member of the American Society for Theatre Research, International Federation for Theatre Research, African Literature Association, Association of Literary Scholars and Critics, among others.

Reginald Eric Vance, M.A. is currently pursuing his Ph.D. in Public Policy from the Nelson Mandela School of Public Policy and Urban Affairs at Southern University and A&M College located in Baton Rouge, Louisiana. Since June of 2000, Vance has worked for the Department of the Interior as a Chief of Administration trainee for the National Park Service. Vance is currently on detail in Denali National Park and Preserve where he performs the duties of a Program Analyst for Budget and Finance.

INDEX

G

H

I

J

K

Q

R

S

T